KT-484-445

5 6 7 8

9 10 11 12

"A little of what other people fancy does you good!"—G. K.

THE GRAHAM KERR COOKBOOK

GRAHAM KERR

MEMBER OF
GOURMET
INTERNATIONAL

Dear Friend,

    If you have taken the plunge and purchased me — congratulations.

    I trust that I shall serve you well. If you have still to make a decision — this may help.

    I am known mostly for my television show 'The Galloping Gourmet'. On this show Treena and I try to entertain you (whatever that may mean). Because of this you may rightly say "Is he a performer or a cook".

    I hope I am both — at least I try.

    However, of one thing I am certain. I realise that the time for laughter stops when you risk your time, money and reputation on somebody else's recipe.

    In this book I have done my serious best to eliminate that risk of failure.

    So relax — and have fun.

        God Bless you,

               Graham Kerr

P.O. BOX 185, NORTH SYDNEY 2060 — TELEPHONE: 92-4523.

THE
Graham Kerr
COOKBOOK

by
The Galloping Gourmet

Photography
HUBERT SIEBEN

W. H. ALLEN
LONDON
1971

The Gold Medal reproduced here was awarded to Graham Kerr for THE GRAHAM KERR COOKBOOK published in Australia by A. H. and A. W. Reed. With editorial changes and additions it is now published for the British market under the title THE GRAHAM KERR COOKBOOK by The Galloping Gourmet.

© Graham Kerr, 1966, 1969
First British edition, 1971.
Printed and bound in Great
Britain by Butler & Tanner Ltd,
Frome, Somerset, for the publishers
W. H. Allen & Co. Ltd, A Division of
Howard & Wyndham Ltd.

ISBN 0 491 00269 6

Acknowledgments

When a book has taken over ten years to prepare it is hard to say thank you for every kindness. It's rather like throwing a party—you always leave someone out!

My parents—for their training. Monsieur André Simon—for his early tuition. Alex Taylor—for his somewhat strenuous education in Hotel Management. Andy Silk—for his perseverance. Shirley Maddock—for starting me off in New Zealand. Elsie Lloyd—for keeping me going. John Berry—for his criticisms. Ash Lewis—for his considerable TV assistance. Monté Holcroft—for his literary advice. Messrs. Shankland and Palmer—for assistance with pilot tapes. WNTV-1 staff—for all their wonderful help. Michael Pritchard—for building my studio. Hubert Sieben—for really fine photography. Jennifer Hepburn—my assistant for this book. Helen Watson—my typist. Ray Richards—my editor. John Reed—for his friendship and support. Don Sinclair—for his artistic advice. All my friends—for testing the recipes. John Moreland—for his guidance on the fish section. Mrs. Hill and Miss Bellet—for herbs and enthusiasm. Len Evans, Tony Bohdan, Frank Christie, Rudy Komon, and Max Lake. T.E.N. 10 staff. Barbara Small—my food assistant and "water bearer." Ron Way with whom we created The Galloping Gourmet format. All at 1500 Merivale Road—Messrs. Y & R in New York, especially Colgan and Peter. Our very dear friend Wilbur Freifeld and Paul Talbot—Vern Ferber, and by no means least the tenacious Clara Claasen of Doubleday.

My wife Treena—TV producer—major critic—reader and checker—coffee maker—official taster—and washer up!

And everyone else. I thank you.

INTRODUCTION

Work began on this book in 1959, although I did not realize it at the time.

I had been taught to cook in the postwar *La Cuisine Française* style of London, England, where I had been born into the hotel industry.

It was different from the prewar French kitchen—there were fewer provisions, fewer trained staff, and much more enthusiasm.

The great desire was to shrug off wartime restrictions and return to happier days—the good old days. So great was the desire that the speed of execution provided a foundation of *status* rather than *stability*; a situation that has only recently been questioned.

I have no doubt whatsoever that, had I remained a hotelier in England, I would still adhere to the basic traditions of the trade.

Traditions are useful as armor against professional attack—they are also a form of self-induced contentment created by stamping up and down on one spot—getting nowhere, risking little, and achieving an immortal zero.

I regard my move to New Zealand as the most important step in my life.

New Zealand, unlike any other "Western" nation, did not have a culinary tradition to return to—that is, apart from her rich farming heritage. There was no establishment to carp, criticize, or snigger. There was a desire to learn and, above all, a love for the practical. New Zealanders are essentially a great practical people who are not in the least concerned with status.

I lived and worked in this refreshing climate of opinion for seven years, and it was during that time that this book was written. It was born from a desire to question, to compare, to experiment, and to decide—an equation of great importance to all cooks.

It had occurred to me that all cookery could be broken down into three simple stages.

The ingredients.
Their preparation before cookery.
Their assembly by using a method of cookery.

It was the last stage that interested me most—after all, the ingredients are a matter of taste, cutting a matter of skill, but a method of cookery should be a practical matter and not necessarily subject to international culinary traditions.

I set to work to examine every possible "method" by which food is cooked and attempted to reduce the variety to a few basic, often used "methods."

I then undertook a study of comparative tests in which I literally conducted my own bake-off. Eventually, after some four years, I discovered those methods that suited me best.

Over the years that have followed, these "methods" have been constantly revised in an attempt to keep them practical.

At the date of publication of this book I know of no easier, no more satisfactory method of achieving a well-cooked dish. But I am equally certain that, in the years to come, our advances in food technology and kitchen appliances will require revision being made.

So, until that day comes along, I present to you my experience and enthusiasm—for it is all I have to offer.

Graham Kerr

This is the Section of every cookbook that nobody ever reads, yet it is the most important. So read and succeed or pass on and risk failure!

HOW TO GET THE MOST FROM THIS BOOK

Firstly I would like you to spend five minutes of your valuable time and turn over each page of this book—keep them turning, don't stop—just scan each one.

You will note that there are a great many step-by-step pictures. These are designed to help you over some of the hard-to-describe practical issues. Wherever you have pictures, you have a basic method. There are ... basic methods.

In practically every case the recipes given to achieve the "basic" method are as simple and inexpensive as possible. On the pages that follow each basic method you will find two other recipes. These make use of the same method but get progressively harder.

Finally—you will note that each method has a **GRADUATE** recipe identified by Ⓖ These are the most difficult to achieve and have their own section in the book starting on page 194.

To help with the construction of a menu I have added some first courses and desserts. Where basic methods apply you will find a page reference.

HOW TO USE THE RECIPES

This is **vital!**

Each recipe is broken down into four stages.

The entire recipe should be read through at least once before you start.

STAGE ONE – "RECIPE TO PRODUCE—PORTIONS"

Under this heading are listed the ingredients. Be sure to weigh or measure each item *before you do anything else.* The measurements are in United States (cup and tablespoon measures), Imperial (weighing scales and pint [20 fluid ounces] measures), Metric (kilos, etc.).

STAGE TWO – "METHOD OF PREPARATION"

It is essential to prepare each ingredient as shown under this heading before you start to cook. The French call this *mise en place,* to put everything in its proper place.

STAGE THREE – "METHOD OF COOKERY"

This is **IT**—the bare bones of the business where you simply assemble all the ingredients— which in other words means you cook.

STAGE FOUR – "SERVING"

Under this heading you have purely suggestions, but please heed one plea. **Don't forget the vegetables.** Often, with a new dish, they tend to get subjugated—they must get your full and creative attention.

And now I feel as I am sure I shall feel when our children finally leave home.

I would like to write and write about the pitfalls that face you, to try to describe what each will be like and how to avoid them. I could chat on for the rest of this and a dozen more books and still not achieve complete protection for you because this you learn properly only through experience.

Just remember—only the creative person risks.

Good luck!

CONTENTS

About Appetizers and First Courses

The Curtain Raiser: Shakespeare understood it best, that sublime piece of integrated nonsense that allowed his audience to settle down. A bridge between the cares of the world and escape into dramatic reality.

So it is with the appetizer and to a lesser extent with the first course.

Now that we have come of age and developed a healthy regard for diet, the old order of endless courses has rightfully disappeared. The main emphasis is right where it belongs—with the main dish.

It takes only two steps to get there. The minute, refreshing "something" to nibble with predinner drinks and the still lighthearted, stimulating first course.

Hostesses who provide nuts, potato chips, and olives before dinner announce to the world their total indifference. The remainder of the meal is a "show" that, regardless of its excellence, is without warmth. It is cultivated hospitality, looking-glass humanity.

Study the great restaurateur; he cares for his guests the instant they set foot in his establishment.

So should it be with one's home, and nuts are not the best greeting!

Albeit, the appetizers must be very small, not overgarnished, always bite-size, easy to handle, and never more than two per head!

Which gets us to the first course.

Your guests are seated, and this is where the fun or failure begins.

The first dish needs to be light and should stimulate the appetite rather than depress it through blandness. It should have color but not be oversauced. Usually I prefer a cold first course unless the weather is really boisterous.

But above all, and this may seem odd to you, my essential prerequisite is that it be plated in individual portions. There is nothing so tedious as the continuous clatter of serving spoons and forks.

CONTENTS OF SECTION

APPETIZERS

1 New Yorker Onion Sandwich

RECIPE TO PRODUCE 2 PORTIONS	U.S.A.	IMPERIAL	METRIC
Brown bread	4 rounds	4 rounds	4 rounds
Mayonnaise	1 tbsp.	1 tbsp.	15 milliliters
Onion slices	4 thin	4 thin	4 thin
Salt, black pepper	To season	To season	To season
Tomato	2 slices	2 slices	2 slices
Parsley	To garnish	To garnish	To garnish

METHOD OF PREPARATION
1. Slice onion.
2. Cut rounds of bread.
3. Slice tomato.

METHOD OF COOKERY
1. Lightly spread the bread with mayonnaise.
2. Place the onion slices on one slice of bread and season. Sandwich bread together.
3. Spread edges of bread with mayonnaise—roll in parsley.
4. Decorate with slice of tomato and sprig of parsley.

SERVING
Serve as savories with vodka-based creations.
At heart this is a dish that everyone enjoys except those with ulcers and those who have a romantic meeting with someone who isn't at the party.

2 Huevos Rancheros

RECIPE TO PRODUCE 4 SERVINGS	U.S.A.	IMPERIAL	METRIC
Eggs	4	4	4
Green pepper	1	1	1
Pimientos (tinned)	2	2	2
Egg tomatoes (tinned Italian style)	14 oz.	14 oz.	420 grams
Chili powder	2 tsp.	2 tsp.	2 grams
Salt, black pepper	To season	To season	To season
Oregano	20 leaves	20 leaves	20 leaves
Onions	2 medium	2 medium	2 medium
Garlic clove	1	1	1
Cumin	2 pinches	2 pinches	2 pinches
Cheddar cheese (mild)	¼ cup	2 oz.	60 grams
Clarified butter	2 tbsp.	1 oz.	30 grams

METHOD OF PREPARATION
1. Slice peppers into fine strips and cut pimiento into strips.
2. Put tomatoes through a sieve.
3. Finely slice onions.
4. Grate cheese.
5. Peel garlic clove. Preheat oven to 450° F.

METHOD OF COOKERY
1. Place clarified butter in frying pan and when hot add the garlic clove. Allow garlic to sweat to release oil and then discard garlic. Add the pepper strips and the onions—toss in the butter and allow to fry gently. Add the tomatoes and season with salt and pepper, the cumin, chili powder, and the oregano. Cook until the mixture has thickened (about 2 minutes).
2. Place the vegetable mixture into a shallow oven dish—make 4 hollows and break an egg into each. Decorate eggs with slices of pimiento in crisscross fashion and cover the entire surface with cheese. Bake in 450° F. oven for 7½ minutes. Serve immediately.

SERVING
Suitable as a snack dish around the fire in winter or as a light brunch on Sundays.

3 Sesame Scallops

RECIPE TO PRODUCE 6 PORTIONS	U.S.A.	IMPERIAL	METRIC
Butter	¼ cup	2 oz.	60 grams
Lemon juice	1 tbs.	1 tbs.	15 milliliters
Salt, black pepper	To season	To season	To season
Scallops	1 lb.	1 lb.	.5 kilo
Bacon slices	8	8	8
Sesame seeds	1 oz.	1 oz.	30 grams

METHOD OF PREPARATION

Melt butter and mix with lemon juice—season with salt and pepper—place scallops in this mixture. Cut bacon into slices large enough to wrap around scallops—place sesame seeds in dish—preheat oven to medium.

METHOD OF COOKERY

1. Wrap bacon around scallop. Secure with a toothpick and roll bacon in sesame seeds.
2. Place on greased oven tray and broil about 5 inches from the heat until the bacon is crisp (about 5 minutes).

SERVING

Serve with general cocktails.

12

4 Empanada Mariscada

RECIPE TO PRODUCE 20 LITTLE PIES	U.S.A.	IMPERIAL	METRIC
Crabmeat	½ cup	5 oz.	150 grams
Shrimp (raw)	½ cup	5 oz.	150 grams
Mussels	12	12	12
Dry white wine	2 tbsp.	1 fl. oz.	30 milliliters
Green pepper	1	1	1
Pimientos (tinned)	2	2	2
Salt, black pepper	To season	To season	To season
Lemon thyme	To season	To season	To season
Onion	½ medium	½ medium	½ medium
Clarified butter	1 oz.	1 oz.	30 grams
Olive oil	5 cups	2 pints	{ 1 liter / 150 milliliters
Parmesan cheese	To dust	To dust	To dust
Egg white	1	1	1
Pastry:			
Baking powder	½ tsp.	½ tsp.	2 grams
Sugar	1½ tsp.	1½ tsp.	6 grams
Salt	½ tsp.	½ tsp.	2 grams
Egg	1	1	1
Butter (melted)	1½ oz.	1½ oz.	45 grams
Sherry	¼ cup	2 fl. oz.	60 milliliters
Flour	⅝ cup	6½ oz.	195 grams

METHOD OF PREPARATION

Make dough—see method below—and chill 1 hour—roll out thinly. Place olive oil into deep fryer and set at 370° F. Dice onion finely—dice green pepper finely—finely slice shrimp—finely slice crab—finely dice pimiento. Place mussels in saucepan with dry white wine. Cover with lid and place on heat, shaking from time to time—cook 2 minutes—take mussels from shells—remove beard and finely slice—grate Parmesan.

METHOD OF COOKERY

1. Place clarified butter in frying pan and add green pepper and onion. Sauté gently and then add raw shrimp with pimiento. Stir until shrimp are pink and then add crab and mussels. Season with salt, pepper, and lemon thyme. Remove mixture from heat and allow to cool completely.
2. Cut pastry into 1½ x 3-inch pieces. Brush lightly with egg white and place a teaspoon of filling in the center of each. Dab your fingers in a little flour and fold pastry over and secure by pressing gently around edges. Drop empanadas into the hot oil and cook 3½ minutes or until puffed and golden. Turn them once.
3. Place on dish covered with paper doily and dust with grated Parmesan.

Pastry method of cookery

In a bowl mix flour with baking powder, sugar, and salt. Make a well in the center of flour and add egg, sherry, and the melted butter. Mix quickly with a spatula, forming a smooth dough. Knead lightly and then place in the refrigerator for 1 hour.

SERVING

Serve hot with a chilled dry sherry.

5 Cheese and Anchovy Crostini

RECIPE TO PRODUCE 4 PORTIONS	U.S.A.	IMPERIAL	METRIC
White bread slices	8 thin	8 thin	8 thin
Anchovy fillets	32	32	32
Mozzarella cheese	½ lb.	½ lb.	240 grams
Clarified butter	½ cup	4 oz.	120 grams
Oregano	Little	Little	Little

METHOD OF PREPARATION

1. Slice mozzarella cheese.

2. Remove crusts from bread.

3. Cut each slice into 4 fingers.

METHOD OF COOKERY

1. Place a thin slice of mozzarella cheese on each bread slice and top with anchovy fillet. Add a little oregano. Sandwich with another finger of bread.

2. Heat butter in pan and fry sandwiches on both sides until golden brown. Serve warm.

SERVING

Serve as appetizers with a white Italian chianti (they are most thirst provoking!).

6 Canadian Rolls

RECIPE TO PRODUCE 48 PIECES	U.S.A.	IMPERIAL	METRIC
Ham slices (thin)	6 oz.	6 oz.	180 grams
Smoked salmon	6 oz.	6 oz.	180 grams
Dill butter:			
Butter	½ cup	4 oz.	120 grams
Dill	4 tbs.	4 tbs.	10 grams
Horseradish butter:			
Butter	½ cup	4 oz.	120 grams
Horseradish (grated)	3 tbs.	3 tbs.	42 grams

METHOD OF PREPARATION

1. Blend butter and dill together.
2. Blend butter with horseradish.

METHOD OF COOKERY

1. Spread ham with horseradish butter. Spread smoked salmon with dill butter.
2. Roll up into small rolls. Wrap rolls in aluminum foil and place in the refrigerator.
3. Cut rolls into thin slices before serving 1-inch pieces.

SERVING

Serve skewered with cocktail sticks accompanied by general cocktails (or colonel hors d'oeuvres).

7 Mrs. Enid Small's Brandied Prunes

RECIPE TO PRODUCE 6 PORTIONS	U.S.A.	IMPERIAL	METRIC
Prunes (large dessert)	18	18	18
Brandy	¼ cup	2 fl. oz.	60 milliliters
Philadelphia cream cheese	½ cup	4 oz.	120 grams
Preserved ginger	2 oz.	2 oz.	60 grams

METHOD OF PREPARATION

1. Stone the prunes and allow to macerate for 1 hour in brandy.
2. Drain.
3. Finely chop ginger.
4. Measure cream cheese.

METHOD OF COOKERY

1. Cream cheese until soft and add ginger. Combine.
2. Place a small quantity of cream cheese mixture in each prune.

SERVING

Serve accompanied by Pisco (Argentinian grape brandy) sour.

8 Fish and Bacon Rolls

RECIPE TO PRODUCE 6 PORTIONS	U.S.A.	IMPERIAL	METRIC
Bacon slices	6	6	6
Lemon juice	1 lemon	1 lemon	1 lemon
Black pepper	To season	To season	To season
Sole fillets	12 small	12 small	12 small

METHOD OF PREPARATION

1. Remove rind from bacon if necessary.
2. Trim fillets.
3. Preheat oven to 375° F.

METHOD OF COOKERY

1. Season fish fillets with lemon juice and pepper. Roll up fillets and wrap in one thickness of bacon (approx. $4\frac{1}{2}$ inches long).
2. Arrange rolls in a lightly greased fireproof dish and cook quickly in a hot broiler.

SERVING

Serve skewered with cocktail stick and garnished with parsley and lemon wedges. Accompany with a dry white wine (Riesling style).

FIRST COURSES

9 Little Patti Tomatoes

RECIPE TO PRODUCE 4 PORTIONS	U.S.A.	IMPERIAL	METRIC
Tomatoes	8 medium	8	8
Tarragon wine vinegar	1 cup	8 fl. oz.	240 milliliters
Olive oil	¾ cup	6 fl. oz.	180 milliliters
Dry mustard	¼ tsp.	¼ tsp.	1 gram
Cayenne pepper	½ tsp.	½ tsp.	2 grams
Onion	1 medium	1	1
Garlic clove	1	1	1
Sugar	1 oz.	1 oz.	30 grams
Parsley stalks, chopped	2 tbsp.	2 tbsp.	10 grams

METHOD OF PREPARATION

1. Skin tomatoes.
2. Peel garlic clove.
3. Measure oil and vinegar.
4. Finely dice onion.

METHOD OF COOKERY

1. Mix mustard, cayenne, onion, garlic, sugar, and olive oil. Add vinegar and shake sauce well.
2. Place tomatoes in a bowl. Scatter top with chopped parsley stalks and cover with the dressing. Place in the refrigerator and leave overnight.

SERVING

As a first course with crisp hearts of lettuce and triangular pieces of finely sliced and buttered whole-wheat bread.

10 Potted Shrimp

RECIPE TO PRODUCE 2 LARGE SERVINGS	U.S.A.	IMPERIAL	METRIC
Shrimps cooked and peeled	8 oz.	8 oz.	240 grams
Butter	6 tbsp.	3 oz.	90 grams
Mace	¼ tsp.	¼ tsp.	1 gram
Nutmeg	¼ tsp.	¼ tsp.	1 gram
Cayenne pepper	To season	To season	To season
Clarified butter	To seal	To seal	To seal

METHOD OF PREPARATION

1. Measure butter.
2. Grease small pots (demitasse coffee cup size).

METHOD OF COOKERY

1. Melt fresh butter. Add the mace and nutmeg and add a good dash of cayenne pepper.
2. Add the shrimp and coat in the aromatic butter. Place in pots and when cool pour over them a little clarified butter. Refrigerate.
3. To serve, turn shrimps onto a lettuce leaf. Serve with thin slices brown bread and butter and lemon wedges. Accompany by cayenne pepper in pot.

SERVING

As a first course.

11 Poached Eggs with Chartreuse Sauce

RECIPE TO PRODUCE 4 PORTIONS	U.S.A.	IMPERIAL	METRIC
Eggs	8	8	8
Potatoes	3 lb.	3 lb.	1.5 kilos
Egg	1	1	1
Butter	¼ cup	2 oz.	60 grams
Salt, black pepper	To season	To season	To season
Nutmeg	To season	To season	To season
Butter	1 tbsp.	1 tbsp.	1 tbsp.
White Sauce			
Milk	2½ cups	1 pint	.5 liter
Butter	¼ cup	2 oz.	60 grams
Flour (all purpose)	2 tbsp.	2 tbsp.	30 grams
Salt, white pepper	To season	To season	To season
Nutmeg	To season	To season	To season
Green chartreuse	2 tbsp.	2 tbsp.	30 milliliters
Tarragon	Pinch	Pinch	Pinch
Lobster	6 oz.	6 oz.	180 grams
Paprika	To garnish	To garnish	To garnish
Dill	To garnish	To garnish	To garnish
Pimiento (tinned)	To garnish	To garnish	To garnish

METHOD OF PREPARATION

1. Make the White Sauce (pp. 256-57, rec. 216 for Basic Method).
2. Bake potatoes in their jackets and mash.
3. Finely chop dill and slice pimiento.
4. Heat broiler unit.
5. Slice lobster into thin round slices (collops).

METHOD OF COOKERY

1. Add 1 egg and ¼ cup butter to mashed potatoes and season with salt, pepper, and nutmeg. Pipe a ring of mashed potatoes onto scallop shells or small ovenproof dishes. Place under broiler unit to brown.
2. Add sliced lobster to sauce, season with the tarragon, and add the chartreuse. Simmer 2 minutes.
3. In a frying pan filled with boiling salted water place the tablespoon of butter and when melted break in the eggs—remove pan from the heat and allow eggs to set. Remove, drain, and place 2 eggs in each dish. Cover with lobster sauce. Garnish with paprika, chopped dill, and slices of red pimiento.

SERVING

As a first course or for a Sunday supper.

12 Melon Treena

RECIPE TO PRODUCE 2 PORTIONS	U.S.A.	IMPERIAL	METRIC
Canteloupe (rock melon)	1 small	1 small	1 small
Sour cream	3 tbsp.	3 tbsp.	45 milliliters
Preserved ginger	1 oz.	1 oz.	30 grams
Ginger syrup	2 tbsp.	2 tbsp.	30 milliliters

METHOD OF PREPARATION

1. Finely chop ginger into slivers.
2. Cut cantaloupe in half and remove seeds.
3. Mix sour cream with ginger.

METHOD OF COOKERY

1. Fill cantaloupe halves with sour cream.
2. Decorate with ginger slivers and pour over a little ginger syrup. Chill.

SERVING

As a first course with a late-picked Rhine wine, Riesling style. This flexible dish can also be served as a dessert.

13 Grapefruit and Orange Cocktail

RECIPE TO PRODUCE 4 PORTIONS	U.S.A.	IMPERIAL	METRIC
Grapefruit	2	2	2
Oranges	2	2	2
Superfine granulated sugar	2 tbsp.	2 tbsp.	60 grams
Mint (chopped)	To season	To season	To season
Light rum	⅛ cup	1 fl. oz.	30 milliliters

METHOD OF PREPARATION

Halve grapefruit and remove flesh in segments—cut oranges into segments—finely chop mint.

METHOD OF COOKERY

1. Combine orange and grapefruit segments. Add the sugar and rum.
2. Place mixture into grapefruit shells. Garnish with chopped mint and chill.

SERVING

As a first course.

14 Spaghetti con Salse di Vongole

RECIPE TO PRODUCE 6 PORTIONS	U.S.A.	IMPERIAL	METRIC
Spaghetti	1 lb.	1 lb.	.5 kilo
Sauce:			
Clams (tinned)	10 oz.	10 oz.	300 grams
Parsley	3 tbsp.	3 tbsp.	15 grams
Capers	1 tbsp.	1 tbsp.	5 grams
Salt, black pepper	To season	To season	To season
Tomatoes	1 lb.	1 lb.	1 lb.
Olive oil	3 tbsp.	3 tbsp.	45 grams
Garlic clove	1	1	1

METHOD OF PREPARATION

Bring 1 gallon (4.5 liters) of salted water to the boil and place the ends of the spaghetti in the pot, bending the strips as they soften—make sure strands are separated by prodding gently around with a fork—cook spaghetti for 7 minutes—then take 1 pint (.5 liter) ice water and pour into spaghetti in the pot—remove from heat and pour into a colander—place spaghetti back in pan, toss with a little olive oil, and keep warm—peel garlic clove—finely chop capers—finely chop parsley—skin, seed, and chop tomatoes.

METHOD OF COOKERY

1. Place oil in a frying pan and when hot add the capers and crushed garlic. Sauté gently—don't brown.
2. Add tomatoes and parsley and cook 5 minutes over gentle heat.
3. Add the clams to tomato sauce—season with salt and black pepper. Cook uncovered to heat clams in sauce.
4. Place spaghetti on serving dish and pour sauce over it.

SERVING

As a filling first course during the winter or as a casual main dish with a dry chianti.

About Soup

Soup is international, often easy to prepare, filling, and homely.

For most of the year our climate is too mild for hot creamy soups. In the winter they come into their own. Essentially soup is either thick or thin. Thick soups are filling. Thin soups should have a stimulating effect upon the appetite. Because of this I feel that thick soups must be highly nutritious—especially when they are used to replace, in part, a substantial element of the main course.

Thick soups filled with fresh vegetables and moistened with meat or fish stocks are a luxury when made in the home. Canned and packet soups should be used when time is short or the raw material is out of season or hard to buy.

Thin soups should be a great delicacy. Traditionally the famous *consommé* is the product of many hours' slow cooking; the result is almost beyond effective description—amber and golden liquids, crystal clear, smooth, and succulent to the taste. Today, without old-fashioned stoves, it is difficult to find space for a large stockpot, and only the fanatics leave their stoves on for twenty-four hours at a stretch to produce "but a pint of shining innocence."

By far the easiest alternative is the preprepared soup. A well-made *bouillon* can fill the bill. After all, its real purpose is to stimulate and not satisfy—if it stimulates, then the appetite is more capable of absorbing maximum goodness from the following dishes.

I have found that many people still have the feeling that soup is only soup when prepared in the home, and therefore I have given, on page 26, recipe 15, Thin Soups—Basic Method a compromise technique by which a "stimulating" soup can be prepared in thirty minutes. The soup shown in the photograph on pages 34-35 is made by the same method. It is clear, golden, and aromatic but lacks the smooth rich flavor obtained from the slow simmering of many bones.

I believe that our best choice of soups is made from fish or shellfish—especially when thickened with fresh vegetables and cream. I am dedicated to the proposal that no more than three courses should be attempted at one meal, and a fish soup provides an excellent answer to the merger of soup and fish course. I have included my favorite seafood soups so that you can experiment. When you think about it, there are more famous fish soups than there are soups based on meat, poultry, or vegetables. *Moules marinière* (mussels), *bisque d'Homard* (lobster), *bouillabaisse* (all in), *clam chowder,* and *shark's fin* are but a few. If you find mine interesting, then we could well add to these international soup stars with *sea truffle* (abalone, paua), *kaikoura* (crayfish or lobster), and *toheroa* (giant green clam).

CONTENTS OF SECTION

15 THIN SOUPS

RECIPE TO PRODUCE 1 PINT

	U.S.A.	IMPERIAL	METRIC
Shin of beef	8 oz.	8 oz.	.25 kilo
Oil	1 tsp.	1 tsp.	1 tsp.
Salt	To season	To season	To season
Carrot	2-in. piece	½ oz.	15 grams
Celery	3-in. stalk	½ oz.	15 grams
Parsnip	2-in. piece	½ oz.	15 grams
Onion	4 thin slices	½ oz.	15 grams
Cold water	2¼ cups	1 pint	570 milliliters
Bay leaf	1	1	1
Clove	1	1	1
Garlic	Size of pea	Size of pea	Size of pea
Parsley	1 stalk	1 stalk	1 stalk
White of egg	1	1	1

Step 1
The meat selected depends upon the end use. If you want a light negative stock, then use veal neck meat. In this case the meat is shin of really old beef. Sprinkle it liberally with salt to draw out the natural juices.

Step 2
In oil, fry the vegetables, meat, and garlic together until a golden brown. You can see the pan base where the juices have adhered and become browned.

COMMENT ON METHOD

I'm not at all sure that the famous consommé isn't on the way out—that is, when it is prepared at home. Yards of bones, a three-gallon pot, and at least twelve hours of pot watching don't make much sense. In this recipe I have tried to produce a seasoned liquid capable of being used as a soup, stock, or sauce base. You could call it a last-ditch stand by the "do-it-yourselfer" to the can.

METHOD OF PREPARATION

1. Chop or mince beef finely.
2. Finely slice carrots, celery, and parsnips.
3. Measure water.
4. Crush garlic.

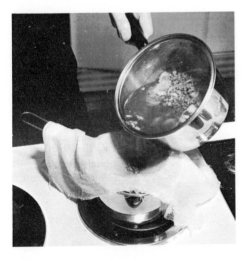 

Step 3
Add water and remaining herbs; cover and cook for 30 minutes. Now strain off the seasoned liquid through muslin into a clean saucepan.

Step 4
Add 1 white of egg and whip it to a froth in the stock. Bring to the boil, take it off the heat for 2 minutes, then boil again. Now skim the egg white off the top. This clears the liquid and it can now be used or frozen ready for future use.

16 Billabong

RECIPE TO PRODUCE 4 PORTIONS	U.S.A.	IMPERIAL	METRIC
Rich beef stock (p. 26, rec. 15)	2½ cups	1 pint	570 milliliters
Onion	1 small	2 oz.	60 grams
Garlic cloves	1	1	1
Tomato	½ small	3 oz.	85 grams
White pepper	To taste	To taste	To taste
Sorrel*	3 leaves	3 leaves	3 leaves
Salt	To season	To season	To season
Parsley	1 tbsp.	1 tbsp.	5 grams

*If sorrel is not available substitute 3 fresh spinach leaves and add 1 teaspoon lemon juice.

METHOD OF PREPARATION
1. Make and clarify beef stock.
2. Slice onion ⅟₁₆-inch thick.
3. Crush garlic.
4. Skin and slice tomato and sorrel finely.
5. Chop parsley.

METHOD OF COOKERY
1. Place onion and crushed garlic in a saucepan and cover with stock. Simmer 8 minutes until onion is tender.
2. Lay tomato slices in soup plates, dust with salt and white pepper, finely sliced sorrel and parsley.
3. Pour boiling soup and onions over tomatoes and herbs.

SERVING
Soup can be poured or ladled at the table, the warm soup plates being placed in front of the guests with tomato and herbs added.

17 Chicken Pepper Pot

RECIPE TO PRODUCE 4 PORTIONS	U.S.A.	IMPERIAL	METRIC
Roast chicken carcass	1	1	1
Onion	1 small	2 oz.	60 grams
Cloves	3	3	3
Bay leaf	1	1	1
Lemon thyme	1 sprig	1 sprig	1 sprig
Carrot	1 small	2 oz.	60 grams
Water	10 cups	4 pints	2.4 liters
Egg white	1	1	1
Celery	1 stalk	2 oz.	60 grams
Green bell pepper	1	1	1

METHOD OF PREPARATION

1. Peel onion and stick with cloves.
2. Peel and finely slice carrot.
3. Shred celery and green pepper very finely.

METHOD OF COOKERY

1. Cover carcass with 10 cups water, add onion and herbs and simmer 4 hours. Boil down to 2½ cups; remove fat.
2. Clarify with whipped egg white.
3. Add shredded vegetables and simmer until just tender.
4. Taste and adjust seasoning if necessary.

SERVING

Best when served with hot whole-wheat rolls and butter.

Ⓖ **For Oyster Soup see page 196.**

Farmhouse Vegetable Soup

RECIPE TO PRODUCE 4 PORTIONS	U.S.A.	IMPERIAL	METRIC
Carrots	2 medium	6 oz.	170 grams
Kumera or turnip	½ small	3 oz.	85 grams
Parsnips	1 small	3 oz.	85 grams
Onions	1 medium	4 oz.	115 grams
Clarified butter	4 tbsp.	2 oz.	60 grams
Garlic	1 clove	1 clove	1 clove
Stock	1¾ cups	15 fl. oz.	430 milliliters
Cream	½ cup	4 fl. oz.	115 milliliters
Salt	To season	To season	To season
Black peppercorns	9	9	9
Bay leaf	3	3	3
Parsley stalks	4	4	4
Lemon thyme sprigs	3	3	3

Step 1
Add to your sliced vegetables a collection of vegetable peelings saved from the day or meal before. Keep them in a plastic bag in the refrigerator.

Step 2
Melt the clarified butter in a frying pan; add the chilled sliced vegetables and cook gently for 4 minutes.

COMMENT ON METHOD

Surprising as it may seem, we had a farmhouse vegetable soup on the menu at the fashion-able Royal Ascot Hotel. As a soup it was the best seller, beating real turtle and royal game. This basic method is the recipe we used. The kumera is a Maori vegetable grown in New Zealand—a type of sweet potato.

METHOD OF PREPARATION

1. Peel chilled vegetables or, if good skins, then just wash well and slice.
2. Measure out stock and cream.
3. Tie herbs together.

Step 3
Add soup stock or broth (see page 26 for quick method). Add herbs and simmer for 20 minutes until vegetables are tender. Remove herbs.

Step 4
Place liquid and vegetables into a blender or a rotary sieve. Whip or sieve and finish with the cream. Season to taste and serve.

19 Toheroa
(Giant Green Clam from New Zealand—the Rarest Food Item in the World)

RECIPE TO PRODUCE 4 PORTIONS

	U.S.A.	IMPERIAL	METRIC
Butter	1 tbsp.	½ oz.	15 grams
Flour	½ oz.	½ oz.	15 grams
Fish stock (p. 196, rec. 146)	1¼ cup	10 fl. oz.	285 milliliters
Milk	10 tbsp.	5 fl. oz.	140 milliliters
Minced toheroas*	4 oz.	4 oz.	115 grams
Lemon juice	To taste	To taste	To taste
Salt	To season	To season	To season
White pepper	To season	To season	To season
Chopped parsley	To garnish	To garnish	To garnish
Cream	2 tbsp.	1 fl. oz.	30 milliliters

*Local clams can be used but the true delicacy demands this very rare shellfish that can be purchased in canned form at very good stores.

METHOD OF PREPARATION

1. Prepare fish stock and measure.
2. Boil milk.
3. Open tin of toheroa or mince fresh toheroa.
4. Measure butter and flour.

METHOD OF COOKERY

1. Melt butter and combine with flour. Stir in fish stock.
2. Add boiling milk with minced toheroa—beat until smooth.
3. Add lemon juice and seasoning to taste.
4. Dust surface with chopped parsley and pour in a drop of cream.

SERVING

Serve, if possible, in rough glazed pottery bowls with lemon wedges and thin-sliced and buttered brown bread.

20 Sea Truffle
(Abalone)

RECIPE TO PRODUCE 5-6 PORTIONS

	U.S.A.	IMPERIAL	METRIC
Milk	1½ cups	12 fl. oz.	340 milliliters
Water	1½ cups	12 fl. oz.	340 milliliters
Onion	1 medium	3 oz.	85 grams
Celery	3 stalks	6 oz.	170 grams
Butter	3 tbsp.	1½ oz.	45 grams
Garlic cloves	3 small	3 small	3 small
Minced abalone*	1 lb.	1 lb.	.5 kilo
Meat or vegetable protein extract	3 tbsp.	3 tbsp.	55 milliliters
Arrowroot	3 tbsp.	3 tbsp.	30 grams
Lemon juice	3 tbsp.	3 tbsp.	55 milliliters
Fresh parsley	3 tbsp.	3 tbsp.	25 grams

*Available canned in specialty stores.

METHOD OF PREPARATION

1. Mince abalone finely.
2. Mix milk and water.
3. Peel and slice finely the onion and celery.
4. Peel and crush garlic.
5. Measure arrowroot, lemon juice, and meat extract.
6. Chop parsley.

METHOD OF COOKERY

1. Melt butter in pan and shallow fry vegetables with garlic to soften.
2. Put in blender† with milk and water, and blend.
3. Add abalone and blend again.
4. Place back over heat and add extract and lemon juice. Bring to boil and stir in the arrowroot paste until it thickens and becomes glossy.
5. Taste and add more lemon and seasonings if necessary.

†A food mill can be used just as well.

SERVING

Serve in the same way as the toheroa soup but add, if possible, some chilled sprigs of watercress. These are eaten with the fingers and **not** dunked into the soup!

Billabong Soup, recipe page 28

About Fish

Although we are well known for our production of meat, by far the greatest volume and variety of foods are available from the sea. At least 200 separate species of edible fish and shellfish live around our shores.

Our failure to eat fish is only a habit. We are used to the preparation of meat and basically lack knowledge on how to process seafoods.

If you study our eating habits you will come up with an extremely interesting discovery. We eat fish in large quantity from restaurants, and hotels. But if you relate this consumption to the home we should be eating at least three fish meals a week! Why aren't we?

There are two main reasons: firstly, you must have heard the comment "I don't like to handle it." Secondly, regardless of religious belief, we have become accustomed to the habit of eating fish on Fridays and disregarding it during the remainder of the week.

Fish preparation need not be a messy business. At this date there are a few packs of filleted fish sold in aroma-proof plastic bags. There is no preparation. Some people regard this method of purchase as expensive. On face value I'd agree, but if you dig a little deeper and buy a whole fish, weigh it, cut off the fillets, and then compare their cost with an equal quantity of packaged fillets, you will be surprised how little extra you're paying for the fillets.

I support this type of packaging because it overcomes the basic problem of handling. However, I still want to be able to buy some whole fish for baking, fillets with their skins left on for frying and broiling, and heads, bones, and trimmings for fish stocks, soups, and sauces. By the way, the suggestion that your hands smell of fish is rubbish—a good rinsing under the cold tap will get rid of the smell instantly.

By far the greatest problem is the "fish for Friday" habit. For those who have no religious restrictions fish is served on Friday because people feel that it is fresher—there is very little fact to support this theory, especially now that ships stay at sea longer and refrigerate their catch almost immediately after it is taken from the water.

What I don't like is that fish is regarded as a "change" from beef, lamb, pork, veal, or poultry, and yet, in my opinion "fish" is not just "fish." It is the same as saying that "I'm going to eat 'meat' from Saturday through to Thursday."

There are fish in our waters that differ in taste, texture, and appearance in just as marked a way as the different meats vary. I know a lot of people who get just as much satisfaction by ringing the changes with fish as they get by changing the Sunday roast!

I suppose that all this adds up to the fact that we just don't *know* a great deal about our local fish and especially how to cook it. Generally speaking, there are few housewives who can tell one piece of fish from another, few that can name more than five varieties of fresh fish, and when the fish is purchased there are few that know more than three ways to cook it.

The other day I overheard a discussion between two country lads. One said to the other, "Saw yer eatin' fish 'n' chips t'other day, mate." The other replied indignantly, "Give over, Charlie—it wasn't fish, yer know—'twas scallops!"

Perhaps we are getting somewhere after all!

CONTENTS OF SECTION

21 DEEP-FRIED FISH

RECIPE TO PRODUCE 4 PORTIONS	U.S.A.	IMPERIAL	METRIC
Codfish	1½ lb.	1½ lb.	.75 kilo
Cold milk	To cover	To cover	To cover
Flour	To coat	To coat	To coat
Salt	To season	To season	To season
White peppercorns			
Yeast frying Batter (p. 254-55, rec. 213)			
Oil for deep frying			

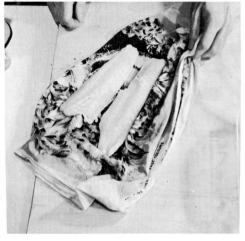 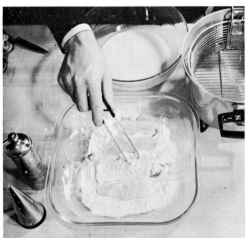

Step 1
Dry the fish well with a clean cloth or paper towel. The soaking period in milk both enhances the flavor and obviously whitens the flesh.

Step 2
Toss the fillets in the seasoned flour until they are all thoroughly coated.

COMMENT ON METHOD

Before I started my television career I used to buy my children fish and chips from an excellent local fish shop. This habit ended abruptly one day when a fellow customer pointed at me and yelled with much mirth, "Ah, now we know what you eat at home." The overfull shop dissolved in laughter. We now prepare our own and, frankly, I'm delighted.

METHOD OF PREPARATION

1. Soak fish in cold milk before cookery, about 1 hour.
2. Season the flour.
3. Heat oil in deep fryer to 370° F.

Step 3
Using a pair of tongs, place floured fillets in the batter—allow excess to drip off and then transfer to the hot oil.

Step 4
Cook at 370° F. for 4 minutes, turning them after 2 minutes. Place on a dish covered with paper doilies and serve with deep-fried parsley.

22　Thames Whitebait

RECIPE TO PRODUCE 4 PORTIONS	U.S.A.	IMPERIAL	METRIC
Whitebait*	1 lb.	1 lb.	5 kilo
Milk	1¼ cups	10 fl. oz.	285 milliliters
Salt	To season	To season	To season
White peppercorns	To season	To season	To season
Flour	6 tbsp.	1½ oz.	45 grams
Lemon	1	1	1
Oil	To deep fry	To deep fry	To deep fry

*A very small whole fish approximately 2 inches long
  cooked whole.

METHOD OF PREPARATION

1. Use fresh whitebait if possible. If deep frozen, then defrost—soak in milk for ½ hour and dry thoroughly.
2. Slice lemon for service.
3. Heat oil to 350° F.

METHOD OF COOKERY

1. Season whitebait with salt and freshly ground white peppercorns.
2. Dust with flour; separate each fish and drop them into heated fat.
3. Deep fry until light brown—approximately 1½ minutes.
4. Remove, drain, and serve with slices of lemon.

SERVING

An ideal first course. Serve with fine slices of buttered brown bread. A light dry white wine goes well, or even a very cold Mateus rosé.

23 South Australian Shellfish Cakes

RECIPE TO PRODUCE 2 PORTIONS	U.S.A.	IMPERIAL	METRIC
Crayfish* meat—preferably uncooked	¼ cup	2 oz.	60 grams
Flounder fillets	¼ cup	2 oz.	60 grams
Mushrooms, diced	1 cup	2 oz.	60 grams
Clarified butter	3 tbsp.	1½ oz.	45 grams
Lemon juice	2 tbsp.	1 fl. oz.	30 milliliters
White Sauce (p. 256-57, rec. 216)	¾ cup	6 fl. oz.	170 milliliters
Paprika	¼ tsp.	¼ tsp.	¼ tsp.
Flour	6 tbsp.	1½ oz.	45 grams
Egg } mix together	1	1	1
Oil }	2 tbsp.	2 tbsp.	30 milliliters
Breadcrumbs	½ cup	2 oz.	60 grams
Oil for deep frying			

*Lobster meat or shrimp may be used instead.

METHOD OF PREPARATION

1. Make white sauce very thick, using an extra ounce each of butter and flour to basic recipe—use half stock from poached flounder, half milk.
2. Finely dice flounder, crayfish, and mushrooms.
3. Measure flour and breadcrumbs.
4. Mix egg and oil.
5. Heat oil in deep fryer to 400° F.
6. Toss mushrooms in butter with 1 tablespoon lemon juice.

METHOD OF COOKERY

1. Mix crayfish, flounder, and mushrooms into thick sauce. Add butter in which mushrooms were cooked.
2. Add remaining lemon juice and paprika.
3. Weigh mixture and divide into 6 equal portions.
4. Roll in flour, dip in egg and oil mixture, and then coat thoroughly in breadcrumbs.
5. Deep fry for 1 minute until golden brown.

SERVING

These are wonderful when served with Golden Coast Sauce (p. 68, rec. 52) and a crisp green salad with an oil and vinegar dressing (p. 263). A chilled Moselle-type white wine would belance well.

© For Fairfield Flounder Fillets see page 197.

RECIPE TO PRODUCE 2 PORTIONS

	U.S.A.	IMPERIAL	METRIC
Large flounder or turbot	2 lb.	2 lb.	1 kilo
Flour	To coat	To coat	To coat
Salt	To season	To season	To season
White peppercorns	To season	To season	To season
Butter	$\frac{1}{4}$ cup	2 oz.	60 grams
Parsley	To garnish	To garnish	To garnish
Lemon wedges	To garnish	To garnish	To garnish

Step 1
Remove fins and detach the head as shown. Carefully peel back the skin from the tail with a sharp knife. Dip fingers in salt and give the skin a sharp even tug. Clean the area from which the head has been taken with a salt-dipped cloth.

Step 2
Coat fish with seasoned flour. Add butter to a moderate-heat pan (350° F.).

COMMENT ON METHOD

Most recipe methods for shallow-fried fish begin with the miller's wife technique given below. According to legend, the miller was up to his hocks in the nearby stream fishing, when his wife (hard at work) heard him shout "Mon Dieu, j'ai une truite"—literally, "My God, I've got a trout." She sped to his side, clasped the trout to her ample flour-covered bosom, ran for the kitchen, and flopped it into foaming butter—hence the method. Surely a lesson in good feminine behavior?

METHOD OF PREPARATION

1. Season flour with freshly ground white peppercorns and salt.
2. Heat frying pan to 350° F.

Step 3
Place the fish in the pan skinned side down. Cook for approximately 4 minutes and then turn and cook for a further 4 minutes, until the flesh can be lifted from the bone.

Step 4
Lay the cooked fish on a dish, dust with freshly chopped parsley and add some extra butter to the pan. Raise the heat until the butter just begins to go light brown—pour this over the fish. The parsley will sizzle; the result—delicious. The fish can be neatly divided into two portions by cutting down the middle with chicken scissors. Serve with lemon wedges.

25 Nelson Flounder Fillets

RECIPE TO PRODUCE 4 PORTIONS	U.S.A.	IMPERIAL	METRIC
Flounder fillets	1 lb.	1 lb.	.5 kilo
Flour	To coat	To coat	To coat
Salt	To season	To season	To season
Pepper	To season	To season	To season
Clarified butter	To fry	To fry	To fry
Tomato	1 medium	8 oz.	230 grams
Garlic clove	1	1	1
Parsley	To dust	To dust	To dust

METHOD OF PREPARATION

1. Fillet flounder if bought whole.
2. Season and flour.
3. Skin and slice tomato $\frac{1}{4}$-inch thick.
4. Chop parsley.
5. Crush garlic.
6. Season tomato with salt and pepper.
7. Heat serving dish.

METHOD OF COOKERY

1. Fry fillets as per basic method in clarified butter.
2. Remove from pan and add seasoned tomato and crushed garlic. Fry quickly.
3. Lay fish on serving dish, cover fillets completely with tomato slices. Dust with parsley and serve.

SERVING

Plain boiled herb buttered potatoes (pp. 218-19, rec. 165) and a dressed Salad (pp. 246-47, rec. 207). Quite a robust dry white wine goes well.

26 Grouper Cutlets Island Bay

RECIPE TO PRODUCE 2 PORTIONS	U.S.A.	IMPERIAL	METRIC
Grouper* cutlets (1 inch thick)	2 7-oz.	2 7-oz.	2 200-gram
White peppercorns	To season	To season	To season
Salt	To season	To season	To season
Fresh nutmeg	To season	To season	To season
Flour	¼ cup	1 oz.	30 grams
Clarified butter	¼ cup	2 oz.	60 grams
Shallots†	½ cup	2 oz.	60 grams
Dry white wine	¼ cup	2 fl. oz.	60 milliliters
Chopped parsley	1 tbsp.	1 tbsp.	5 grams

*Haddock or cod.
†Scallions or green onions if shallots are not available.

METHOD OF PREPARATION

1. Dry cutlets and season with salt, freshly ground peppercorns, and grated nutmeg (very little). Dust with flour.
2. Finely slice shallots (or small onions).
3. Chop parsley.
4. Measure wine.
5. Heat frying pan to 300° F.
6. Heat serving dish.

METHOD OF COOKERY

1. Melt butter in pan. Add shallots.
2. Lay cutlets on shallots.
3. Cook 5 minutes either side, reducing heat to 250° F., when cooked on first side.
4. Remove to serving dish.
5. Pour off any excess fat. Add wine and bring to boil.
6. Dust cutlets with parsley and coat them with the reduced wine.

SERVING

Bennet Potatoes (p. 223, rec. 173). Green Beans in winter (p. 236, rec. 190) and a good salad dressed with Blue Vein Salad Dressing in the summer (p. 262, rec. 226). A cool white wine can be served.

Ⓖ **For Potts Point Fish Pot see page 198.**

27 BROILED FISH

RECIPE	U.S.A.	IMPERIAL	METRIC
Gurnard (filleted)*	1 per head	1 per head	1 per head
Flour	To coat	To coat	To coat
Salt	To season	To season	To season
White peppercorns	To season	To season	To season
Clarified butter	To brush	To brush	To brush

*Or small rainbow trout (9 inches maximum).

Step 1
Make diagonal incisions into the fleshy part of the fillet, cutting deeper where the flesh is thickest. This helps to speed cookery.

Step 2
Season the fillets and brush on the clarified butter.

COMMENT ON METHOD

Apart from certain flat fish such as sole and flounder, there is an infallible rule to apply to broiled fish. The skin must not be removed before cookery. The reason for this is simple. The skin has a layer of natural fat between it and the flesh. This fat bastes the fish and imparts a wonderful taste and aroma. Removing the skin is like taking all the fat off a leg of lamb before roasting—silly, isn't it?

METHOD OF PREPARATION

1. Season the flour.
2. Melt the butter.
3. Heat broiler (medium hot).
4. Grease the rungs of the broiler.

Step 3
Place skin down in the flour and brush the inside surface with butter—flour this side. Shake off any surplus and place onto the broiler.

Step 4
Just before broiling, brush over with butter once more. Broil at medium to hot for 5 minutes either side.

28 Broiled Lemon Sole, Parsley Butter

RECIPE TO PRODUCE 2 PORTIONS	U.S.A.	IMPERIAL	METRIC
Sole	2 8 oz.	2 8 oz.	2 230-grams
Clarified butter	4 tbsp.	2 oz.	60 grams
Salt, white peppercorns	To season	To season	To season
Butter:			
Butter	4 tbsp.	2 oz.	60 grams
Parsley	1 tbsp.	1 tbsp.	5 grams
Cayenne pepper	¼ tsp.	¼ tsp.	¼ tsp.
Lemon juice	1 tbsp.	1 tbsp.	15 milliliters
Garlic clove	½	½	½

METHOD OF PREPARATION

1. Trim sole as per fried flounder (p. 42).
2. Remove white skin only.
3. Loosen fillets from bone.
4. Heat broiler to moderate.
Butter:
5. Soften butter.
6. Chop parsley.
7. Measure pepper, lemon juice.
8. Crush garlic.
9. Grind peppercorns finely.

METHOD OF COOKERY

1. Season sole both sides, brush with clarified butter.
2. Brush broiler rack with butter. Begin cooking skin side uppermost 3 inches away from heat.
3. Give 3 minutes on skin side, turn and brush with butter again. Cook 1 minute longer—until slightly browned.
Butter:
4. Add all ingredients to softened butter—roll in greaseproof paper to form long roll 1 inch in diameter—put in refrigerator until firm.
5. Cut in thin slices and place on fish just before serving.

SERVING

Moreland Potatoes (p. 218, rec. 166), buttered Swiss chard (pp. 236-37, rec. 189). A light dry wine is the best match.

29 Broiled Pebble River Eel

RECIPE TO PRODUCE 1 PORTION

	U.S.A.	IMPERIAL	METRIC
Small silverbelly eel	1	1	1
Flour	To dust	To dust	To dust
Clarified butter	To brush	To brush	To brush
Salt	To season	To season	To season
White peppercorns	To season	To season	To season

METHOD OF PREPARATION

1. Clean eel inside and out. Dust with flour and season with salt, freshly ground peppercorns.
2. Melt butter.
3. Preheat broiler to medium heat, rack on top shelf.

METHOD OF COOKERY

1. Curl eel in a circle, fixing mouth to the tail with wire.
2. Brush eel with clarified butter.
3. Place in broiler and cook 10 minutes or until tender right through and skin falls back.
4. Pull skin away, remove wire, and serve quite plain.

SERVING

The eel has been broiled in a circle shape. Fill the center of this circle with Ngauruhoe Potatoes (p. 222, rec. 172) and surround the eel with freshly cooked peas. This is a perfect dish for the barbecue. Serve with well-chilled light lager-type beer.

Ⓖ **For Taupo Trout Steaks with Herb Butter see page 199.**

30 POACHED FISH

RECIPE TO PRODUCE 4 PORTIONS

	U.S.A.	IMPERIAL	METRIC
Young scrod or North Sea cod	2 lb.	2 lb.	1 kilo
Stock	⅝ cup	5 fl. oz.	140 milliliters
Milk	⅝ cup	5 fl. oz.	140 milliliters
Butter	2 oz.	2 oz.	60 grams
Flour	½ cup	2¼ oz.	70 grams
Milk—for sauce	1¼ cup	10 fl. oz.	285 milliliters
Dry white wine	¼ cup	2 fl. oz.	60 milliliters
Salt	To season	To season	To season
White peppercorns	To season	To season	To season

Step 1
Place the fillets in a shallow dish and add the 5 fluid ounces of milk. Leave to soak for 1 hour.

Step 2
Place on a gentle heat (or in an oven set at 250° F.) and add 5 fluid ounces of fish stock (made from the bones cooked for 30 minutes). Cover and cook for 8 minutes—do not boil. Test for doneness by easing away the flesh with a knife point.

COMMENT ON METHOD

I think that the poaching method of cooking fish is excellent. It is a pity that it is so seldom used. So many varied flavors and garnishes can be added to the sauce, and the whole task, including the sauce, is over in 20 minutes. One word of warning. Some fish sauces that include white wine go gray when cooked in an *aluminum* pot. To be on the safe side use good Teflon.

METHOD OF PREPARATION

1. Brush the poaching dish with butter.
2. Combine stock and milk for poaching liquid.
3. Measure butter, flour, wine.

Step 3
While fish is poaching, make up basic White Sauce with milk (pp. 256-57, rec. 216) but do not add herbs. Strain off cooking liquid from fish into the sauce. Add the wine and beat well.

Step 4
Add whatever seasoning or garnishes you wish to the sauce and pour it over the fillets.

51

31 Cod, Capers, and Egg Sauce

RECIPE TO PRODUCE 4-6 PORTIONS	U.S.A.	IMPERIAL	METRIC
Young scrod or North Sea cod	2 lb.	2 lb.	1 kilo
Stock	⅝ cup	5 fl. oz.	140 milliliters
Milk	⅝ cup	5 fl. oz.	140 milliliters
Butter	2 tbsp.	1 oz.	30 grams
Flour	5 tbsp.	1¼ oz.	35 grams
Eggs	2	2	2
Capers	1 tbsp.	1 tbsp.	10 grams
Dry matured grated cheese	½ cup	2 oz.	60 grams
Parsley	To dust	To dust	To dust
Paprika	To dust	To dust	To dust

METHOD OF PREPARATION

1. Butter the poaching dish.
2. Boil eggs until center is just moist (6 minutes) and roughly chop.
3. Measure butter, flour, capers, and poaching liquid.
4. Chop parsley.

METHOD OF COOKERY

1. Poach fish in stock and milk in greased dish for about 8 minutes.
2. Make a roux with butter and flour while fish is poaching; pour off poaching liquid from fish (10 fluid ounces) and make a quick sauce.
3. Add chopped eggs, capers, and pour fish on serving dish. Scatter with cheese and brown under grill.
4. Dust with parsley and paprika and serve.

SERVING

Either peas, stringless beans, or asparagus go well when cooked completely plain. Neither potato nor rice go well—it is really best to leave all starches alone. A very light dry white wine.

32 Bay of Plenty Pie

RECIPE TO PRODUCE 4-6 PORTIONS	U.S.A.	IMPERIAL	METRIC
Lemon sole fillets	1 lb.	1 lb.	.5 kilo
White wine	½ cup	4 fl. oz.	115 milliliters
Milk	1¼ cups	10 fl. oz.	285 milliliters
New Zealand spinach*	1 lb.	1 lb.	.5 kilo
Salt	To season	To season	To season
Potatoes	2 lb.	2 lb.	1 kilo
Asparagus	6 spears	6 spears	6 spears
Egg	1	1	1
White peppercorns	To season	To season	To season
Lemons	1	1	1
Parsley	1 good spray	1 good spray	1 good spray
Paprika	To garnish	To garnish	To garnish
Butter, melted	½ cup	4 oz.	115 grams

*Or regular spinach.

METHOD OF PREPARATION

1. Measure wine, milk. Marinate fillets in this mixture for 30 minutes.
2. Wash spinach thoroughly.
3. Butter dish.
4. Peel and boil potatoes.
5. Chop parsley.
6. Cut lemon wedges and dip ends in water and then in parsley.
7. Melt butter.
8. Preheat broiler to moderate.

METHOD OF COOKERY

1. Poach fish fillets in its marinade of wine and milk for 8 minutes.
2. Finely slice the spinach, season and cook in a little butter in a covered saucepan for 3 minutes.
3. Place half the spinach in a buttered casserole, cover with the poached fillets, add a further layer of spinach.
4. Heat up potatoes in milk, butter, and freshly ground peppercorns. Add raw egg and cooked asparagus and cream well until mushy.
5. Put potato mix into a pastry bag and decorate entire surface of pie.
6. Broil to brown the surface. Serve with lemon wedges cut to overlap dish. Dust with parsley and paprika.

SERVING

Serve with a colorful tossed Salad (pp. 246-47, rec. 207)—it already has its potato and vegetable in the pie. Best when served with sparkling cold beer.

Ⓖ **For Tarakihi Tauranga see page 200.**

33 BAKED FISH

RECIPE TO PRODUCE 4 PORTIONS	U.S.A.	IMPERIAL	METRIC
Butterfish, trout, or small salmon	2½-3 lb.	2½-3 lb.	1-1.5 kilo
Salt	To season	To season	To season
Black peppercorns	To season	To season	To season
Clarified butter	4 tbsp.	2 oz.	60 grams

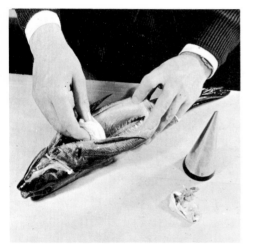 

Step 1
Wipe inside fish with a muslin pad dipped in salt. All whole fish should be cleaned in this way.

Step 2
Cut through thickest part of the body with diagonal strokes to a depth of ½ to 1 inch. Season well with salt and freshly ground black peppercorns. Rub the seasonings into the incisions.

COMMENT ON METHOD

A whole baked fish can be delicious, and if you can't lay your hands on a trout then there are many commercially available fish that make a good substitute. The butterfish shown in this basic method is a wonderful purchase and when served with lemon butter sauce—boy oh boy! If you can get a trout, then toss away the wet newspaper and try this method—it works.

METHOD OF PREPARATION

1. Prepare a muslin pad for cleaning fish.
2. Wash fish thoroughly and dry inside and out.
3. Preheat oven to 350° F.

Step 3
Baste thoroughly with melted clarified butter. You will note that the fish is placed on grill bars in a roasting dish. This provides all-round heat and helps to turn the fish onto the serving dish.

Step 4
Bake the fish at 350° F. for 8 minutes either side until the flesh comes easily from the bone. Turn the fish onto an oval dish and strip off the skin.

34 Baked Striped Mullet

RECIPE TO PRODUCE 2 PORTIONS	U.S.A.	IMPERIAL	METRIC
Mullet (not less than 12 inches long)	1 per head	1 per head	1 per head
Clarified butter	1/4 cup	2 oz.	60 grams
Onion	1 small	2 oz.	60 grams
Tomato	1 small	4 oz.	115 grams
Sweet green pepper	1/2 cup	2 oz.	60 grams
Ground fennel seeds	1/2 tsp.	1/2 tsp.	1/2 tsp.
Salt	To season	To season	To season
Ground black peppercorns	To season	To season	To season
Dry red wine	6 tbsp.	3 fl. oz.	85 milliliters
Parsley	To garnish	To garnish	To garnish

METHOD OF PREPARATION

1. Clean and scale mullet and leave whole. Make gashes in sides.
2. Finely slice onion.
3. Blanch and remove tomato skins. Chop roughly.
4. Very finely slice green pepper.
5. Preheat oven to 350° F.
6. Chop parsley.

METHOD OF COOKERY

1. Melt buter in casserole dish.
2. Add onion, then tomato, then green pepper.
3. Season with salt, black pepper, and fennel seeds.
4. Season the mullet, brush with melted clarified butter and lay on cooked vegetables.
5. Add wine.
6. Bake at 350° F. for 15-20 minutes, basting occasionally.
7. Slit open belly a little and remove gut before serving. Coat fish with the wine-flavored vegetables and garnish with parsley.

SERVING

I like to see these fish served whole (heads on). It may seem like a lot of fish but there are a lot of bones and a smaller fish is simply not worth the struggle. Plain Boiled Potatoes (p. 218, rec. 165) and peas, both buttered, and a very dry cold white wine go well.

35 Gourmet Grouper

RECIPE TO PRODUCE 4 PORTIONS	U.S.A.	IMPERIAL	METRIC
Whole striped grouper, head and tail removed (keep tail)	3 lb.	3 lb.	1.5 kilo
Water	1¼ cups	10 fl. oz.	285 milliliters
Parsley	1 spray	1 spray	1 spray
Celery	3 leaves	3 leaves	3 leaves
Bay leaf	½	½	½
Large white potatoes	2 lb.	2 lb.	1 kilo
Salt and freshly ground white peppercorns	To season	To season	To season
Spring onions	2	2	2
Clarified butter, melted	6 tbsp.	3 fl. oz.	85 milliliters
Celery hearts	1 lb.	1 lb.	.5 kilo
Cream	10 tbsp.	5 fl. oz.	140 milliliters
Arrowroot	1½ tsp.	1½ tsp.	5 grams
Capers	1 tbsp.	1 tbsp.	10 grams
Stuffed olives	12	12	12
Parsley	2 tbsp.	2 tbsp.	10 grams

METHOD OF PREPARATION

Measure water—tie herbs together—peel potatoes—finely slice spring onions—measure butter and cream—cut off hearts of celery so that length between base and cut is 9 inches—mix arrowroot with a little milk—cut olives in half—chop parsley—preheat oven to 350° F.

METHOD OF COOKERY

1. Boil potatoes for 10 minutes in salted water.
2. Place tail in saucepan with water, celery leaves, bay leaf and parsley spray. Simmer for 30 minutes.
3. Make ½-inch diagonal cuts on flanks of fish and season inside and out with salt and white pepper.
4. Cut potatoes in ½-inch slices, lay in roasting pan (no more than 2 slices deep), leaving space for fish.
5. Strain fish stock over these and place fish on top.
6. Brush with butter, place on top shelf in the oven, bake 10 minutes per pound (30 minutes). Brush with oil each 10 minutes.
7. When cooked, place fish on serving dish, surround with potatoes.
8. Mix cream into fish residue. Bring to boil, thicken with arrowroot paste, add other garnish ingredients, and pour over fish.

SERVING

As potatoes are already provided, no additional starch is suggested. Some Buttered Spinach (p. 240, rec. 197) is an excellent accompaniment. Serve a chilled Moselle-type wine.

Ⓖ **For Baked Trout with Taupo Stuffing see page 201.**

36 JUMBO SHRIMP

Step 1
Shrimp must be perfectly fresh. When shrimp has been "sitting about," the head shell goes a very dark color. Beware of these. Grasp the head firmly and break it downward from the tail.

Step 2
Strip off the outer shell by loosening it first from the underside.

37 Shrimp Cocktail

RECIPE TO PRODUCE 4 PORTIONS	U.S.A.	IMPERIAL	METRIC
Jumbo shrimp, cooked	16	16	16
Lettuce heart	¼	¼	¼
Mayonnaise (pp. 262-63, rec. 225)	½ cup	4 fl. oz.	115 milliliters
Concentrated tomato paste	2 tbsp.	1 fl. oz.	30 milliliters
Cream	2 tbsp.	1 fl. oz.	30 milliliters
Lemon juice	1 tsp.	1 tsp.	5 milliliters
Cayenne pepper	To dust	To dust	To dust
Parsley	1 tbsp.	1 tbsp.	5 grams
Lemon	1	1	1

METHOD OF PREPARATION

Shell shrimp and remove waste tract—cut each into 3 equal pieces—slice lettuce finely—make mayonnaise—measure cream—squeeze lemon—chop parsley—cut lemon in quarters, ends squared off—cut under skin half way up so that a tab is made to assist in hanging lemon on glass.

METHOD OF COOKERY

1. Toss lettuce in lemon juice and place equal portions in 4 glasses. They should be half filled.
2. Lay shrimp on the lettuce. Place glasses into refrigerator.
3. Add cream to mayonnaise and then add tomato paste until a light pink color is reached. Consistency should be thick and smooth.
4. Just before serving, place a good spoonful of mixture over shrimp. Dust well with cayenne and chopped parsley.
5. Hang a lemon wedge on side of glass and serve.

SERVING

This makes a first-class starter for a good meal. Serve brown bread in very thin slices and a very light dry white wine well chilled.

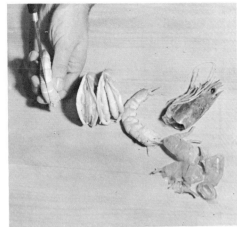

Step 3
Cut into the back of the tail with a sharp knife. Do not cut deeply—only the slightest pressure is needed.

Step 4
Peel back the flesh to uncover the waste tract. In this photograph you have, on the right, a clear view of the tract—remove this completely. On the left you can see the tract covered with coral. Remove the tract but retain the coral for use as a garnish or for incorporation in a cocktail sauce.

38 Shrimp in Sherry Sauce

RECIPE TO PRODUCE 4 PORTIONS

	U.S.A.	IMPERIAL	METRIC
Jumbo shrimp, raw ("green")	16	16	16
Salt	To season	To season	To season
White peppercorns	To season	To season	230 milliliters
Butter	7 tbsp.	3 oz.	To season
Medium dry sherry	½ cup	4 fl. oz.	85 grams
Egg yolks	3	3	115 milliliters
Cream	1 cup	8 fl. oz.	3
Lemon	To garnish	To garnish	To garnish
Parsley	To garnish	To garnish	To garnish
Cayenne pepper	To garnish	To garnish	To garnish

METHOD OF PREPARATION

Cut shrimp in half lengthways—warm the sherry—mix cream and yolks—cut lemon into wedges—finely chop parsley.

METHOD OF COOKERY

1. Season shrimp well with ground peppercorns and salt.
2. Toss in butter in frying pan until well coated.
3. Add sherry. Boil rapidly to reduce.
4. When almost boiled away, add yolks and cream, stirring all the time **off** the heat. When all is added, return to a gentle heat. Do NOT boil.
5. When thickened, spoon shrimp and sauce into a rice nest. Dust with cayenne and parsley.
6. Serve with lemon wedges.

SERVING

Serve with plain Boiled Rice (pp. 226-27, rec. 177) and a tossed green Salad (pp. 246-47, rec. 207). Serve a good dry white wine, nicely chilled.

39 CRABS

COMMENT ON METHOD

Ian Fleming once wrote of his hero, James Bond—Secret Agent 007, sitting down to a meal of buttered stone crabs accompanied by a pint of iced champagne served in a pewter tankard. Since this highly descriptive piece of writing, I am told that crabs have nearly doubled their price! Fact or fiction? I don't know, but whenever I'm in Sydney or northern Florida I run my

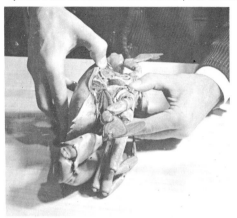

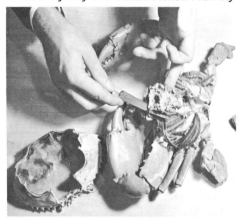

Step 1

Crabs should be cooked the same way as crayfish or lobster (pp. 62-63, rec. 42). Cook rapidly and break open the shell from the rear. It will come apart easily.

Step 2

Remove the head stomach just behind the eyes. Detach the "dead man's fingers"—the long curled pieces immediately behind the point of my knife.

40 Crab Mayonnaise

RECIPE TO PRODUCE 4 PORTIONS

	U.S.A.	IMPERIAL	METRIC
Cooked crabmeat	1 cup	8 oz.	230 grams
Mayonnaise	½ cup	4 fl. oz.	115 milliliters
Gherkin, fine-diced	1 tsp.	1 tsp.	1 tsp.
Capers	1 tsp.	1 tsp.	1 tsp.
Chopped parsley	1 tbsp.	1 tbsp.	7.5 grams
Eggs	4	4	4
Paprika	1 tbsp.	1 tbsp.	7.5 grams

METHOD OF PREPARATION

Slice cooked crabmeat into ¼-inch rounds—hard boil eggs—prepare mayonnaise or use purchased mayonnaise—finely dice gherkin—measure capers—chop parsley—separate yolks and whites of hard-boiled eggs—slice whites into short strips.

METHOD OF COOKERY

1. Mix yolks of hard boiled eggs to a paste.
2. Add paprika and mayonnaise.
3. Mix until smooth.
4. Add capers, diced gherkins, chopped parsley, and last of all the julienne strips of egg white.
5. Combine with the sliced crab and serve, if possible, from the empty head shell.

SERVING

This makes an ideal summer salad dish. Especially excellent when served with a fruity dry white wine —well chilled.

own detective agency, tracking down this delicious dish. Be careful, however, that the crab weighs heavy in the hand and that when you shake it, there is no sound of liquid. Crabs have an unpleasant habit of being empty!

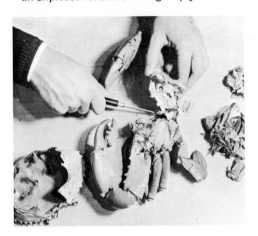 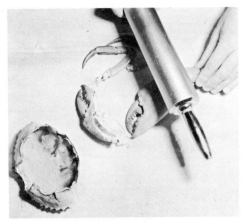

Step 3
Cut the body in two and lever out all the fleshy parts.

Step 4
Break the heavy claws with a gentle rap from a rolling pin. Peel off the shell and take out the meat.

41 Hot Cracker Crab

RECIPE TO PRODUCE 4 PORTIONS

	U.S.A.	IMPERIAL	METRIC
Crabmeat, cooked	1 cup	8 oz.	230 grams
Celery	1 stalk	2 oz.	60 grams
Green pepper	½	2 oz.	60 grams
Shallots	8	2 oz.	60 grams
Parsley	¾ cup	1 oz.	30 grams
Water biscuits	¾ cup	3 oz.	85 grams
Salt	To season	To season	To season
Dry mustard	To season	To season	To season
Cayenne pepper	¼ tsp.	¼ tsp.	¼ tsp.
Clarified butter	½ cup	4 oz.	115 grams
Cream	¼ cup	2 fl. oz.	60 milliliters
Butter	To brush	To brush	To brush

METHOD OF PREPARATION

Cook crabmeat lightly and slice—very finely slice celery, shallots, and green pepper—finely chop parsley—crush water crackers roughly—melt butter to brush—preheat oven to 350° F.

METHOD OF COOKERY

1. Melt 2 oz. clarified butter in saucepan. Add shallots, then green pepper, then celery, then crabmeat.
2. Season with salt, mustard, cayenne. Stir in 1 oz. cracker crumbs, cream and parsley.
3. Place in shallow casserole or baking dish. Top with remaining crumbs, brush with remaining melted butter. Bake at 350° F. for 25 minutes.

SERVING

This makes a very good first course. Serve with a little salad and a cold dry white wine.

42 CRAYFISH OR LOBSTER

COMMENT ON METHOD

There are at least eight different ways to kill a crayfish. I'm a coward when it comes to dealing with a live crayfish, and the one on this page was not only active but quite large. The method chosen here shows the boiling process. You can, however, stop at Step 3 if you want to go on

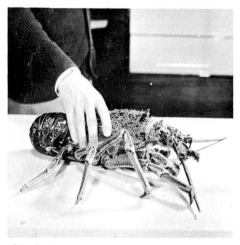 

Step 1

When buying live shellfish it is best to order your requirements well in advance. Before you leave the shop ensure that its tail moves vigorously when the shellfish is held in the air. Never cook a dead crayfish.

Step 2

All edible crustacea die at 98.6° F. What I do is place the crayfish in the sink and allow warm water to run in slowly. I have found that in this way the crayfish does not struggle and appears to pass away peacefully.

43 Crayfish Melbourne

RECIPE TO PRODUCE
4 FIRST-COURSE PORTIONS

	U.S.A.	IMPERIAL	METRIC
White Sauce (pp. 256-57, rec. 216)	1¼ cups	10 fl. oz.	285 milliliters
Dry white wine	½ cup	2 oz.	60 grams
Cooked crayfish or lobster meat	¼ cup	1 oz.	30 grams
Mushrooms, finely chopped	½ cup	1 oz.	30 grams
Lemon juice	1 tsp.	1 tsp.	5 milliliters
Parsley	1 tbsp.	1 tbsp.	5 grams
Potato	1 baking size	8 oz.	.25 kilo
Butter	2 tbsp.	1 oz.	30 grams
Milk	3 tbsp.	1½ fl. oz.	45 milliliters
White peppercorns, salt	To season	To season	To season
Cheddar cheese	¼ cup	1 oz.	30 grams
Chopped parsley and cayenne pepper	To garnish	To garnish	To garnish

METHOD OF PREPARATION

Prepare sauce with 50 per cent fish stock and 50 per cent milk. Measure wine—slice crayfish meat thinly —chop mushrooms finely—chop parsley—cook potato, add butter and milk, mash and beat well. Grate cheese finely—preheat broiler very hot—prepare 4 scallop shells.

METHOD OF COOKERY

1. Add wine to sauce. Place one spoonful of the sauce in each shell. Cover with crayfish slices.
2. Mix mushrooms, lemon juice, parsley, salt, and pepper, sprinkle over crayfish. Top with sauce.
3. Pipe potato in a border round shells. Dust top of sauce with cheese, place under hot broiler to brown the surface. Garnish with chopped parsley and a little cayenne pepper.

SERVING

This is a perfect first course. A glass of chilled sherry blends well.

and broil or shallow fry the flesh. Another simple way to deal with a live crayfish is to place it into a deep freeze. It keeps very well and the method appeals to my nature.

Step 3
For the most flavorsome results prepare a lightly salted water mixture containing the following ingredients for each 3 pints: 8 ounces carrot, 2 shallots or 1 medium onion, 1 bay leaf, 1 sprig thyme, 1 ounce salt, ¼ pint white vinegar, 6 stalks parsley, 6 black peppercorns. Boil this for 30 minutes before you add the crayfish.

Step 4
Boil for 7 minutes for a 1½-pound crayfish if you wish to reheat the flesh for a made-up dish. If you prefer to eat it cold, then cook for 10 minutes. In both cases transfer the cooked crayfish straight into a bowl of very cold water. This prevents the crayfish from continuing to cook by the "Haybox" principle.

44 Broiled Crayfish Tails, Lemon Butter Sauce

RECIPE TO PRODUCE 2 PORTIONS

	U.S.A.	IMPERIAL	METRIC
Crayfish or lobster tails (must be uncooked)	2 10-oz.	2 10-oz.	2 285-grams
Clarified butter	To brush	To brush	To brush
Salt	To season	To season	To season
White peppercorns	To season	To season	To season
Lemon Butter Sauce (pp. 260-61, rec. 222)	½ quantity	½ quantity	½ quantity
Parsley	To dust	To dust	To dust

METHOD OF PREPARATION

Detach tail from head—lay tail flat on board, shell uppermost. With serrated knife, cut through shell lengthways down center—**don't** cut right through. Put thumbs into cut made in shell and bend shell open. The soft shell on the underside of the tail will hold the halves together. Remove the digestive tract. Preheat broiler to medium heat—rack on top rung—prepare sauce—grind peppercorns.

METHOD OF COOKERY

1. Brush tails with melted clarified butter and season with salt and pepper.
2. Place, shell side up, under flame for 5 minutes, then turn, brush again with melted butter, and grill for a further 8 minutes.
3. Ladle sauce over the crayfish flesh and dust with parsley before serving.

SERVING

This is an extremely rich and wonderful dish. It is best when served with plain Boiled Potatoes (pp. 218-19, rec. 165) and a good Salad (pp. 246-47, rec. 207). A well-chilled rosé-type wine goes very well.

45 OYSTERS

COMMENT ON METHOD

Oysters should, by right, only be eaten raw—straight from the shell. This is how to open them, but if you prefer them cooked, well here is one suggestion below.

Step 1
When buying oysters in the shell, buy only those that are tightly closed. The one on the right could be said to be all right but I wouldn't touch it with a barge pole!

Step 2
Scrub the outer shells thoroughly in cold water.

46 Angels in Orbit

RECIPE TO PRODUCE 4 SNACK PORTIONS	U.S.A.	IMPERIAL	METRIC
Salami	½ lb.	8 oz.	230 grams
Raw oysters	2 doz.	2 doz.	2 doz.
Parsley, chopped	To garnish	To garnish	To garnish

METHOD OF PREPARATION

Slice salami thinly—leaving the skin on—into 24 rounds.

METHOD OF COOKERY

1. Heat frying pan until moderately hot (375° F.).
2. Drop salami onto hot surface and leave until slices curl up into cups.
3. Remove and serve with a raw oyster in each salami cup. Dust with chopped parsley.

SERVING

These make wonderful snacks at a cocktail party and also provide a good first course. They can be served either hot or cold. For hot service, serve salami straight from pan; for cold, chill salami cups on tray in normal refrigerator before adding the oyster.

Step 3
Use a cloth and a sharp steel knife exactly as shown here. You can cut yourself to ribbons if, you don't take adequate precautions. Cut into the hinge end and feel along the flat shell until the muscle is detached.

Step 4
With the top shell removed, you can release the oyster from the bottom and turn it over. The underneath side looks better, but gourmets prefer to cut them from the shell at the table. Please keep the natural juice surrounding the oyster in the shell. Serve with wedges of lemon or a shaker of cold dry white wine.

47 Rock Oyster Pasty

RECIPE TO PRODUCE 4 PORTIONS

	U.S.A.	IMPERIAL	METRIC
Pastry:			
Butter	¾ cup	6 oz.	170 grams
Flour	2 cups	8 oz.	230 grams
Salt	1 tsp.	1 tsp.	5 grams
Water	6 tbsp.	3 fl. oz.	85 milliliters
Filling:			
Oysters	2 doz.	2 doz.	2 doz.
Bacon	4 slices	4 slices	4 slices
Tomatoes	2	2	2
Salt	To season	To season	To season
Black peppercorns	To season	To season	To season
Parsley	1 tbsp.	1 tbsp.	5 grams
Egg	1	1	1
Flour	¼ cup	2 oz.	60 grams

METHOD OF PREPARATION

Cut butter into 1-inch square pieces, ¼-inch thick—sift flour with salt—measure water—drain oysters—fry bacon until crisp and drain well—slice tomatoes—chop parsley—beat egg.

METHOD OF COOKERY

1. Shake butter pieces in flour to coat, then pinch in quickly and lightly.
2. Mix in water. Roll out ⅛-inch thick, cut into 4 7-inch rounds.
3. Roll oysters in flour; season. Place in pastry center raw.
4. Cover with 1 bacon slice and 3 slices of tomato; season with salt, pepper, and chopped parsley.
5. Mold up edges, moistened with beaten egg. Brush with egg and bake for 35 minutes at 400° F.

SERVING

Oyster Pasties should be eaten hot, as a supper-type dish. Cold beer is perfect.

48 SQUID

COMMENT ON METHOD

Squid is used mostly for bait. This seems to me to be a gross waste of a delicious seafood.

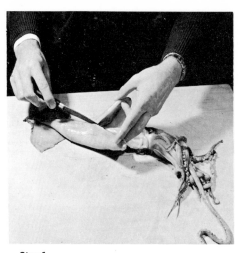

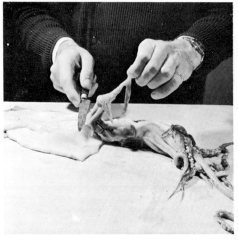

Step 1
Open the hood down the back with a sharp knife. Lay the hood open flat.

Step 2
Starting at the top, gently detach the gut and ink sac and cut through at the base of the hood. Cut off the tentacles just below the beak and throw the center portion away (or freeze it ready for the next fishing trip!).

49 Lyall Bay Casserole

RECIPE TO PRODUCE 4 PORTIONS

	U.S.A.	IMPERIAL	METRIC
1 squid hood			
Rice	13 oz.	13 oz.	370 grams
Garlic cloves	¾ cup	3 oz.	85 grams
Clarified butter	2	2	2
Onion	4 tbsp.	2 oz.	60 grams
Green pepper	1 small	2 oz.	60 grams
Tomato flesh	½	2 oz.	60 grams
Parsley stalks	½ cup	2 oz.	60 grams
Black peppercorns	2 tbsp.	2 tbsp.	5 grams
Salt	To season	To season	To season
Water	To season	To season	To season
New Zealand Sauce (p. 258, rec. 220)	5 cups	2 pints	1.2 liters
	1¼ cups	10 fl. oz.	285 milliliters

METHOD OF PREPARATION

Remove hood from squid—take out all insides without cutting hood open—wash thoroughly. Remove all outer skin. Prepare filling—boil rice 5 minutes—finely dice onion and green pepper—remove skin and pips of tomato—roughly chop parsley stalks—make New Zealand sauce.

METHOD OF COOKERY

1. Melt butter, fry onion, add garlic, green pepper, parsley, and tomato. Soften and season well.
2. Add strained rice. Fill hood (it should not be completely full), sew up as for duck (p. 93, step 8).
3. Add all trimmings from green pepper, tomato, and onion to water and fill saucepan so that the stuffed hood is covered.
4. Cover and simmer for 1 hour until tender. Remove and slice into ½-inch slices.
5. Lay the slices flat on a heated serving dish and coat each one with the New Zealand sauce.

SERVING

Best when served with buttered Pasta (pp. 230-31, rec. 183) and a well-chilled Italian dry white wine.

In some countries it is a luxury. I admit that it looks utterly repulsive at first, but as you will see from Steps 3 and 4 when it is properly prepared, it looks highly edible—and it is!

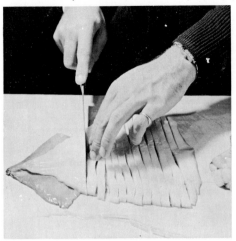

Step 3
Rub the outer skin with a coarse salt-dipped cloth to remove the skin. Peel out the backbone (seen at the bottom of the picture) and then slice into ½-inch-wide strips.

Step 4
Place hood and tentacles together in a steamer and steam gently for 45-60 minutes. Remove when completely tender and use in casserole or fried dishes. It tastes like a combination of oyster and chicken.

50 Strip Dip

RECIPE TO PRODUCE 6 PORTIONS

	U.S.A.	IMPERIAL	METRIC
Squid	1½ lb.	1½ lb.	.75 kilo
Flour	¾ cup	3 oz.	85 grams
Salt	To season	To season	To season
Pepper	To season	To season	To season
Frying batter (pp. 254-55, rec. 213)	1¼ cups	10 fl. oz.	285 milliliters
Frying oil	10 cups	4 pints	2.25 liters
Tomato sauce	¾ cup	6 fl. oz.	170 milliliters
Garlic cloves	2	2	2
Parsley	To garnish	To garnish	To garnish

METHOD OF PREPARATION

Cut squid down back of hood—remove ink sac and cut off just above eyes. Rub purple outside skin with salt or strip off—remove membrane spine—cut tentacles from hood just below beak—remove serrated edge of suckers. Season flour—heat oil to 380° F.—measure batter ingredients—prepare small bowl and doily for serving.

METHOD OF COOKERY

1. Place sliced squid in double steamer with a little water below. Cover, steam gently 45-60 minutes, until it gives easily to touch.
2. Make batter with the liquid in the steamer base in lieu of fish stock.
3. Add crushed garlic to tomato sauce and place in small bowl in the center of a doily-covered serving dish.
4. Flour squid pieces, dip in batter, and deep fry until crisp and golden.
5. Dust with salt and parsley.

SERVING

Excellent as a dunk dish for a cocktail party, especially when the guests don't know what they are eating. They will rave about its oyster and chicken flavor and when they have drunk as much as you can afford—tell them!

51 SCALLOPS

COMMENT ON METHOD

Scallops are one of our finest seafoods. Keen types like to buy them in the shell, and if you should want to join them, this is the method of opening and basic preparation.

Step 1

Scrub the shells well in cold water. The shells don't close as tightly as oysters, but it is obvious when they are dead. In Step 2 the acceptable ones are those on the top shelf—the ones below are very dead.

Step 2

One way of opening scallops is to put them into an oven set at 200° F. for 5 minutes and then cut them open by detaching the muscle from the flat shell. I'm not completely sold on this technique as they are really quite easy to open with a knife without heating.

52 Golden Coast Scallops

RECIPE TO PRODUCE 2 PORTIONS

	U.S.A.	IMPERIAL	METRIC
Scallops	1 doz.	1 doz.	1 doz.
Breadcrumbs	¼ cup	1 oz.	30 grams
Flour	¼ cup	1 oz.	30 grams
Egg	1	1	1
Olive oil	¼ cup	2 oz.	60 milliliters
Golden Coast Sauce:			
Mayonnaise	1½ cups	12 fl. oz.	340 milliliters
Parsley	1 tbsp.	1 tbsp.	5 grams
Gherkin	1 tbsp.	1 tbsp.	5 grams
Capers	1 tbsp.	1 tbsp.	5 grams
Cayenne pepper	½ tsp.	½ tsp.	½ tsp.
Lemon juice	1 tbsp.	1 tbsp.	15 milliliters

METHOD OF PREPARATiON

Prepare scallops as shown above—remove from wine and dry well—mix egg with oil—heat frying oil in deep fryer— to 375° F.—place flour, egg and oil mixture, and breadcrumbs in separate bowls. Measure mayonnaise—chop parsley, gherkin, and capers.

METHOD OF COOKERY

1. Season and then dip scallops in flour, egg, and breadcrumbs. Deep fry 2½-3 minutes at 375° F.

2. Drain and serve with **Golden Coast Sauce.**

Sauce:

3. Mix all ingredients and put into serving dish. There will be ample for this dish, enough in fact for 8-10 people. The remaining sauce can be bottled and kept in the refrigerator for at least 14 days.

SERVING

Serve with a tossed salad and lemon wedges. This makes a wonderful lunch dish and when served with a chilled Moselle-type wine, it's fantastic!

Step 3
Open the scallops over a bowl containing ½ cup dry white wine, 1 ounce sliced onion, 1 sprig thyme, 6 black peppercorns, and 1 crumbled bay leaf. Any juices will mix with this poaching liquid and help the finished flavor.

Step 4
Cut the scallop from the curved shell and strip off the beard, leaving only the trimmed center core and the bright orange flap as seen on left of picture. Put the trimmed scallops into the wine mixture and poach gently for 4 minutes; remove and use as the recipe requires.

53 Scallops Whakatane

RECIPE TO PRODUCE 4 PORTIONS

	U.S.A.	IMPERIAL	METRIC
Scallops	1 doz.	1 doz.	1 doz.
Flour	To dust	To dust	To dust
Salt, white peppercorns	To season	To season	To season
Lemon juice	1 tbsp.	1 tbsp.	15 milliliters
Clarified butter	6 tbsp.	3 oz.	85 grams
Garnish:			
Mushrooms, finely sliced	1 cup	2 oz.	60 grams
Spring onions	2	2 oz.	60 grams
Tomato	1 small	5 oz.	140 grams
Green pepper	½	2 oz.	60 grams
Parsley	1 tbsp.	1 tbsp.	5 grams
Garlic clove	1	1	1

METHOD OF PREPARATION

Dry scallops well, season, and flour—finely slice green peppers—chop spring onions—white and green parts—quarter tomato—chop parsley—peel garlic.

METHOD OF COOKERY

1. Melt 2 tablespoons clarified butter in saucepan; add crushed clove of garlic, green pepper, and spring onions. Fry for 2 minutes.
2. Add mushrooms and stir gently.
3. Add tomato. Cook 3 minutes more.
4. Shallow fry scallops in another pan with 4 tablespoons butter for 4 minutes, tossing them over several times in this period.
5. Lift scallops onto serving dish, sprinkle with lemon juice, and cover with vegetables and chopped parsley.

SERVING

As a first course this takes a lot of beating. Serve with brown bread and butter and a wedge of lemon. A good light dry white wine is most suitable.

Brisbane Prawn Soufflé, recipe page 87

About Eggs

A chicken needs grit and determination to produce an egg—with a shell, that is. Yet what do you care—familiarity breeds contempt. You crack it like a child breaks its first toy—golden yolk, liquid white—one of nature's masterpieces. What do you care—if you don't crack it, you overcook it and shatter another day of domestic harmony.

The egg is the most valuable of all foods—whenever you find it—it improves—just look.

A **whole egg** makes sponges, cakes of all kinds—fruity and light. Batters are lighter and crisper. Pancakes too frail to toss. They can be scrambled, poached, boiled, baked, fried, shirred, coddled, and stuffed inside, or have stuffing outside. They add luxury to salad—a bloom to a loaf of bread. A golden gloss to pastry. They make omelets—flat or fluffy. Soufflés too high for the oven. Griddlecakes that warm golden butter, waffles all dripping with honey. They provide decorative fun at Easter and consolation on a winter's morning.

A **yolk** can thicken a sauce when added with cream—cracked into a raw beef dish. It makes a good cocktail—or health drink, even a pick-me-up taken raw with Worcestershire sauce. A yolk makes mayonnaise, hollandaise, Béarnaise, Choron, and many other sauces—whipped raw as a dunk dish for Asian foods or crumbled when cooked as a garnish.

The **white** makes meringues—even Pavlovas (God help us). It clarifies stock—can be used as a garnish for soups. Makes a mousse or a jelly, icing or a cream—quite delicious. When used for fresh fruit whips—it's fantastic!

Once I said, "Where would we be without eggs?"—why, they're even good for your hair.

CONTENTS OF SECTION

54 BOILED EGGS

COMMENT ON METHOD

I have two great ambitions in life. One is to be the Brigade of Guards officer who actually troops the Colour at the famous Horseguards Parade ceremony. The other is to eat my daily breakfast of two boiled eggs in a heavily encrusted, elegant silver egg cup—with a long,

Step 1
No matter which way you like to cook eggs, they should **always** be taken from the refrigerator the night before. **Cold eggs don't cook well.** Prick the "sharp end" of the egg with a pin. This helps equalize pressure and stops shell from cracking.

Step 2
Bring water to the boil. Place eggs in a wire basket. By doing this you run less risk of cracking and they all get the same time. Take the pan from the heat and add the eggs. Return pan to heat and boil. DO NOT ADD VINEGAR TO WATER—PLEASE.

55 Salmon Eggs

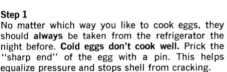

RECIPE TO PRODUCE 4 PORTIONS	U.S.A.	IMPERIAL	METRIC
Eggs	4	4	4
Cooked salmon	8 oz.	8 oz.	230 grams
Butter	1 tbsp.	½ oz.	15 grams
Flour	2 tbsp.	½ oz.	15 grams
Fish stock	3 tbsp.	1½ fl. oz.	45 milliliters
Eggs	2	2	2
Salt	To season	To season	To season
Black peppercorns	To season	To season	To season
Nutmeg	To season	To season	To season
Breadcrumbs	½ cup	2 oz.	60 grams
Parsley	To garnish	To garnish	To garnish
Lemon	To garnish	To garnish	To garnish

METHOD OF PREPARATION

Hard boil 4 eggs—shell and place in cold water—flake salmon free from skin and bones—chop (not too finely)—beat the 2 eggs—grind peppercorns finely—grate fresh nutmeg—measure butter, flour, fish stock—chop parsley—slice lemon into 4 wedges.

METHOD OF COOKERY

1. Melt butter, stir in flour. Cook over low heat for 2 minutes, add stock, and stir until it thickens.
2. Still stirring, add chopped salmon, mix thoroughly with half the beaten egg; season with salt, ground peppercorns, and grated nutmeg. When hot pour onto plate, flatten, and cool.
3. Divide into 4 even portions, flatten again, and wrap around eggs. Brush with beaten egg, roll in breadcrumbs. Shallow fry in clarified butter for 8 minutes or deep fry for 4 minutes.
4. Drain, cut in halves, place in lettuce nests. Place a sprig of parsley in the center of each yolk.

SERVING

Basically this is either a first course for four hogs or a good supper dish either hot or cold.

slender silver egg spoon. As I am unlikely to achieve the former, have you by chance got such an egg cup to spare?

Step 3
The egg on the extreme right has had 3 minutes—it is still very runny. The next has had 3½ minutes—the white has just set. The last opened has received 4½ minutes and the yolk is just soft but not runny. On the left is my method of opening an egg. My children request that I perform this skillful operation every morning—when will they grow up and get married!

Step 4
In our family we eat the egg before the cereal. In this way the eggs are eaten at their best and we can all sit down together. It makes a refreshing change actually and we think it's sensible.

56 Eggs in Spiced Mushroom Sauce

RECIPE TO PRODUCE 4 PORTIONS

	U.S.A.	IMPERIAL	METRIC
Eggs	4	4	4
Tomato purée	6 tbsp.	3 fl. oz.	85 milliliters
Dry white wine	6 tbsp.	3 fl. oz.	85 milliliters
Parsley stalks	½ tbsp.	½ tbsp.	5 grams
Rice	1 cup	6 oz.	170 grams
Butter	½ tbsp.	½ tbsp.	10 grams
Garlic clove	½	½	½
Mushrooms, sliced	1 cup	2 oz.	60 grams
Parsley	To garnish	To garnish	To garnish

METHOD OF PREPARATION

Boil eggs for 6 minutes—place in cold water and gently remove shells—measure purée and wine—chop parsley stalks and parsley separately—boil rice as per basic method (pp. 226-27, rec. 177).

METHOD OF COOKERY

1. **Make up sauce:** Melt butter, add crushed garlic then tomato purée and wine. Boil to reduce to half volume to sauce consistency. Add parsley stalks.
2. Shallow fry mushrooms in a little butter—turn into the sauce.
3. Place boiled rice on a plate and mold into a nest. Place shelled eggs in sauce and heat through.
4. Pour eggs and sauce into rice nest.
5. Dust with parsley and serve.

SERVING

A perfect dish for a cold winter round-the-fire supper.

57 POACHED EGGS

COMMENT ON METHOD

In one of my parents' hotels we kept chickens (not in the hotel, you understand) and when their eggs were poached they were perfectly formed. To get a perfect poached egg you really need a very fresh egg. I have found a way to reproduce this shape and avoid one that looks like a map of North America!

Step 1
Leave the eggs out of the refrigerator overnight. Place a frying pan on low heat and brush on a little melted butter.

Step 2
Bring water to the boil and lower the eggs into the water in a basket. Boil for exactly 10 seconds and then remove them. Pour the boiling water into the buttered pan.

58 Flatiron Rarebit

RECIPE TO PRODUCE 4 PORTIONS

	U.S.A.	IMPERIAL	METRIC
Eggs	4	4	4
Swiss or Monterey Jack cheese	4 2-oz. slices	4 2-oz. slices	4 60-gram slices
Bacon	4 slices	4 slices	4 slices
Bread slices for toast	4	4	4
Tomatoes	4	4	4
Parsley	To garnish	To garnish	To garnish
Butter	To spread	To spread	To spread

METHOD OF PREPARATION

Slice cheese 1/4 inch thick—cut bread—trim edges—halve tomatoes—chop parsley—trim rind from bacon —heat broiler to medium hot—put on water for poached eggs.

METHOD OF COOKERY

1. Toast bread slices.
2. Spread with butter and place cheese slice on top.
3. Broil until the cheese bubbles. Cover with bacon, broil again until bacon is just cooked (approximately 4 minutes).
4. Meanwhile, poach eggs as per basic method. Slip onto bacon. Decorate with tomato halves and chopped parsley.

SERVING

I find this makes a perfect Sunday night snack around the fire in the winter. Coffee called for here?

It is given below. As a matter of interest, I haven't broken one yolk since I adopted this technique, and best of all there is no salt or vinegar added to the water.

Step 3
Crack the eggs into the pan and keep them at a low heat (just before simmer) until the white sets.

Step 4
Lift the eggs with a perforated spoon. Where the eggs are required for a made-up dish, they can be slipped into a bowl of cold water (on left) and re-heated later. For normal use, however, I don't recommend this precookery, as it does tend to reduce some of the egg's fabulous food value.

59 West Coast Eggs

RECIPE TO PRODUCE 4 PORTIONS

	U.S.A.	IMPERIAL	METRIC
Cheese Sauce (half recipe, p. 256, rec. 217)	1¼ cups	10 fl. oz.	285 milliliters
Swiss chard or spinach	2 lb.	2 lb.	1 kilo
Eggs	4	4	4
Cheese to garnish	6 tbsp.	1½ oz.	45 grams
	4 tbsp.	1 oz.	30 grams

METHOD OF PREPARATION

Prepare sauce using 1 ounce cheese—strip off leaves from vegetable—grease 8-inch flan tin—heat serving plate—grate cheese—preheat grill to very hot.

METHOD OF COOKERY

1. Cook Swiss chard or spinach as per basic method (p. 240, rec. 197).
2. Lay cooked leaves in flan tin and place in oven to keep hot.
3. Poach eggs.
4. Turn Swiss chard or spinach onto hot serving plate, place poached eggs on top.
5. Coat with thick cheese sauce.
6. Dust with grated cheese.
7. Place under heated grill just to brown the sauce.
8. Serve at the table by cutting into wedges.

SERVING

Some people serve this as a first course—in my view it is far too filling. Best as another supper dish.

60 JENA EGGS

COMMENT ON METHOD

This is an unusual method of cooking eggs, but I hope it may catch on. They can be cooked only in a special container called an Eierkocher made by the Jenaer Glaswerk Schott & Gen., Mainz, Germany. As you will see, the possibilities for variety are unlimited, but my favorite

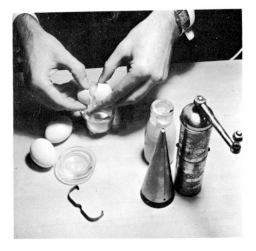 

Step 1
Place 1 fluid ounce cream in bottom of the container. Add some freshly ground **black** peppercorns and a little salt. For variety you can add a little salmon, liver sausage, creamed shrimp, or mushrooms, etc. Break an egg on top.

Step 2
Hold the container firmly and fix the spring clip.

61 Jena Eggs with Salmon

RECIPE TO PRODUCE 4 PORTIONS

	U.S.A.	IMPERIAL	METRIC
Eggs	4	4	4
Cream	¼ cup	2 fl. oz.	60 milliliters
Salmon	½ cup	4 oz.	115 grams
White peppercorns	To season	To season	To season
Lemon juice	4 tsp.	4 tsp.	15 milliliters
Parsley stalks	4 tsp.	4 tsp.	10 grams
Paprika	To garnish	To garnish	To garnish
Parsley	To garnish	To garnish	To garnish
Single-egg-size Jena containers	4	4	4

METHOD OF PREPARATION

Measure cream—chop parsley stalks—chop parsley garnish.

METHOD OF COOKERY

1. Cream salmon with lemon juice, parsley stalks, and ground pepper. Do not add salt.
2. Place equal amount in bottom of each container.
3. Add ½ fluid ounce cream per container.
4. Drop an egg into each on tóp of cream.
5. Seal and place in boiling water.
6. Cook for 7 minutes.
7. Dust with paprika and chopped parsley.

SERVING

An excellent and unusual first course.

is the one used here to describe the basic method—just cream, seasoning, and a touch of parsley—perfection. I'm delighted that I can write, rather than talk, about the container; you try to pronounce it!

Step 3
Place in boiling water; the level of which just comes to the base of the clips. Cover with a lid. Cook for 4 minutes soft and 5 minutes medium.

Step 4
Serve in the glass with a sprinkle of fresh chopped parsley.

62   Jena Eggs with Bacon and Mushrooms

RECIPE TO PRODUCE 4 PORTIONS	U.S.A.	IMPERIAL	METRIC
Bacon slices	4	4	4
Mushrooms	4	4	4
Chives	1 tbsp.	1 tbsp.	7½ grams
Lemon juice	1 tbsp.	1 tbsp.	15 milliliters
Cream	¼ cup	2 fl. oz.	60 milliliters
Eggs	4	4	4
Double-egg-size Jena containers	4	4	4

METHOD OF PREPARATION
Finely slice bacon slices—very finely slice mushrooms—chop chives.

METHOD OF COOKERY
1. Fry bacon until crisp—remove.
2. Fry mushrooms lightly in bacon fat with lemon juice for 1 minute only.
3. Mix bacon and mushrooms—add no salt—and divide between 4 containers. Press down.
4. Add ½ fluid ounce cream per container.
5. Drop an egg into each. Seal on top and cook 7 minutes.
6. Serve dusted with chopped chives.

SERVING
Another good first course.

63 SCRAMBLED EGGS

COMMENT ON METHOD

At the time of writing, my young son Andrew has just started to cook. His first attempt was scrambled egg. He made it exactly as shown on this page—it was perfect, wonderfully soft,

Step 1
Leave the eggs out of the refrigerator overnight. The recipe given here is for two people. Place ½ ounce butter into a small pan and melt.

Step 2
Cut up another ½ ounce butter into small pieces. Beat 4 eggs in a bowl and add salt and freshly ground white peppercorns.

64 Karewai Eggs

RECIPE TO PRODUCE 4 PORTIONS

	U.S.A.	IMPERIAL	METRIC
Lean bacon	4 slices	4 slices	4 slices
Tomatoes, medium	4	4	4
Parsley stalks	4 small	4 small	4 small
Butter	½ cup	4 oz.	115 grams
Lemon	1	1	1
White bread for toast	4 slices	4 slices	4 slices
Eggs	8	8	8
Cream	½ cup	4 fl. oz.	115 milliliters
White peppercorns, freshly ground	To season	To season	To season
Garlic salt	To season	To season	To season
Cayenne pepper	To garnish	To garnish	To garnish
Parsley sprays	4	4	4

METHOD OF PREPARATION

Slice bacon into small pieces—skin, pip, and chop tomatoes—chop parsley stalks roughly—squeeze 1 lemon—cut crusts from bread and cut into large round fancy shapes—measure cream—prepare parsley for garnishing each portion.

METHOD OF COOKERY

1. Melt half butter in frying pan, add chopped bacon, and cook until pieces separate. Add chopped tomato and lemon juice.
2. When heated and combined (not sloppy), turn out and keep warm.
3. Melt a little more butter in pan and fry bread both sides—remove and keep warm.
4. Make scrambled eggs as shown in basic method above, using garlic salt instead of regular salt.
5. Add bacon, tomatoes, and parsley.

SERVING

Turn out onto fried bread, dust with cayenne, garnish with parsley, and serve as a breakfast or snack dish. I don't think that wine is applicable—do you?

creamy, and seasoned fit for the gods. Confidentially, I'm a little worried about my pride in his achievement. Usually fathers get all steamed up over their son's first black eye!

Step 3
Pour beaten eggs onto the melted butter and stir with a wooden spoon. Add the pieces of butter from time to time during setting period.

Step 4
When the eggs are just set, add ¼ cup cream and stir in well until the mixture is hot. By adding cold cream at the end you arrest cookery at just the right moment; otherwise the eggs can rapidly become dry, even in the time they take to serve.

65　Gruyère and Anchovy Eggs

RECIPE TO PRODUCE 4 PORTIONS	U.S.A.	IMPERIAL	METRIC
Eggs	8	8	8
Cream	½ cup	4 fl. oz.	115 milliliters
Butter	4 tbsp.	2 oz.	60 grams
Gruyère cheese	2 oz.	2 oz.	60 grams
Fillets anchovy	8	8	8
White peppercorns, freshly ground	To season	To season	To season

METHOD OF PREPARATION

Halve butter and divide 2 tablespoons into small pieces—cube cheese into ½-inch squares—measure cream—soak anchovy fillets in a little milk for 30 minutes (this reduces the salt content).

METHOD OF COOKERY

1. Make scrambled eggs as shown in basic method above.
2. Stir with a spurtle.*
3. At very last moment, lightly stir in cheese cubes and anchovy fillets. Serve at once.

SERVING

This is a very unusual supper dish. Test it on yourself first. I think it is a delicious but acquired taste.

*A spurtle is a Scottish wooden stirring stick.

66 SAVORY OMELETS

COMMENT ON METHOD

The omelet is the perfect instant meal for the do-it-yourselfer. You can add virtually anything that happens to be lying around, and the result is filling and extremely good for you. Some

Step 1
Break eggs into a small bowl. Heat a 7-inch frying pan and add ½ ounce of butter. Note the plates sitting on top of the saucepan of boiling water on the right of the picture. This is the best way of keeping them hot and at hand when each omelet is cooked.

Step 2
Beat 2 eggs gently with 2 tablespoons cream so that the cream blends with the yolks. Don't beat to a froth. Season with garlic salt and freshly ground white peppercorns.

67 Graham Kerr Omelet

RECIPE TO PRODUCE 4 PORTIONS

	U.S.A.	IMPERIAL	METRIC
Basic omelet mixture	4	4	4
Bacon slices	4	4	4
Tomatoes	4 medium	4 medium	4 medium
Parsley stalks	1 tbsp.	1 tbsp.	7½ grams

METHOD OF PREPARATION

Prepare omelet mixture (do not add salt). Slice bacon into ¼-inch squares. Skin and cut tomatoes in quarters—chop parsley stalks fine.

METHOD OF COOKERY

1. Place bacon in small saucepan. Heat until pieces separate.
2. Add tomatoes and simmer until tender (4 minutes).
3. Remove saucepan from heat. Add parsley stalks.
4. Make omelet in normal way.
5. Fill with prepared mixture, turn out, brush over melted butter, and serve.

SERVING

This is my only departure from two boiled eggs for breakfast!

people are scared of omelets. I hope these instructions will cure this lack of confidence and that you will share in this "instant gastronomy."

Step 3
When the butter in the pan starts to go a very light brown, add the eggs and stir vigorously with a fork, moving the pan at the same time. Fold both edges into the center when the top of the mixture is still runny.

Step 4
If the bottom of the omelet should stick, then run a little butter along the edge (as shown above) and slip a spatula underneath to loosen. Turn onto hot plate and brush with a little butter. Serve and insist that it is eaten—immediately!

68 West Coast Omelet

RECIPE TO PRODUCE 4 PORTIONS

	U.S.A.	IMPERIAL	METRIC
Shrimps (usually tinned)	¾ cup	6 oz.	170 grams
White cabbage, shredded	1 cup	6 oz.	170 grams
Cabbage stalk (white center core)	1 small wedge	1 oz.	30 grams
Green chili	1	1	10 grams
Parsley stalks	1 tsp.	1 tsp.	5 grams
Onion	¼ medium	1½ oz.	45 grams
Eggs	8	8	8
Cream	1 cup	8 fl. oz.	230 milliliters
Soya sauce	3 tbsp.	3 tbsp.	45 milliliters
Butter	2 tbsp.	1 oz.	30 grams
Clarified butter, melted	¼ cup	2 fl. oz.	60 milliliters
White peppercorns	To season	To season	To season
Garlic salt	1 pinch	1 pinch	1 pinch

METHOD OF PREPARATION

Cut stalk of cabbage into matchstick size—pip and chop chili very fine—chop parsley stalks—add soya sauce to cabbage stalk, chili and parsley—let stand 1 hour—open shrimps—measure cream, butter and clarified butter—slice onion finely.

METHOD OF COOKERY

1. Place clarified butter in heated heavy frypan, add onions and toss lightly. Add cabbage. Toss 1 minute, add soya sauce mixture. Toss again.
2. Add shrimps, stir lightly with fork, cover saucepan, and remove from heat.
3. Make omelets as per basic method above. When still moist on top, add a spoonful of the filling, turn omelet out, butter the top, and garnish with parsley.

SERVING

Serve with freshly warmed bread, rolls, or hot toast. Serve with a tossed salad and chilled beer.

69 SWEET OMELETS

COMMENT ON METHOD

There are very few classical exceptions to the rule "savory omelets are solid in texture and sweet omelets are fluffy." If there is anything that I really detest, it is fluffy savory omelets. Hence I dedicate this recipe to that grand array of luxurious edibles—"afters."

Step 1
Whip whites of 4 eggs in a basin, adding 1 tablespoon water and ¼ teaspoon salt. Add 1 fluid ounce of liqueur of your choice and 1 ounce superfine granulated sugar to the yolks and beat together. When the whites are very stiff, fold in the yolk mixture gently.

Step 2
Add a small piece of butter to a heated pan and wait until the edges of the butter froth (see Step 1). Add mixture all at once and stir quickly using a spatula. Bang the pan onto the element a couple of times to settle the mixture. Smooth the surface with the knife.

70 Sweet Peach Omelet

RECIPE TO PRODUCE 2 PORTIONS

	U.S.A.	IMPERIAL	METRIC
Eggs	4	4	4
Superfine granulated sugar	¼ cup	2 oz.	60 grams
Clarified butter	2 tbsp.	1 oz.	30 grams
Salt	1 pinch	1 pinch	1 pinch
Water	1 tsp.	1 tsp.	5 milliliters
Filling:			
Peaches, sliced	2¼ cups	6 oz.	170 grams
Butter	2 tbsp.	1 oz.	30 grams
Ground cardamom	¼ tsp.	¼ tsp.	5 grams
Soft brown sugar	1 tsp.	1 tsp.	5 grams

METHOD OF PREPARATION

Separate eggs—use fresh peaches if available—peel and slice—if using tinned peaches, omit Demerara sugar—preheat broiler to medium.

METHOD OF COOKERY

1. Cream yolks with sugar.
2. Add salt and cold water to whites and whip till stiff.
3. Fold yolks into whites.
4. Melt clarified butter and add omelet mixture. Stir hard with spatula and bang pan down on stove to settle. Cook over not-too-high heat.
5. Finish under medium heat.
6. Meanwhile toss sliced peaches in butter over moderate heat. Dust with sugar and cardamom to glaze.
7. Place peaches in center of omelet. Fold out onto hot plate. Dust with superfine granulated sugar.

Step 3
Place immediately under a moderate heat broiler and lightly cook surface until small bubbles or blisters appear and the level has risen.

Step 4
After the mixture leaves the broiler you can add your filling to the center of the omelet. Loosen the edges and carefully fold it out of the pan with the spatula. This recipe serves two people. Serve sprinkled with sugar.

71 Strawberry Liqueur Omelet

RECIPE TO PRODUCE 2 PORTIONS

	U.S.A.	IMPERIAL	METRIC
Large eggs	4	4	4
Strawberries, sliced	1 cup	8 oz.	230 grams
Brandy	¼ cup	2 fl. oz.	60 milliliters
Butter	2 tbsp.	1 oz.	30 grams
Water, cold	1 tsp.	1 tsp.	15 milliliters
Salt	1 pinch	1 pinch	1 pinch
Grand Marnier	¼ cup	2 fl. oz.	60 milliliters
Superfine granulated sugar	1 cup	4 oz.	115 grams

METHOD OF PREPARATION

Separate yolks from whites—place brandy bottle in hot water—measure butter, water, salt, Grand Marnier, and sugar.

METHOD OF COOKERY

1. Halve the strawberries, dust with 2 ounces sugar and sprinkle with 1 fluid ounce Grand Marnier. Stand for only 10 minutes—no more.
2. Add salt and cold water to egg whites. Beat very stiff.
3. Add remaining sugar and Grand Marnier to egg yolks; beat well.
4. Make Sweet Omelet as shown above in basic method. Add strawberries just before the omelet is turned from pan.

SERVING

Turn onto hot oval serving dish, dust with sugar, and pour on heated brandy. Light with a match at the table—very impressive. Serve a chilled sweet white wine.

85

72 SOUFFLES

COMMENT ON METHOD

I had the honor once to attend a luncheon given for me by the Home Science class of Te Puke High School in the Bay of Plenty, New Zealand. The students decided that I should be served with a cheese soufflé. The Te Puke Soufflé was so good that I asked one Maori student

Step 1
Make a basic White Sauce with 4 tablespoons butter and 5 tablespoons plain flour (pp. 256-57, rec. 216). Add 1¼ cups milk. Season highly with salt and freshly ground white peppercorns. Cool the sauce and then mix in the yolks of 6 eggs. Finally add 1 cup finely shredded Cheddar cheese. Beat until very smooth.

Step 2
Very gently add the sauce to the whipped whites of 7 eggs. Do not overdo this mixing—many a soufflé is ruined at this point.

73 Sweetcorn Soufflé

RECIPE TO PRODUCE 4 PORTIONS

	U.S.A.	IMPERIAL	METRIC
Butter	2 tbsp.	1 oz.	30 grams
Flour	¼ cup	1 oz.	30 grams
Milk	1 cup	8 fl. oz.	230 milliliters
Corn, cream style	1 cup	8 oz.	230 grams
Eggs	4	4	4
White peppercorns	To season	To season	To season
Salt	To season	To season	To season
Nutmeg	To season	To season	To season
Cayenne	To season	To season	To season
Mustard (dried)	1 tbsp.	1 tbsp.	5 grams

METHOD OF PREPARATION

Divide corn into 6 ounce and 2 ounce portions—measure butter, flour, milk, mustard—separate eggs—preheat oven and baking sheet to 350° F.—rack on lowest rung. Butter soufflé dish.

METHOD OF COOKERY

1. Make sauce with butter, flour, and milk. Season with white peppercorns, cayenne, nutmeg, salt. Allow to cool.
2. Add 4 yolks, beat well; add ¼ cup creamed corn and mustard.
3. Whip whites and pour over sauce. Spoon together.
4. Spoon half into dish, cover with ¾ cup creamed corn and spoon remaining mixture over top.
5. Bake at 375° F. for 35 minutes.

SERVING

Serve with slices of grilled bacon and a tossed green salad. Wine is not really suitable as an accompaniment.

if I might have the recipe. She immediately brought me back a second helping—a happy mistake on her part—I got the recipe later.

Step 3
Butter a soufflé dish and fix a band of foil about the dish, raised 3 inches from the rim. Scrape the mixture into the dish and smooth the surface.

Step 4
Place on the bottom shelf of an oven preheated to 350° F. with a solid baking sheet. Place soufflé on this sheet and bake **undisturbed** for 30 minutes. To test doneness, give the baking sheet a sharp tug. If the soufflé top wobbles, give it a little longer.

74 Brisbane Prawn Soufflé

RECIPE TO PRODUCE 4 PORTIONS

	U.S.A.	IMPERIAL	METRIC
Butter	2 tbsp.	1 oz.	30 grams
Flour	2 tbsp.	½ oz.	15 grams
Milk	1 cup	8 fl. oz.	230 milliliters
Eggs	3	3	3
Cheese	6 tbsp.	3 oz.	85 grams
Brandy	1 tbsp.	½ fl. oz.	15 milliliters
Prawns (shelled weight), large shrimp	3	6 oz.	170 grams
Butter	2 tbsp.	1 oz.	30 grams
Brandy	2 tbsp.	1 fl. oz.	30 milliliters
Salt, white peppercorns, cayenne, nutmeg	To season	To season	To season

METHOD OF PREPARATION

Measure butter, flour, milk, separate eggs—whip whites stiffly—grate cheese—measure brandy—cut prawns into ½-inch pieces—grease soufflé dish well. Preheat baking sheet in oven at 375° F.

METHOD OF COOKERY

1. Melt butter, add flour to make a roux, then add milk gradually, see White Sauce (pp. 256-57, rec. 216).
2. Allow to cool. Beat in yolks and cheese until smooth.
3. Chop 1 ounce prawns very fine and add to sauce, also add ½ fluid ounce brandy. Season quite highly with salt, pepper, cayenne, nutmeg.
4. Fold into stiffly-beaten whites.
5. Sauté remaining prawns in clarified butter for 1 minute; add brandy and set alight.
6. Place half soufflé mixture in dish, place flamed prawns on top, and cover with remaining mixture.
7. Place in 375° F. oven and bake 40 minutes.

SERVING

Serve with plain boiled and buttered herb potatoes (pp. 218-19, rec. 165) and a colorful tossed salad. A very good dry white full-bodied wine goes well.

75 PANCAKES

COMMENT ON METHOD

Pancakes can be made quite some time before they are served—in fact up to 12 hours in advance, providing they are prepared and kept in the way shown below. I think they are a

Step 1
Make up a batter mixture (pp. 254-255, rec. 214). Allow to stand. Melt 2 tablespoons butter in the pancake pan and add this to the batter, mixing it in well. This provides each pancake with its own buttering and saves repeated greasing of the pan. It also helps to keep the pancake over a period.

Step 2
Pour the mixture into the heated pan and roll it around so that it covers the pan base. Do not allow it to creep up the sides, otherwise you will get hard crisp edges.

76 Te Puke Pancakes

RECIPE TO PRODUCE 4 PORTIONS

	U.S.A.	IMPERIAL	METRIC
Plain flour	1 cup	4 oz.	115 grams
Salt	1 pinch	1 pinch	1 pinch
Eggs	2	2	2
Milk	1¼ cups	10 fl. oz.	285 milliliters
Grand Marnier	2 tbsp.	1 fl. oz.	30 milliliters
Butter	1 tbsp.	½ oz.	15 grams
Very red rose petals	40	40	40
Superfine granulated sugar	To dust	To dust	To dust

METHOD OF PREPARATION

Sift flour with salt—use yolk of 1 egg and 1 whole egg—melt butter—measure Grand Marnier—pluck rose petals.

METHOD OF COOKERY

1. Combine all dry ingredients, make a well, add eggs and milk gradually. Beat well.
2. Add Grand Marnier and melted butter.
3. Beat and allow to stand, covered, for 4 hours.
4. Heat a little butter in omelet pan, add batter, and rock pan to cover surface. Place 4 petals on batter. When bubbles form, flip over. DO NOT TOSS.
5. Pile pancakes on plate, brushing melted butter on top. Wrap in serviette and place in refrigerator to keep.
6. Reheat in warming oven before service.

SERVING

Fill with vanilla ice cream chopped up with fresh fruit. Dust with superfine granulated sugar and serve. The rose petals give the dish a most unusual and attractive appearance.

very valuable asset in any repertoire of recipes and can be used for sweet and savory purposes.

Step 3
Cook until small waxy bubbles appear on the surface. Then push a spatula under the pancake in one smooth movement; lift the pancake and turn it over. This is a much less demanding technique than trying to toss the beastly thing!

Step 4
When the second side is cooked, slide out onto a hot plate and brush the surface with a little melted butter and cover with a clean cloth. You can keep them covered in the refrigerator for up to 12 hours. Reheat in the warming oven and serve.

77 Citrus Pancakes

RECIPE TO PRODUCE 4 PORTIONS

	U.S.A.	IMPERIAL	METRIC
Plain flour	1 cup	4 oz.	115 grams
Salt	1 pinch	1 pinch	1 pinch
Eggs	2	2	2
Milk	1¼ cups	10 fl. oz.	285 milliliters
Orange zest	1 pinch	1 pinch	1 pinch
Lemon zest	1 pinch	1 pinch	1 pinch
Butter, melted	1 tbsp.	1 tbsp.	15 milliliters
Pancakes	8	8	8
Sauce:			
Butter	4 tbsp.	2 oz.	60 grams
Superfine granulated sugar	4 tbsp.	4 tbsp.	60 grams
Orange zest, grated	1 tbsp.	1 tbsp.	7.5 grams
Lemon zest, grated	1 tbsp.	1 tbsp.	7.5 grams
Oranges	2	2	2
Lemon	1	1	1

METHOD OF PREPARATION

Sift flour with salt—use yolk of one egg plus 1 whole egg—measure milk—melt butter for pancakes—juice oranges and lemon for sauce.

METHOD OF COOKERY

1. Mix dry ingredients, make a well, add eggs and milk gradually, beating all the time.
2. Add melted butter, beat and stand, covered, for 4 hours at least. Make pancakes as shown above.
Sauce:
3. Place butter and sugar in a hot pan and make a light fudge.
4. Add orange and lemon zests and juice, the latter a little at a time. Stir until boiling.
5. Add pancakes and fold into quarters in the sauce. Serve coated with sauce.

About Poultry

Go back over twenty years and anyone who told you that chicken would be an economy food would have been locked up.

Now it is a fact. Apart from fish in certain areas, it is the lowest cost protein available.

We have, however, suffered along the way. The battery-fed and fattened chicken lacks flavor when compared to the hard-to-find farm bird. The flavor loss in fact, in some cases, is so marked that special steps have to be taken with seasonings to give them a lift.

Every chicken dish in this section has been tested with a particularly negative brand of frozen chicken.

I hope the reasoning isn't too obtuse—it is just that I cannot see any improvement being made within the next couple of years, and so if rape is inevitable, we had better get cracking and do something about it!

CONTENTS OF SECTION

COMMENT ON METHOD

The most fascinating experience in hotel kitchens is the first time you are permitted to sew up a chicken. When I went through this part of my early training, I was as excited as a young surgeon after completing a neat appendectomy. With great pride I presented it to

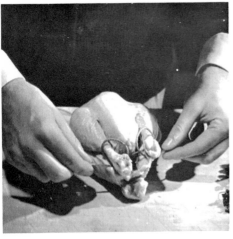

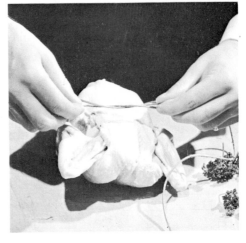

Step 1
Having first thoroughly dried the bird, cut a piece of string about 2 feet long. Loop the center piece of the string over the drumsticks and pull tight.

Step 2
Turn the bird over and tie the string in the center of the backbone.

Poultry Stuffing

Step 5
This stuffing is for roast duck and is sufficient for a 3½-4 pound bird. Fry 1 small finely sliced onion in a little butter; add 1 cup breadcrumbs when onions are tender.

Step 6
Mix in 12 soaked and pitted prunes and a small apple peeled and cut into small cubes. Add the juice of ½ lemon and season with ¼ teaspoon of sage (12 leaves fresh sage), salt, and freshly ground black peppercorns. Combine with 1 egg.

the chef for his approval. His comment was "Very good—now do it in under thirty minutes." I have had a complex ever since about using needle and thread. I have now overcome this problem by devising a tying-up method that requires no needle. It's quicker and just as neat.

Step 3
Pass the ends around the wing pieces next to the breast.

Step 4
Bring the string up and tie it in the middle. Tuck the neck flap under the knot. The chicken is now perfectly tied for roasting or boiling.

Step 7
Place one-third of the mixture in the neck end, pressing it in well with the back of a spoon. Put the remainder of the stuffing into the vent.

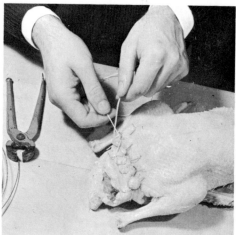

Step 8
A neat way of avoiding the use of needle and thread is to make up pins with stainless steel wire and push these through the two sides of the vent. Take a piece of fine string and lace it up, tying tightly at the far end. Complete recipe for Christmas Duckling (p. 98, rec. 81).

79 CARVING POULTRY

COMMENT ON METHOD

Ladies—protect your males from obscurity and let them carve. The joint **must** be carved by the man of the house and it is better to do this at the table in all cases but that of duck for the reasons shown below.

Step 1
Remove string from bird. Place carving fork into thickest part of thigh. Cut through between breast and inside leg until joint is reached. Lever leg away with the fork and detach the whole piece at the ball and socket joint.

Step 2
Take a thin slice off the breast—holding the bird firmly with a fork pressed into the wing.

Step 5
Remove string and pins. Cut thin slices from the breast on both sides, laying the slices onto the hot serving dish.

Step 6
Cut down from the top of the wishbone right through to the joints of the wings. This provides easier access to the slices nearer the breastbone.

Step 3
Continue to slice the breast, laying the pieces onto the carving dish. It follows that the dish must be very hot—in this way the thin slices stay hot and, as you will see, they sit in the natural juices of the bird.

Step 4
When the bird has been thoroughly "picked over," put the carcass in a plastic bag and, if you have space, deep freeze it. Later you can prepare a delicious thin soup.

Step 7
Cut the leg away, pulling it down with the fork. Detach at the ball and socket joint seen just in front of the knife blade.

Step 8
Lay carved pieces on a hot serving dish with stuffing down center. Pour juices over meats and serve. Duck is one joint that should be "attacked" in the kitchen until you are thoroughly proficient. Keep the carcass for use later on as a soup base.

80 ROAST POULTRY

RECIPE TO PRODUCE 4 PORTIONS

	U.S.A.	IMPERIAL	METRIC
Chicken	3½ lb.	3½ lb.	1.75 kilos
Onion	1 medium	1 medium	1 medium
Cloves	4	4	4
Flour	To coat	To coat	To coat
Fresh ginger	To season	To season	To season
Salt	To season	To season	To season
White peppercorns	To season	To season	To season
Clarified butter	To baste	To baste	To baste
Brandy (if you feel expensive just pour the brandy into the bird immediately before you close the oven door—delicious!)	1 tsp.	1 tsp.	1 tsp.

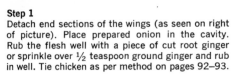

Step 1
Detach end sections of the wings (as seen on right of picture). Place prepared onion in the cavity. Rub the flesh well with a piece of cut root ginger or sprinkle over ½ teaspoon ground ginger and rub in well. Tie chicken as per method on pages 92–93.

Step 2
Always weigh the bird before you roast and then calculate the time with great accuracy. At 375° F. a chicken of this size will be perfectly cooked if given 25 minutes per pound.

COMMENT ON METHOD

Roasting is an extremely expensive method of cookery. It gets ridiculous when you try to economize by buying an "old bird" and part boil, part roast it. The older the bird the greater the weight of fat it carries, and I have proved the point time and time again that it is as cheap to buy an under 12-week-old bird as it is to pick up a so-called pot roaster, and the texture is far superior.

METHOD OF PREPARATION

Peel onion, stud with cloves—dry chicken thoroughly—prepare seasoning and flour—preheat oven to 375° F.—melt butter.

Step 3
If you are at all doubtful as to the age of your "roaster," cut up 1 small onion, 1 medium carrot, and 2 slices of bacon into thick pieces; add a little butter and simmer for 2 minutes. Add the trussed chicken, fix a lid on top, and steam for 10 minutes. Remove the now plump bird and dry thoroughly.

Step 4
Season the bird with salt and pepper and dust with flour. Brush well with clarified butter and place on a wire rack or on the oven rungs with a tray underneath. Brush during cookery. When cooked, remove, cut strings, and serve.

81 Christmas Duckling

RECIPE TO PRODUCE 4 PORTIONS	U.S.A.	IMPERIAL	METRIC
Duckling—preferably Long Island			
or Brome Lake	3½ lb.	3½ lb.	1.5 kilos
Stuffing:*			
Onion	1 small	2 oz.	60 grams
Prunes	12	12	12
Green apple	1 small	4 oz.	115 grams
Breadcrumbs	1 cup	4 oz.	115 grams
Lemon	½	½	½
Sage	¼ tsp.	¼ tsp.	1 gram
Egg	1	1	1
Butter	2 tbsp.	1 oz.	30 grams
Salt	To season	To season	To season
Black peppercorns	To season	To season	To season
Clarified butter	½ cup	4 oz.	115 grams

*See step-by-step method of preparation on pages 92-93.

METHOD OF PREPARATION

Slice onion finely—cube apple into ½-inch pieces—soak prunes 10 minutes in water, then remove stones—juice ½ lemon—use powdered sage or 12 leaves of fresh sage—beat eggs—grind peppercorns finely—dry duck thoroughly inside and out—detach wings at last joint—preheat oven to 350° F.

METHOD OF COOKERY

1. Gently sauté onion in butter to soften; add to stoned prunes, apple, breadcrumbs, sage. Moisten with lemon juice and egg.
2. Season to taste.
3. Spoon a quarter of the stuffing into the neck cavity. Place remainder into vent cavity. Pin vent together and lace up with fine string (pp. 92-93).
4. Tie bird carefully, pulling neck skin right back under middle knot.
5. Season with salt and pepper. Brush with clarified butter.
6. Place on oven shelf with roasting dish underneath. Roast 2 hours at 350° F. When cooked, remove—take out pins and string. Brush with butter and set for 20 minutes in warming oven.

SERVING

Buttered new potatoes with herbs (pp. 218-19, rec. 165), green peas, and an orange salad made with fine-diced cucumbers, celery, and chopped walnuts—peel off orange rind and pith, cut out segments—delicious! Although oranges spoil good wine, I suggest at least a reasonably full-bodied red wine.

82 Roast Turkey with Parsnip Stuffing

RECIPE TO PRODUCE 8-10 PORTIONS

	U.S.A.	IMPERIAL	METRIC
Turkey (frozen weight) (stripped weight 8 lb.)	10½ lb.	10½ lb.	15.25 kilos
Onion	1 large	10 oz.	285 grams
Parsnips	1 lb.	1 lb.	.5 kilo
Clarified butter	¼ cup	2 oz.	60 grams
Sausage meat	14 oz.	14 oz.	410 grams
Turkey liver	1	3½ oz.	100 grams
Garlic clove	1	1	1
Sesame seeds	1 level tsp.	1 level tsp.	7.5 grams
Apple	1	1	1
Lemon thyme leaves	2 tsp.	2 tsp.	6 grams
Parsley stalks	1 tbsp.	1 tbsp.	7.5 grams
Breadcrumbs	¾ cup	3 oz.	85 grams
Eggs	2	2	2
Salt and black peppercorns	To season	To season	To season
Water	1¼ cups	10 fl. oz.	285 milliliters
Bay leaves	2	2	2
Parsley	1 stalk	1 stalk	1 stalk
Bacon slices	4	4	4

METHOD OF PREPARATION

Peel and finely slice onion and parsnips—melt butter in pan. Finely dice liver—crush garlic—peel and cube apple—chop thyme leaves and parsley stalks—roughly grind peppercorns—preheat oven 325 °F.

METHOD OF COOKERY

1. Sauté onion and parsnips in butter over low heat for 15 minutes until soft. Remove.
2. Fry together sausage meat, garlic, sesame seeds, and liver for 5 minutes. Stir all the time.
3. Add to parsnips in mixing bowl. Crush together well with a potato masher. Beat to blend well; add apple, eggs, crumbs, parsley, and thyme.
4. Season inside turkey with salt. Stuff neck area only. Tie as shown on pages 92-93. Brush melted butter over flesh. Season with salt, ground peppercorns. Cover breast and top of thighs with fat bacon slices.
5. Cook for 3 hours at 325° F.* Baste occasionally during cooking, remove bacon when shrunken and crisp.
6. If too brown, recover with water-dampened brown paper.

*Most references suggest 4 hours for a turkey weighing "8 lb.—stripped, unstuffed." Mine takes 3 hours.

SERVING

Remove turkey 20 minutes before service and if you can get it into the warming oven—do so. Make gravy with liquid obtained by browning and simmering the giblets and neck in 1¼ cups water with 2 bay leaves. Serve with roast vegetables, Brussels sprouts.

Ⓖ **For Roast Wild Duck: Cream and White Sauce see page 202.**

83 BOILED POULTRY

RECIPE TO PRODUCE 8 PORTIONS

	U.S.A.	IMPERIAL	METRIC
Boiling fowl	4 lb.	4 lb.	2 kilos
Chicken stock	5½ cups	2½ pints	1.5 litre
Bay leaf	1	1	1
Thyme	1 sprig	1 sprig	1 sprig
Lemon slices	To cover breast	To cover breast	To cover breast
Onion	1 medium	3 oz.	85 grams
Carrot	1 large	3 oz.	85 grams
Bacon	1 slice	1 rasher	1 rasher

Step 1
If a really old bird has been selected then place the sliced vegetables with a rasher of bacon in the bottom of a saucepan. Place the fowl on this vegetable base, cover the pan tightly and cook over a moderate heat for 10 minutes.

Step 2
After this initial "Tenderizing" process (you can see how the bird has swollen) and add the stock, (or water if you must) you the herbs.

COMMENT ON METHOD

Chicken can be made to go a very long way if you boil it. Cool the carcass and then strip off every vestige of flesh. It can then be made into many delicious dishes by using the stock as a base for a quick, creamy, soft white sauce. You can also carve up the chicken like a roasted bird if you wish, but I consider this a gross failure in home economics.

METHOD OF PREPARATION

1. Peel and slice vegetables.

2. Dry chicken well and tie up.

3. Prepare stock.

Step 3
The fowl is then simmered with a lid on for approximately 23-25 minutes per pound. Keep a check on the liquid level and top up from time to time. In most family-size saucepans, the breast will not be covered. If this should happen to you, just keep it covered with thinly sliced lemons.

Step 4
Skim off the chicken fat and foam during cookery. When the chicken is cooked, strip off all the flesh, strain, and clarify (pp. 264-65, rec. 228) the cooking liquid and proceed with making a good White Sauce (pp. 256-57, rec. 216), using the clear chicken broth as the liquid.

84 Hunter River Chicken

RECIPE TO PRODUCE 4 PORTIONS	U.S.A.	IMPERIAL	METRIC
Spring chicken	2 lb.	2 lb.	1 kilo
White Sauce (see pp. 256-57, rec. 216 for basic method):			
Milk	1¼ cups	10 fl. oz.	285 milliliters
Plain flour	7 tbsp.	2 oz.	60 grams
Butter	3 tbsp.	1½ oz.	45 grams
Dry white wine	¼ cup	2 fl. oz.	60 milliliters
Black grapes	2 doz.	2 doz.	2 doz.

METHOD OF PREPARATION

1. Clean chicken and dry.
2. Measure white sauce items.
3. Peel and pit grapes.

METHOD OF COOKERY

1. Boil chicken with bacon, onion and carrot as per basic method.
2. Simmer for 45 minutes. Remove chicken and skim fat from cooking liquid. Strain and boil down to 10 fluid ounces.
3. Make sauce using a roux base of flour and butter. Add equal quantities of reduced stock and milk.
4. Strip skin off cooked chicken. Cut bird into primary joints (2 legs and thighs—2 breasts). Keep hot.
5. Add wine and grapes to sauce and pour over jointed chicken.

SERVING

Serve with asparagus tips and Bennet Potatoes (p. 223, rec. 173). A good fruity white wine goes perfectly.

85   Chicken Treenestar

RECIPE TO PRODUCE 6 PORTIONS	U.S.A.	IMPERIAL	METRIC
Roasting chicken	3½ lb.	3½ lb.	1.75 kilos
Onion, medium	1	1	1
Carrot, medium	1	1	1
Bay leaf	1	1	1
Clove essence	2 drops	2 drops	2 drops
Parsley sprays	3	3	3
Salt	To season	To season	To season
White pepper	To season	To season	To season
Butter	½ cup	4 oz.	115 grams
Flour	1 cup	4 oz.	115 grams
Milk	1¼ cups	½ pint	285 milliliters
Dry white wine	½ cup	4 fl. oz.	115 milliliters
Rice	2⅛ cups	1 lb.	.5 kilo
Shrimp (or 5 diced fresh jumbos)	1 small tin	1 small tin	1 small tin
Asparagus tips	1 cup	8 oz.	230 grams
Cayenne pepper	To dust	To dust	To dust

METHOD OF PREPARATION

1. Peel and leave onion and carrot whole.
2. Rub butter and flour together until sandy (kneaded butter).
3. Measure wine and milk.
4. Wash rice well.
5. Drain shrimps.
6. Cook asparagus until tender.

METHOD OF COOKERY

1. Place chicken, onion, carrot, herbs and clove essence in saucepan of cold water to cover just by 1 inch. If saucepan is not large enough, cover breast with slices of lemon.
2. Bring to boil, remove foam, reduce to a simmer, cover, and cook for 1 hour.
3. Test chicken by moving legs. Remove chicken and strip entire bird while still warm. Cover pieces with strained cooking liquor and cool in refrigerator.
4. Place carcass back in remaining liquor and crush. Bring to boil and reduce liquid by half. Skim off fat and strain off ½ pint. Add milk to this, bring to a boil and add kneaded butter. Stir well. DO NOT BOIL after addition is made. Season to taste.
5. Strain liquor from cooled chicken, add 1 pint water and use this to boil the rice (see pp. 226-27, rec. 177 for method). Add half asparagus and half shrimps to rice.
6. Cut chicken flesh into pieces, add to sauce with remaining asparagus (chopped), shrimps, and wine. Heat through.
7. Steam rice to heat, place on serving dish with chicken in center. Dust with cayenne pepper and chopped parsley.

SERVING

No potatoes or extra rice are needed, only a plain green salad with crusts of garlic toast (pp. 246-47, rec. 207). A really good full-bodied white wine is justified.

Ⓖ **For Oriental Bay Pancakes see page 203.**

86 BRAISED POULTRY

RECIPE TO PRODUCE 4 PORTIONS	U.S.A.	IMPERIAL	METRIC
Duckling, preferably Long Island or Brome Lake	3½ lb.	3½ lb.	1.75 kilos
Salt	To season	To season	In season
Black peppercorns, freshly ground	To season	To season	In season
Carrot	1 large	3 oz.	85 grams
Onion	1 medium	3 oz.	85 grams
Garlic clove	2	2	2
Clarified butter			
Apricot juice from the can*	½ cup	5 fl. oz.	140 milliliters
Bay leaf	1	1	1
Thyme	2 sprigs	2 sprigs	2 sprigs
Parsley	1 sprig	1 sprig	1 sprig
Arrowroot	2 tbsp.	½ oz.	????
Water	3½ cups	1½ pints	855 milliliters
Apricots	1 20-oz. can	1 20-oz. can	600-gram can

*Two pounds of fresh apricots can be gently poached in a light syrup when in season.

Step 1
Season the duck well inside and out. Place a little butter in the casserole dish, brown the sliced vegetables, and add crushed garlic. In a frying pan brown the duck well in some more very hot clarified butter.

Step 2
Place the duck on the browned vegetables and add the apricot juice and water. Add the herbs and place in an oven set at 375° F. to cook, with lid on, for 1½ hours.

COMMENT ON METHOD

My main "grouse" with duck is that when it is roasted, there appears to be very little meat left. My favorite method is to braise duckling, and if this is done carefully, the results are fabulous, filling, and tender. Tenderness is quite a point with me because I once planned a dinner for New Zealand's Governor-General. The roast Aylesbury duckling was so tough that even a fiercely wielded viceregal fork could not penetrate its golden crust!

METHOD OF PREPARATION

1. Peel and slice vegetables and cloves of garlic.
2. Measure apricot juice and water.
3. Preheat oven to 375° F.
4. Prepare arrowroot paste for thickening sauce.
5. Tie up herbs.
6. Dry duck inside and out and tie up.

Step 3
Skim off the fats from the surface and then remove the duck. Strain the liquor and bring it to the boil; add the arrowroot thickening and stir until it clears. If not dark enough, add some vegetable or meat flavor concentrate.

Step 4
Take the string off the duck and, holding it with a wooden spoon, give it a little extra golden crispness by placing it under a very hot broiler for a couple of minutes. Serve on a carving dish surrounded with the apricot halves.

Braised Duck in Apricot Sauce (Basic Method), recipe page 104

Roast Ginger Chicken (Basic Method), recipe page 96

87 Chicken Whakatane

RECIPE TO PRODUCE 4 PORTIONS	U.S.A.	IMPERIAL	METRIC
Roasting chicken	3 lb.	3 lb.	1.5 kilo
Tomatoes	1 lb.	1 lb.	.5 kilo
Sweet green pepper, sliced	3 cups	12 oz.	340 grams
Spring onions	8 oz.	8 oz.	230 grams
Garlic cloves	4	4	4
Dry white wine	½ cup	4 fl. oz.	115 milliliters
White peppercorns	To season	To season	To season
Salt	To season	To season	To season
Flour	½ cup	2 oz.	60 grams
Mace	¼ tsp.	¼ tsp.	¼ tsp.
Butter	4 tbsp.	2 oz.	60 grams
Parsley	To garnish	To garnish	To garnish

METHOD OF PREPARATION

1. Cut chicken in manner shown for broiling on pages 116-17. Dry chicken pieces well.
2. Place flour and seasonings in a bag.
3. Skin, pip, and chop tomatoes.
4. Skin and slice onions fine.
5. Crush garlic.
6. Measure wine and butter.
7. Chop parsley.
8. Preheat oven to 325° F.

METHOD OF COOKERY

1. Toss chicken pieces in bag containing flour and seasonings, including ground mace. Remove and shake off excess flour.
2. Gently sauté chicken in melted clarified butter until just colored.
3. Remove and keep warm.
4. In same pan, lightly fry spring onions, green peppers, and garlic for 3 minutes, then tip into casserole dish. Place chicken on vegetables. Add wine and sufficient water just to cover. Cover and place in oven set at 325° F. for 40 minutes.*

*You may thicken the sauce with a little arrowroot and water if you wish—I prefer it thin!

SERVING

Remove any surface fats, dust with parsley and serve from the dish. Serve with Otaki Potatoes (p. 219, rec. 167). A vigorous dry white wine would blend well.

88 Queensland Duckling

RECIPE TO PRODUCE 4 PORTIONS	U.S.A.	IMPERIAL	METRIC
Duckling	2½ to 3 lb.	4½–5 lb.	2 to 2.5 kilos
Water	12 cups	5 pints	3 liters
Salt	1 tbsp.	½ oz.	15 grams
Clarified butter, melted	½ cup	4 fl. oz.	115 milliliters
Pineapple pieces	1 30-oz. can	1 30-oz. can	720-gram can
Sweet green peppers	2	2	2
Fresh ginger or ground	1 tsp.	1 tsp.	45 grams
Pineapple juice (from can)	1 cup	8 fl. oz.	230 milliliters
Soya bean sauce	2 tbsp.	2 tbsp.	30 milliliters
Black peppercorns, freshly ground	1 tsp.	1 tsp.	10 grams
Arrowroot	2 tbsp.	¾ oz.	20 grams
Long grain rice	1½ cups	10 oz.	285 grams

METHOD OF PREPARATION

1. Cut duck into 4 even-size pieces.
2. Measure butter.
3. Strain juice from can of pineapple and keep.
4. Skin, pip, and dice green peppers to same size as pineapple.
5. Peel and grate fresh ginger or measure ground ginger.
6. Mix juice from can, soya bean sauce, ground peppercorns, and arrowroot.
7. Dissolve arrowroot.

METHOD OF COOKERY

1. Place duck in cold water in a large saucepan. Add salt. Bring to boil, reduce to simmer, cover with a lid, and cook 45 minutes.
2. Remove duck and dry with cloth.
3. Strain cooking liquid and remove fat from surface.
4. Shallow fry duck in butter for 15 minutes to color.
5. Put pieces back in saucepan, add 1¼ cups of cooking liquid, pineapple, green pepper, and ginger. Cover. Simmer 15 minutes. Remove duck to serving casserole and keep hot.
6. Skim fat from cooking liquid, bring to boil, thicken with arrowroot mixture, and stir until clear. Adjust seasoning if necessary. Pour over duck.

SERVING

Serve with plain Boiled Rice (pp. 226-27, rec. 177) tinted with turmeric by placing 1 level teaspoonful with the water for the initial boiling. Serve also some whole green beans lightly tossed in butter. Serve a very lightly chilled full-bodied white wine.

89 Masterton Chicken
(Braised Poultry)

RECIPE TO PRODUCE 2 PORTIONS	U.S.A.	IMPERIAL	METRIC
Tender roasting chicken	1½ lb.	1½ lb.	.75 kilo
Clarified butter	4 tbsp.	2 oz.	60 grams
Olive oil	¼ cup	2 fl. oz.	60 milliliters
Brandy	¼ cup	2 fl. oz.	60 milliliters
Dry red wine	2½ cups	1 pint	570 milliliters
Small mushrooms	2 cups	4 oz.	115 grams
Cooked ham, finely diced	¼ cup	2 oz.	60 grams
Salt and black peppercorns	To season	To season	To season
Parsley stalks	4	4	4
Thyme (or 2 sprigs lemon thyme)	¼ tsp.	¼ tsp.	¼ tsp.
Bay leaf	1	1	1
Peppercorns	6	6	6
Onions	6 small	6 small	6 small
Arrowroot	2 tbsp.	2 tbsp.	30 milliliters
Parsley	1 tbsp.	1 tbsp.	5 grams

METHOD OF PREPARATION

1. Cut chicken in half down back, cut away back bones—place in paper bag with seasonings and shake well.
2. Melt butter with oil.
3. Warm brandy and red wine.
4. Peel mushrooms and leave whole.
5. Place parsley stalks, thyme, bay leaf, peppercorns in muslin bag.
6. Peel onions.
7. Mix arrowroot with a little water.
8. Chop parsley.
9. Set oven at 350° F.

METHOD OF COOKERY

1. Toss chicken pieces in heated oil and butter until golden.
2. Pour over it warmed brandy; light, douse flames with red wine, and add mushrooms, ham, onions, and bunch of herbs. Wine should just cover all ingredients—if not, add more!
3. Cover casserole tightly.
4. Cook at 350° F. for 45 minutes.
5. Test chicken, remove from sauce, and thicken this with arrowroot. Put back chicken, dust with parsley, serve.

SERVING

Serve only a simple tossed green salad with a good dressing. A really good full-bodied red wine can be purchased to serve with this dish.

90 Chicken with 40 Cloves of Garlic

RECIPE TO PRODUCE 4 PORTIONS	U.S.A.	IMPERIAL	METRIC
Chicken	3½ lb.	3½ lb.	2.5 kilos
Bouquet garni comprising:			
Thyme	1 sprig	1 sprig	1 sprig
Rosemary	1 sprig	1 sprig	1 sprig
Sage	1 sprig	1 sprig	1 sprig
Bay leaf	1	1	1
Parsley stalks	2	2	2
Celery stick	1 small	1 small	1 small
Olive oil	⅞ cup	7 fl. oz.	210 milliliters
Garlic cloves (unpeeled)	40	40	40
Salt, black pepper	To season	To season	To season
Parsley	To garnish	To garnish	To garnish
Butter	3 tbs.	1½ oz.	45 grams
Flour and water dough:			
Flour (all purpose)	2 cups	8 oz.	240 grams
Salt	1 tbsp.	1 tbsp.	15 grams
Water	To dampen	To dampen	To dampen

METHOD OF PREPARATION

1. Cut wings off chicken at the breastbone and dry thoroughly.
2. Tie herbs together with long length of string.
3. Preheat oven to 350° F.
4. Make flour and water dough by mixing flour with salt and then adding enough cold water to make soft dough.
5. With floured hands make a dough ring.
6. Cut parsley finely.

METHOD OF COOKERY

1. Cover the base of a frying pan with olive oil and when hot add garlic cloves and bouquet garni. Toss in the oil and allow cloves to sweat gently for 2 minutes. Remove garlic cloves to an ovenproof casserole and place bouquet garni inside chicken.
2. In the oil remaining in the pan place the chicken and turn to brown lightly all over. Season chicken and then place chicken on top of the bed of garlic. Add more olive oil. Place the lid on the casserole and seal with the flour and water dough. Cook in 350° F. oven for 1½ hours.
3. When cooked, remove lid and dough—cut off chicken legs and then cut off backbone in one slice. Next, remove the bones from the breast and cut the breast in two. Remove all the outer skin from each "quarter." Cover with finely chopped parsley. Heat the fresh butter until foaming and pour over parsleyed chicken. Serve immediately.

SERVING

As a main course accompanied by a salade Niçoise and a light fruity red wine.

91 DEEP-FRIED POULTRY

COMMENT ON METHOD

As this method of preparation needs more illustrations, I shall not list the recipe. A 2-pound chicken will satisfy 4 people and the beaten egg is made up with 1 whole egg and 2 tablespoons oil.

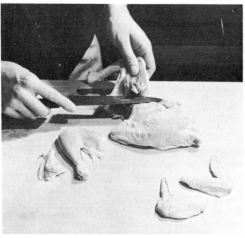 

Step 1
Detach the wing pieces as shown on the right of this picture. Cut off the legs at the thigh joint, just under my left thumb, and then remove the skin.

Step 2
Cut the whole of the breast away from the bony backbone and remove the outer skin.

 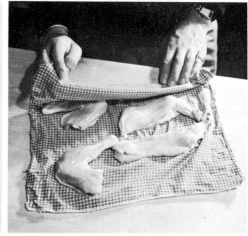

Step 5
You will now have the joints shown above. From a 2-pound bird you get 2 legs (each 4 ounces); 2 breasts (each 3 ounces); 2 wings (each 2 ounces); and 15 ounces of jolly good trimmings for an excellent soup base. Prepare exactly as for the beef stock on pages 26-27, recipe 15—delete beef and use chicken trimmings.

Step 6
Dry the main joints thoroughly in a clean cloth.

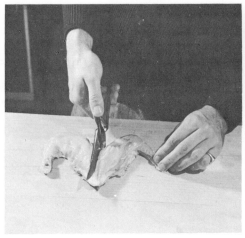

Step 3
Cut the breast in two down the center. Chicken scissors are best for this job but it can be done with a sharp heavy knife.

Step 4
Beat the breast gently with a rolling pin—this will loosen the bones. Now cut out the bones carefully.

Step 7
Toss the pieces in well-seasoned flour in a plastic bag. See extreme left of picture. Now coat the pieces in the egg and oil mixture and finally coat with fine breadcrumbs. Shake to remove surplus.

Step 8
Place chicken into a deep fryer set at 300° F. for 12 minutes. Allow to drain and then serve very hot.

92 Chicken in the Crust

RECIPE TO PRODUCE 4 PORTIONS	U.S.A.	IMPERIAL	METRIC
Chicken	2 lb.	2 lb.	1 kilo
Five-Minute Pastry (pp. 186-87, rec. 140)			
Mushrooms	4 large	4 large	4 large
Clarified butter	4 tbsp.	2 oz.	60 grams
Lemon juice	1 tbsp.	1 tbsp.	15 milliliters
Oil for deep frying			
Egg	1	1	1

METHOD OF PREPARATION

1. Prepare chicken as for deep frying (pp. 112-13, rec. 91)—use breasts only.
2. Prepare pastry.
3. Peel mushrooms.
4. Preheat oil in deep fryer to 400° F.
5. Beat egg for sealing pastry.

METHOD OF COOKERY

1. Lightly fry mushrooms in butter with lemon juice. Drain and pat dry.
2. Roll out pastry and cut into 2 pieces large enough to enclose breasts. Place each piece of chicken on the pastry pieces with 2 mushrooms on top of each.
3. Brush edges of pastry with beaten egg and seal tightly.
4. Deep fry for 10 minutes at 400° F. Drain and serve.

SERVING

One pastry case is sufficient for 2 portions unless the diner is extremely robust, in which case make it 1 case per person. Serve with a colorful salad and a bottle of chilled dry white wine.

114

93 Scotch Duckies

RECIPE TO PRODUCE 4 PORTIONS	U.S.A.	IMPERIAL	METRIC
Cooked duck meat	12 oz.	12 oz.	360 grams
Mushrooms, finely sliced	1½ cups	3 oz.	85 grams
Lemon juice	1 tbsp.	1 tbsp.	15 milliliters
Parsley stalks	1 tbsp.	1 tbsp.	7.5 grams
Duck stock, reduced	1 cup	8 fl. oz.	230 milliliters
Clarified butter	2 tbsp.	1 oz.	30 grams
Flour	5 tbsp.	1¼ oz.	37.5 grams
Shallots	4 tbsp.	4 tbsp.	115 grams
Whisky	2 tsp.	2 tsp.	10 milliliters
White Sauce (pp. 256-57, rec. 216)	8 tbsp.	4 fl. oz.	115 milliliters
Parsley stalks	4 tbsp.	4 tbsp.	30 grams
Breadcrumbs	½ cup	2 oz.	60 grams
Egg	1	1	1
Salt	To season	To season	To season
Black peppercorns	To season	To season	To season

METHOD OF PREPARATION

1. Squeeze lemon juice.
2. Prepare white sauce.
3. Peel and finely chop shallots.
4. Prepare flour, egg, and breadcrumbs in separate dishes.
5. Preheat oil in deep fryer to 400° F.

METHOD OF COOKERY

1. Dice duck meat finely.
2. Boil down the duck stock to 1 cup.
3. Place chopped duck into a saucepan and poach for 8 minutes in the reduced stock.
4. Fry sliced mushrooms with lemon juice in clarified butter. Add to duck.
5. Shallow fry shallots and when very hot—light a match—pour over whisky, and light quickly. When flames die down, add this to duck mixture with white sauce and parsley stalks. Season with salt and ground peppercorns.
6. Mold into 2-ounce portions, dip in flour, egg, and breadcrumbs, and deep fry for 2 minutes until crisp and golden. Drain and serve.

SERVING

Serve with Golden Coast Sauce (p. 68, rec. 52). Otaki Potatoes (p. 219, rec. 167), and a plain green tossed salad. A dry red wine goes down well with this dish.

ⓖ **For Buttered Breast of Chicken see page 204.**

RECIPE TO PRODUCE 2 PORTIONS	U.S.A.	IMPERIAL	METRIC
Chicken	1½ lb.	1½ lb.	.75 kilo
Flour	To season	To season	To season
Salt	To season	To season	To season
White peppercorns, freshly ground	To season	To season	To season
Clarified butter	¼ cup	2 oz.	60 grams

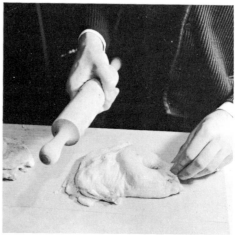

Step 1
Cut the chicken in half, starting by cutting through the backbone. Remove the wing ends and the neck.

Step 2
Beat the chicken lightly with a rolling pin to loosen the **major** bones. Remove only the heaviest bones (found below the thigh nearest to the board in the photograph).

COMMENT ON METHOD

Broiled poultry, especially young, tender chicken is a very attractive method of cookery. A small bird should be chosen—about 1½ pounds.

METHOD OF PREPARATION

1. Preheat broiler (medium hot).
2. Melt butter.
3. Prepare seasoned flour.

Step 3
Toss the halves well in seasoned flour.

Step 4
Brush the rack well with butter, then place the chicken halves on top. Now brush the surface thoroughly and broil outer side for 10 minutes until golden brown; turn over and broil for a further 8-10 minutes. Serve immediately.

95 Broiled Chicken Perth

RECIPE TO PRODUCE 2 PORTIONS	U.S.A.	IMPERIAL	METRIC
Chicken	1½ lb.	1½ lb.	.75-1 kilo
Clarified butter	3 tbsp.	1½ oz.	45 grams
Tomatoes	2	2	2
Garlic cloves	2	2	2
Salt	To season	To season	To season
White peppercorns	To season	To season	To season
Parsley	To garnish	To garnish	To garnish

METHOD OF PREPARATION

1. Cut chicken as shown in basic method—flour and season.
2. Slice tomatoes ¼ inch thick.
3. Crush garlic.
4. Preheat broiler to medium hot, rack 3 inches away from heat.
5. Melt butter.
6. Chop parsley.

METHOD OF COOKERY

1. Brush chicken with melted butter.
2. Place under broiler, skin side up.
3. Broil 10 minutes, turn, butter, and give 10 minutes on reverse side.
4. Brush with butter again.
5. Place tomato slices over cooked upper side, spread squeezed garlic on tomatoes. Dust with salt and ground peppercorns. Broil just to color tomato (3 minutes).
6. Remove. Dust with parsley and serve.

SERVING

Very pleasant dish when served with buttered asparagus and Otaki Potatoes (p. 219, rec. 167). Serve a ''crackling'' rosé wine.

96 Deviled Chicken

RECIPE TO PRODUCE 2 PORTIONS	U.S.A.	IMPERIAL	METRIC
Chicken	1½ lb.	1½ lb.	.75 kilo
Dry mustard	2 tbsp.	2 tbsp.	15 grams
Dry vermouth	1 tbsp.	1 tbsp.	15 milliliters
Clarified butter, melted	1 tbsp.	1 tbsp.	15 milliliters
Black peppercorns, freshly ground	To season	To season	To season
Salt	To season	To season	To season

METHOD OF PREPARATION
1. Trim chicken—prepare 2 sides.
2. Measure mustard, vermouth, butter.
3. Preheat broiler to medium hot.

METHOD OF COOKERY
1. Mix mustard, vermouth, and melted butter. Brush chicken all over.
2. Season with salt and pepper.
3. Broil skin side uppermost for 10 minutes, turn, baste again with mustard mix, and give a further 10 minutes on cut side.
4. Dust with parsley and serve.

SERVING
Serve with grilled tomatoes, corn-on-the-cob, and Bennet Potatoes (p. 223, rec. 173). Serve a light cold beer.

Ⓖ **For Broiled Chicken Carson see page 205.**

About Meat

When I did my compulsory service with the British Army they tried to make me a radar expert. I suppose it was an obvious choice, as I had spent my whole life in the hotel business!

I rebelled, and after spending several months as a pan washer in a very large kitchen (a revolting occupation), I was commissioned as a Specialist Catering Officer. At that time we had a ration scale that allowed 3½ ounces of meat—fat on, bone in—frozen, per man per day. This was considered sufficient and, believe it or not, we managed.

In our Armed Forces there would be a military *putsch* if less than sixteen ounces of meat was provided as a daily ration. We eat a lot of meat because it is a tradition based upon our early farming days—a time when bulk was beneficial and variety was for snobs.

Our current situation has changed the environment but has only had a marginal effect upon our meat-eating habits—there appears to be some room for adjustment. The lion's share of the population now live in towns and cities and work in industry. A small element can still kill their own stock and "live off the land," but the majority buy from the butcher. As a result the plentiful, cheap, excellent cuts of the past are giving way to the still plentiful, but expensive, excellent cuts of today.

As meat costs rise there are only two courses open if you want to avoid a vastly inflated home budget. You can either reduce the quantity eaten or buy cheaper cuts.

My butcher friends tell me that the trend is toward the purchase of cheaper cuts *and* a lesser quantity, at least among their "white collar clients"! The obvious result of these changes is that the incomparable (I really believe this) roast is giving way to a variety of methods suited to cheaper cuts. But here you have an interesting conflict of desire.

"The cheaper the cut, the longer and more involved is the method of cookery." There are very few exceptions to this rule. Our modern way of life, however, suggests that "the quicker the method the better." In other words, to coin a phrase, one jumps out of the frying pan into the casserole!

The answer isn't easy. I believe that chops and steaks will continue to be popular because of their speed. Lesser cuts will be braised, pot roasted, and stewed (or casseroled if you prefer the word). The quantity of meat used in these dishes will be quite large—at least eight ounces per portion. Roasts will gradually drop in popularity because of their high initial cost —coupled with weight loss during cookery. A four-pound leg of lamb will produce almost exactly two pounds of edible meat when cooked—therefore this meat costs exactly twice the purchase cost per pound, and if eight-ounce portions are eaten it is as costly as a half pound tenderloin.

In this section I have given nine methods of cooking meats, five of which are suitable for cheaper cuts. I have also given five preparation techniques for variety meats in the hope that these important foods may become more acceptable—when understood.

CONTENTS OF SECTION

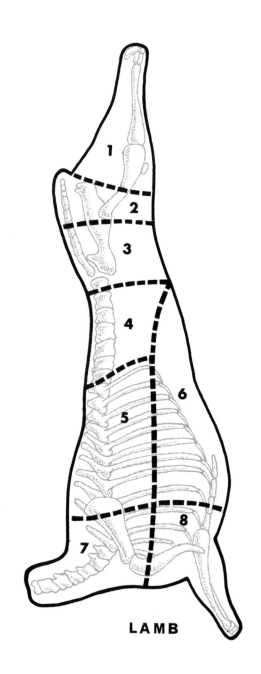

LAMB

LAMB

CUT OR JOINT	POSITION ON CARCASS	METHOD OF COOKING
Whole leg	1 + 2 + 3	Whole leg—roast
Half leg:		
Shank (or lower)	1	
Thick (or upper)	2 + 3	
Shank end half of leg	1	Roast
Thick end half of leg	2 + 3	
Middle fillet	2	
Short leg	1 + 2	
Forequarter or shoulder quarter (mutton or hogget)		
Half forequarter:		
Either raised shoulder	Part of 7 and 8 and	
Neck and breast	Part of 7 and 8, and 8	Roast or braise
Shank end half		
Raised shoulder	Part of 7 and 8	
Half raised shoulder:		
Either shank end half	Part of 8;	
Or blade end half	Part of 7	
Neck and breast	Part of 7 and 8	
Neck	Part of 7	
Spanish neck (neck and shoulder)	7	
Best end of Spanish neck (shoulder blade)	Part of 7	Stewing and braising
Scrag end of Spanish neck	Part of 7	
Framed shoulder (includes some upper ribs)	7 + 8 + part of 5 and 6	
Shank end of framed shoulder	8 + part of 6	
Blade end of framed shoulder	7 + part of 5	
Loin	4 + 5	
Middle loin	4	Roast
Rib end of loin or rack (Saddle is a double rack)	5	
Middle loin chops	4	
Rib chops	5	
Rib loin chops	5	Shallow fry, broil, braise
Chump chops or leg steaks	3	
Leg chops	2 + part of 1	
French cutlets	5	
Shoulder chops or cutlets	7	Stewing and braising
Neck chops	7	Stewing and braising
Best end neck chops	Part of 7	Shallow fry, broil, braise
Shoulder chops	8	
Shoulder cutlets	Part of 8	Stewing and braising
Flap or flank chops	Part of 6	
Flap or flank	6	
Mutton, hogget, or lamb steak	1 + 2 + 3	Shallow fry, Chinese and Japanese cookery

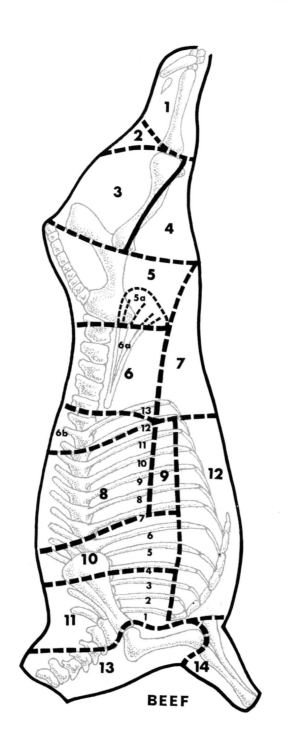

BEEF

BEEF

CUT OR JOINT	POSITION ON CARCASS	METHOD OF COOKING
Rump steak	5	Broil, shallow fry, braise
Tenderloin or eye fillet steak	6a + part of 5a	Broil, shallow fry or finely chop and eat raw
Undercut steak (fillet)	5a	Broil, shallow fry, braise
T-bone steak or porterhouse steak bone in	Part of 6	
Porterhouse steak, bone out or sirloin steak	Part of 6	
Club steak, rib eye steak, or scotch fillet steak	Part of 8	Braise, or marinade and then shallow fry or broil
Round or topside steak	Part of 3	Braise, use for beef olives
Flat bone sirloin steak	4	Braise, use for beef olives
Blade or bolar steak	Part of 11, 12, and 13	Braise, or marinade and then shallow fry or broil
Crosscut blade steak	Part of 11	Shallow fry or broil if well hung — otherwise braise or casserole
Chuck steak	Part of 11	Braise or casserole
Flank steak	7	Braise or casserole
Silverside or bottom round	Part of 3	Corned and poached
Sirloin	6	Roast
Hip of beef	5	Roast (by some considered better value than sirloin)
Rib steak	8	Broil, shallow fry, braise
Back ribs	10	Roast or braised in the piece
Chuck ribs	11	Braise, pot roast, roast (marginal)
Club steak or wing rib	6b	Roast
Short or flat ribs	9	Marinade 24 hours and braise or barbecue as a piece
Set of ribs (standing rib roast)	8 + 9	Roasts and pot roasts
Gravy beef	1, 13	Clear soups, stocks
Shin meat	1, 14	Clear soups, steaks plus very long slow cooking for pies and pudding fillings
Brisket or breast	12	Braise or corn and poach
Leg	1	
Half leg	Part of 1	
Shin	14	
Half shin	Part of 14	General stewing, soup, and stocks
Knuckle end of shin	Part of 14	
Middle cut of shin	Part of 14	
Thick end of shin	Part of 14	
Thin flank	7	

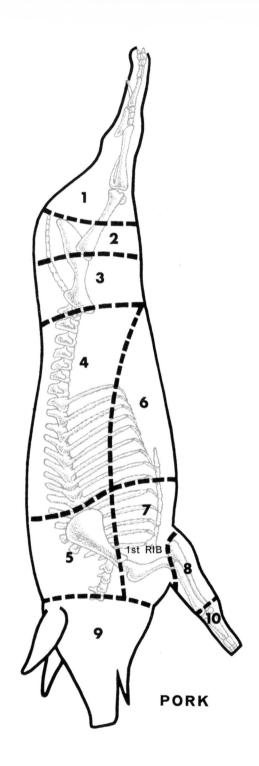

1st RIB

PORK

PORK

CUT OR JOINT	POSITION ON CARCASS	METHOD OF COOKING
Whole leg pork (ham)	1 + 2 + 3	
Half leg of pork:		
Shank (or lower)	1	
Thick (or butt)	2 + 3	
Shank end half of leg	1	Roast
Thick end half of leg	2 + 3	
Middle fillet	2	
Short leg	1 + 2	
Loin	4	Roast on bone or roll and stuff
Boston butt or foreloin (shoulder)	5	Roast or braise
Loin chops, rib chops	4	Broil, shallow fry, braise
Leg chops	1 + 2	Broil, shallow fry, braise
Chump chops or hip chops	3	Braise, shallow fry, broil
Foreloin chops or shoulder chops	5	Braise
Framed shoulder of pork	5 + 7 + 8	Pot roast, braise
Shank end of framed shoulder	7 + 8	Stewing
Blade end of framed shoulder	5	Stewing and braising
Hand of pork	7 + 8	Chinese dishes, stewing
Spring (belly, flap, or flank)	6	Chinese dishes, stewing
Pork slices or salt pork	6	Braise
Forequarter	5 + 7 + 8	Braise or stew
Ham steaks	1, 2, 3	Shallow fry, grill, braise
Rolled pork	5 + 7 + 8 and part of 4 + 6	Roast or pot roast
Trotters	10	Boil, braise, or broil (to finish)
Head	9	Boil, braise, or broil (to finish)
Picnic shoulder	7	Roast
Cushion picnic shoulder	8	Roast
Spareribs	6 + 7	Roast, broil or bake

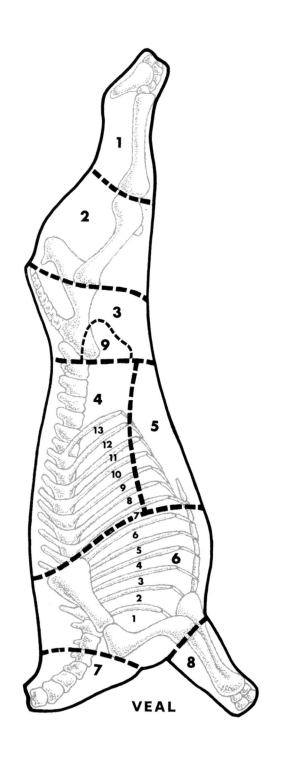

VEAL

VEAL

CUT OR JOINT	POSITION ON CARCASS	METHOD OF COOKING
Veal cutlets or fillets	2	Roast, braise, or slice finely for wiener schnitzel
Veal rump steak or roast	3	Shallow fry or broil
Veal steak	2, 9, part of 4, part of 6	Beat well and fry or braise
Veal undercut (fillet)	9	Shallow fry or broil
Veal T-bone	Part of 4	
Veal cutlets	4	
Veal loin or rib roast	4	Roast
Rolled shoulder, blade, and arm steaks	6	Braise, pot roast
Stewing veal	1, 5, 7, 8	Stews and pies
Veal soup meat	1, 7, 8	Special stocks for use with fish, poultry, and other delicate foods
Breast of veal	3, 5	Braise
Rib chops and roast	4	Roast, shallow fry, or broil
Crown roast	4	Roast

97 CARVING MEATS

COMMENT ON METHOD

I have already commented upon my feeling with regard to carving on page 94. I trust that my statement will help my fellow males to pick up the carving knife and perform. I have concentrated mostly on lamb on this page, because due to its size it tends to be the most complex.

Step 1 SHOULDER OF LAMB

First slice off the top of the shoulder. This is called the Hawke's Bay cut and is very popular with New Zealand farmers in that region. It is usually kept and served cold.

Step 2

Cut the end piece off as shown and then carve out the sweet shoulder cutlets—seen on right of carving dish.

Step 5

Cut straight down onto bone until the aitchbone is reached. About ½-inch-thick slices are best for lamb.

Step 6

Turn the blade flat onto the bone at the last cut and carve along the bone, thus releasing the perfect slices. The remainder of the joint is carved at will!

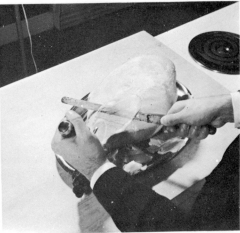

Step 3
Continue through the piece to produce individual cutlets, in each case cutting between the rib bones. The end piece can be sliced as shown on the left of the carving dish.

Step 4 LEG OF LAMB
First slice a small piece from the fleshy side of the leg. This is done so that the joint can balance on this point during carving.

Step 7 HAM
Ham can be carved as shown for leg of lamb, or as illustrated here. My preference is for this method. Cut away the fat first. Use a long thin knife.

Step 8
Slice into very thin pieces, bearing down on the cutting-in stroke, but use no pressure on the back stroke.

RECIPE TO PRODUCE 6-8 PORTIONS

	U.S.A.	IMPERIAL	METRIC
Leg of lamb	5–6 lb.	5–6 lb.	2.25–3 kilos
Garlic cloves	2	2	2
Salt	To season	To season	To season
Black peppercorns	To season	To season	To season
Flour	To dust	To dust	To dust

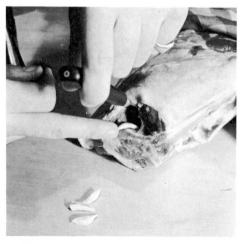

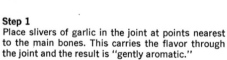

Step 1
Place slivers of garlic in the joint at points nearest to the main bones. This carries the flavor through the joint and the result is "gently aromatic."

Step 2
Rub the joint well with salt and freshly ground black peppercorns, and then dust it all over with sifted flour. The bamboo spikes indicate the position of garlic in a leg of lamb.

COMMENT ON METHOD

In accordance with ancient tradition, many gourmet authors and leading chefs prefer to cook their roasts at a high initial temperature and then reduce heat to roughly 400° F. I am not a traditionalist. It has been proven time and time again that a stable temperature of 300°–325° F. throughout cookery produces a tender, succulent, and above all economic result. The time has now gone when we can afford to let such expensive meat cuts evaporate.

METHOD OF PREPARATION

1. Peel cloves of garlic and cut into thin slices as shown in Step 1.
2. Dry meat with a clean cloth.
3. Preheat oven to 325° F.

Step 3
Place the joint directly on the rungs of your oven shelf with a roasting dish underneath. In this way you get all-round circulation of hot air, and it definitely improves the quality. Always put joint in fat side uppermost. Roast for approximately 30 minutes per pound—internal temperature 168° F.

Step 4
Unless the joint is very lean do not baste during cookery and NEVER add the dripping from one animal to a roast of another, i.e. pork dripping for lamb roast.
You can see the advantage of the oven shelf position here. You can really stack in the vegetables, whereas space is limited with the joint in the same roast tray.

99 Roast Spiced Beef

RECIPE TO PRODUCE 6 PORTIONS

	U.S.A.	IMPERIAL	METRIC
Rolled ribs of beef*	3 lb.	3 lb.	1.5 kilos
Cinnamon, freshly grated	¼ tsp.	¼ tsp.	¼ tsp.
Ground cardamom	¼ tsp.	¼ tsp.	¼ tsp.
Fresh ground ginger	1 tsp.	1 tsp.	1 tsp.
Fresh grated nutmeg	¼ tsp.	¼ tsp.	¼ tsp.
Ground black pepper	¼ tsp.	¼ tsp.	¼ tsp.
Garlic cloves	3	3	3

*Also good with porterhouse roast on the bone, tail removed (see back cover or illustration pp. 142-143) and sirloin roast. In either case cut pockets close to the bone and insert spices on a knife blade.

METHOD OF PREPARATION

1. Untie beef.
2. Mix spices.
3. Make a muslin pad.
4. Slice garlic.
5. Heat oven to 350° F.

METHOD OF COOKERY

1. Dip pad in spices and rub beef well inside and out. Put in garlic slices.
2. Retie and roast at 350° F. for 30 minutes per pound.

SERVING

Serve with roast potatoes and Sesame Crust Parsnips (p. 242, rec. 200). A grilled tomato half adds color and a side salad of chilled watercress adds a perfect touch. Serve a really full-bodied red wine.

100　Roast Leg of Pork and Spiced Peaches

RECIPE TO PRODUCE 8-12 PORTIONS	U.S.A.	IMPERIAL	METRIC
Leg of pork	8 lb.	8 lb.	3.6 kilos
Seasoned Oil:			
Thyme	½ tsp.	½ tsp.	½ tsp.
Caraway seed	½ tsp.	½ tsp.	½ tsp.
Garlic cloves	2	2	2
Olive oil	½ cup	4 fl. oz.	115 milliliters
Salt	To season	To season	To season
Apple Wine Gravy:			
Tart apple	1	1	1
Black peppercorns	To season	To season	To season
Cloves	To season	To season	To season
Dry white wine	½ cup	4 fl. oz.	115 milliliters
Spiced Peaches:			
Peach halves	8	8	8
Wine vinegar	1¼ cups	10 fl. oz.	285 milliliters
Cloves	½ tsp.	½ tsp.	½ tsp.
Cinnamon stick	1 small stick	1 small stick	1 small stick
Allspice berries	½ tsp.	½ tsp.	½ tsp.
Watercress		Large bunch for garnish	

METHOD OF PREPARATION

1. Score outer skin of pork.
2. Simmer oil ingredients together on low heat for 30 minutes. Strain, bottle for use.
3. Peel, core, and finely slice apple.
4. Grind peppercorns.
5. Use canned or bottled peaches—strain off juice.
6. Wash watercress well.
7. Set oven 350° F., drip pan under rack as per basic method.

METHOD OF COOKERY

1. Puncture leg in deepest muscle areas with steel skewer, sprinkle well with salt.
2. Brush joint with seasoned oil.
3. Stand for 1 hour before roasting. Place joint directly on oven rack. Roast 30 minutes per lb. (185° F. internal).
4. Simmer wine vinegar, cloves, cinnamon and allspice in a covered saucepan for 30 minutes.
5. Pour over peach halves; when cold, lift out halves and place them around the joint;* strain and bottle spicy vinegar for later use.
6. Keep roast warm. Pour fat from vegetables in drip pan, and scrape meat residues into a small frying pan.
7. Add cloves, peppercorns, wine, and apple. Simmer until soft. Bring to boil, pass through a sieve. Reheat and serve with the meat.

*Do not keep peaches in spice vinegar.

SERVING

Carve the joint at the table. Provide a spare plate for the crackling. Serve with Brussels sprouts, roast potatoes, and a watercress garnish. Beer is best with pork.

Ⓖ **For Stuffed Saddle of Lamb Roxdale see page 206.**

RECIPE TO PRODUCE 6 PORTIONS

	U.S.A.	IMPERIAL	METRIC
Blade roast	3 lb.	3 lb.	1.5 kilos
Flour	To coat	To coat	To coat
Black peppercorns	To season	To season	To season
Salt	To season	To season	To season
Clarified butter	6 tbsp.	3 oz.	85 grams
Onions	2 medium	8 oz.	.25 kilo
Parsnip	1 medium	4 oz.	115 grams
Carrot	1 large	4 oz.	115 grams
Garlic cloves	2	2	2
Bay leaf	1	1	1
Red wine	½ cup	4 fl. oz.	115 milliliters
Arrowroot	3 tbsp.	3 tbsp.	3 tbsp.

Note: Stock can be used in lieu of wine.

Step 1
Because of its long slow moist heat this method makes a wonderful job of cuts containing a good deal of sinew. The selected roast should be wiped with a clean damp cloth and then dried thoroughly. Now lightly flour the roast.

Step 2
First shallow fry the vegetables with crushed garlic in the saucepan or casserole dish—remove when browned slightly. The size of utensil is important; it should be just large enough for the roast.

COMMENT ON METHOD

Forgive me if I get immodest over the recipe given here. Although it is a basic method it is really very pleasant—no, delicious! The meat is a roast blade of beef (well matured) and it melts in your mouth. Pot roasting should really be reserved for tougher meat cuts—those with a good deal of connective tissue—but I find that now and again a tender cut can be given added flavor when cooked in this fashion.

METHOD OF PREPARATION

1. Peel and cut vegetables into ¼-inch-thick slices.
2. Peel cloves of garlic.
3. Measure wine.
4. Make an arrowroot paste with 3 tablespoons each of arrowroot and water.

Step 3
Add the roast and brown well on both sides over a high heat. This builds up a delicious crust that both flavors and colors the sauce. Replace the fried vegetables and set the roast on top.

Step 4
Add the wine and the bay leaf. Place a lid on top and cook either on the ring or in an oven set at 350° F. to simmer for 40 minutes per pound. When cooked, throw out vegetables (they will be "pappy" and tasteless) and clear the fat from the "sauce." Thicken this with arrowroot paste, correct the seasoning, and serve.
Note: You can add fresh vegetables half an hour before the roast is cooked, removing the old ones. The new vegetables are then served with the roast.

137

102 Rump and Beer Pot Roast

RECIPE TO PRODUCE 6 PORTIONS	U.S.A.	IMPERIAL	METRIC
Joint of well-hung rump	3 lb.	3 lb.	1.5 kilos
Bacon	4 slices	4 slices	4 slices
Onion	1 cup	4 oz.	115 grams
Flat beer	1¾ cups	15 fl. oz.	430 milliliters
Water	1¾ cups	15 fl. oz.	430 milliliters
Vinegar	2 tbsp.	1 fl. oz.	30 milliliters
Brown sugar	1 tbsp.	1 tbsp.	10 grams
Salt	To season	To season	To season
Black peppercorns	6	6	6
Cloves	3	3	3
Bay leaf	1	1	1
Arrowroot	To thicken	To thicken	To thicken
Flour	To dust	To dust	To dust

METHOD OF PREPARATION

1. Ask butcher to lard rump with strips of pork fat and tie up as a joint with *no wood skewers.* *
2. Slice onion.
3. Measure beer, water, vinegar.
4. Prepare brown sugar, herbs, and spices.

*And stand back and see what happens!

METHOD OF COOKERY

1. Flour and season meat.
2. Fry bacon in casserole and remove.
3. Fry onion, remove.
4. Add meat. Brown well and again—remove!
5. Replace onion and bacon, put meat on top. Add vinegar, water, beer, brown sugar, cloves, bay leaf, peppercorns. Cover and simmer 3 hours.
6. Skim the fat from the surface of the cooking liquid and strain it. Thicken the sauce if necessary, with an arrowroot and water paste. Bring back to the boil until the sauce thickens and becomes clear.

SERVING

Carve the meat in the kitchen and lay it in thick overlapping slices on an oval serving dish. Coat with the sauce and surround the plate with freshly cooked Root Vegetables. (pp. 241-42, rec. 198). Serve with beer.

103 Venison Pot Roast with Cream Sauce

RECIPE TO PRODUCE 4 PORTIONS	U.S.A.	IMPERIAL	METRIC
Boned shoulder venison	2 lb.	2 lb.	1 kilo
Salt	1 tsp.	1 tsp.	5 grams
Black peppercorns	1 tsp.	1 tsp.	5 grams
Sugar	2 tsp.	2 tsp.	10 grams
Celery seed	1 tsp.	1 tsp.	2 grams
Ginger	½ tsp.	½ tsp.	1 gram
Clarified butter	¼ cup	2 oz.	60 grams
Bay leaves	2	2	2
Whole allspice	6	6	6
Juniper berries	6	6	6
Black peppercorns	6	6	6
Stock fortified with meat protein extract or soya sauce	2 cups	16 fl. oz.	455 milliliters
Lemon	1	1	1
Dry red wine	½ cup	4 fl. oz.	115 milliliters
Cream	10 tbsp.	5 fl. oz.	140 milliliters

METHOD OF PREPARATION

1. Weigh meat and wipe well.
2. Mix salt, ground pepper, sugar, ginger, and celery seed.
3. Measure butter.
4. Measure wine and cream.
5. Slice lemon peel into very fine strips.

METHOD OF COOKERY

1. Rub seasoning mixture into meat, inside and out. Then tie up.
2. Brown meat in casserole in butter. Add bay leaves, allspice, juniper berries, peppercorns, stock, wine, and sliced lemon.
3. Cook over low heat for 2 hours.
4. When tender, strain off the sauce. Add the cream and heat. If not thickened enough, add a little arrowroot and water paste and boil for 30 seconds.
5. Correct seasoning and pour sauce over meat or serve it from a sauceboat.

SERVING

Carve roast in the kitchen and lay it out on a serving dish. If coated with the sauce, then dust with chopped parsley. Serve with thin potato chips, Sweet Potato Cakes (p. 242, rec. 199), and a green salad. A smooth rich red wine is an excellent accompaniment.

RECIPE TO PRODUCE 4 PORTIONS

	U.S.A.	IMPERIAL	METRIC
Blade steak	1½ lb.	1½ lb.	.75 kilo
Onion	1 medium	4 oz.	115 grams
Carrot	1 large	4 oz.	115 grams
Bay leaf	1 leaf	1 leaf	1 leaf
Parsley stalks	1 spray	1 spray	1 spray
Thyme	2 sprigs	2 sprigs	2 sprigs
Clarified butter	1 oz.	1 oz.	30 grams
Salt	To season	To season	To season
Black peppercorns	To season	To season	To season
Garlic cloves	2	2	2
Meat stock (p. 26, rec. 15 for quick method)	½ cup	4 fl. oz.	115 milliliters
You can also add tomato sauce for additional color			
Flour	To dust	To dust	To dust

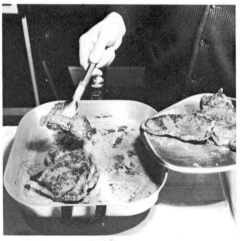

Step 1
Cut the steaks into relatively even-size pieces. Dry them well and then press into the seasoned flour.

Step 2
Melt butter in the frying pan and sear the steaks until beautifully browned. Remove. Add a little more butter and fry the vegetables until they too are browned.

COMMENT ON METHOD

It has been said that there is no difference between braising and pot roasting. They are similar, but a braise should be *covered* with liquid at the beginning of cookery, not just ¼ to ½ way up as is the case with a pot roast.

METHOD OF PREPARATION

1. Tie up bay leaf, parsley, and thyme with a piece of string.
2. Dry steaks thoroughly.
3. Heat frying pan to 400° F.
4. Peel and cut vegetables into ¼-inch-thick slices.
5. Measure stock and tomato sauce.
6. Season the flour well with salt and ground peppercorns.

Step 3
Replace the steaks, add the herbs, and pour in sufficient stock to cover. With a wooden spoon, scrape all residue from pan base into the liquid. Cover and cook at the simmer for 1½ hours.

Step 4
When meat has cooked remove the herbs, skim off the fat, and thicken with an arrowroot paste if necessary. I sometimes add ½ cup of tomato sauce. This improves the color and helps to thicken the cooking liquid. Dust with parsley and serve.

Yorkshire Pudding, recipe page 255

Roast Spiced Beef Porterhouse, recipe page 134

105 Spring Sunshine: Pork

RECIPE TO PRODUCE 4-6 PORTIONS	U.S.A.	IMPERIAL	METRIC
Belly of pork (called spring)	2 lb.	2 lb.	1 kilo
Flour	To coat	To coat	To coat
Onion	1 cup	4 oz.	115 grams
Bay leaf	1	1	1
Parsley stalks	2	2	2
Thyme	1 sprig	1 sprig	1 sprig
Clarified butter	¼ cup	2 oz.	60 grams
Black peppercorns, freshly ground	To season	To season	To season
Salt	To season	To season	To season
Garlic clove	1	1	1
Light beef stock	2½ cups	1 pint	570 milliliters
Green pepper	1½ cups	6 oz.	170 grams
Apple	1¼ cups	5 oz.	140 grams
Large raisins	3 tbsp.	1 oz.	30 grams
Arrowroot	1 tbsp.	1 tbsp.	10 grams

METHOD OF PREPARATION

Remove rind from pork belly and cut into thin strips ½-inch across—dry thoroughly—flour and season—
heat butter to 400° F.—slice onion thickly—cut green pepper into thin 2-inch strips—soak raisins after
measuring—tie herbs together—measure stock—10 minutes before service, slice, core, and chop apple.
Blend arrowroot with a little water.

METHOD OF COOKERY

1. Brown meat thoroughly in frying pan. Remove.
2. Brown onion, replace meat, and add crushed garlic.
3. Add herbs and stock—stir well. Cover and cook 1½ hours at 220° F. (simmer).
4. Thirty minutes before end of cookery, add sliced green pepper. Continue cooking.
5. Remove fat from surface, take out herbs, add apple 10 minutes before serving. Immediately before
   service, add drained raisins. Thicken at boil with arrowroot.

SERVING

Serve with buttered noodles (p. 230, rec. 183) and baby carrots. A glass of cold beer is the best "wine."

106 Beef Tuckerbag
(A "Bird" by Any Other Name)

RECIPE TO PRODUCE 4 PORTIONS	U.S.A.	IMPERIAL	METRIC
Fresh breadcrumbs	1 cup	4 oz.	115 grams
Shredded suet	¼ cup	2 oz.	60 grams
Parsley	4 tbsp.	4 tbsp.	30 grams
Dried marjoram	1 tsp.	1 tsp.	1 tsp.
Grated lemon rind	½ tsp.	½ tsp.	½ tsp.
Eggs	2	2	2
Grated nutmeg	To season	To season	To season
Salt	To season	To season	To season
Ground black peppercorns	To season	To season	To season
Dry red wine	½ cup	4 fl. oz.	115 milliliters
Top side of beef	2 lb.	2 lb.	1 kilo
Onion	1	1	1
Mushrooms	2 cups	4 oz.	115 grams
Clarified butter	4 tbsp.	4 tbsp.	60 grams
Beef stock	2½ cups	1 pint	570 milliliters
Arrowroot	3 tbsp.	3 tbsp.	30 grams
Water	3 tbsp.	3 tbsp.	50 milliliters

METHOD OF PREPARATION

Make fresh crumbs—grate lemon rind—cut beef into thin slices 3 by 4 inches—pound thin—finely chop onion and mushrooms—mix arrowroot and water to thicken—prepare string to tie tuckerbags—chop parsley.

METHOD OF COOKERY

1. Mix breadcrumbs, suet, parsley, marjoram, lemon rind, and eggs.
2. Season well with salt, pepper, and grated nutmeg.
3. Add wine to mix.
4. Spread mixture on flattened, tenderized beef. Roll up and secure with fine string. Do not tie too tightly.
5. Shallow fry onion and mushrooms in melted butter in flameproof casserole until onion is cooked but not colored. Add tuckerbags and brown well on all sides.
6. Pour over stock to cover. Simmer 1½–2 hours until tender.
7. Just before serving, skim off fat, thicken sauce with arrowroot and water, cut strings from tuckerbags, and serve coated with sauce.

SERVING

Serve with very well Creamed Potatoes (p. 222, rec. 171) and Green Beans (p. 236, rec. 190). A side salad of chilled chopped tomatoes and watercress can also be served. I would choose a good full-bodied red wine for this dish.

Ⓖ **For Bluff Bolar: Beef see page 207.**

107 BOILED MEAT

Comment for Recipe on Hams

Boiling:

Put in a large kettle. Cover completely with boiling water. Reduce the heat so that the water barely simmers. Cover. Cook 20-30 minutes per pound.

Baking:

5 lb. ham	2½ hours at 325° F.
9-12 lb. ham	3½ hours at 325° F.
15-20 lb. ham	4 hours at 325° F.

In Foil:

Wrap the ham in foil, place on rack in roasting pan, fat side up, and bake at 325° F. A meat thermometer will register 150° F. when the ham is done.

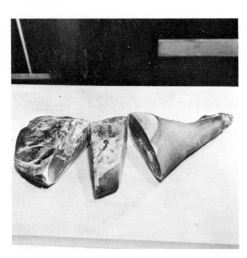

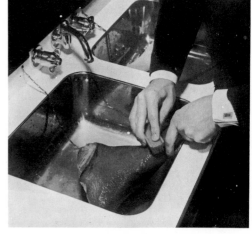

Step 1

Ask your supplier to cut a country-cured ham into 3 pieces as shown above. The hock, or shank, end (on the right) is a good boiling piece, as is the gammon, or butt, end. The middle gammon is excellent for frying or broiling, and by keeping it for this purpose you avoid that frightful business of eating cold ham until you look like one.

Step 2

The first task is to soak the ham for approximately 12 hours. This is becoming less and less necessary as curing techniques improve, but it is better to be on the safe side. This hock end weighed 5 pounds 2 ounces before soaking and 5 pounds 6 ounces after. From this you will gather that it also makes the joint beautifully moist. After soaking, give it a good scrub.

COMMENT ON METHOD

Traditionally thousands upon thousands of people buy a ham for Christmas. It has become as normal a piece of festive fare as the English Christmas pudding. It is boiled in clothes kettles, kerosene cans, or in the baby's bath. Apart from this annual "boil up" there are few roasts cooked in this manner. Because of this I have selected the ham as a "basic" in order to suggest a rather unusual way of approaching the problem.

Step 3
Place the scrubbed ham in cold water with *no added seasoning* and bring to a gentle boil (this means simmer, but I happen to like, the description gentle boil). Leave at this heat for 20 minutes per pound.

Step 4
Allow to half cool in the "poaching" liquid and then strip off the skin. Place the naked joint in the refrigerator to finish cooling.

108 High Country Ham, Red Currant Sauce (Hogget)*

RECIPE TO PRODUCE 4 PORTIONS	U.S.A.	IMPERIAL	METRIC
Cured and smoked leg of hogget†	6 lb.	6 lb.	3 kilos
Red Currant Sauce:			
Red currant jam	½ cup	4 oz.	115 grams
Celery	3 oz.	3 oz.	85 grams
Lemon	1	1	1
Clarified butter	1 tbsp.	1 oz.	30 grams

*In New Zealand the term hogget applies to sheep meat of an age between lamb and mutton. It is highly prized.

METHOD OF PREPARATION

1. Do not cut up in manner illustrated for ham—soak for 24 hours in cold water and then scrub.
Sauce:
2. Slice celery finely.
3. Measure jam.
4. Squeeze lemon.

METHOD OF COOKERY

1. Place meat in cold water to just cover.
2. Bring to boil and cook to 150° F. internal heat for approximately 2 hours.
3. Cool in liquor and wash. Peel off outer skin.
4. Fry celery in butter until just softened.
5. Add red currant jam and lemon to taste.
6. Coat with a little of the sauce and place in an oven set at 350° F. for 20 minutes.
7. Can also be served cold.

†You will have to ask your butcher to cure and smoke a large leg of lamb—it is worth the effort. Even he will be surprised.

SERVING

Serve hot in very thin slices with a spoonful of the sauce with each portion. A light dry red wine blends well.

109 Ox Tongue and Raisin Sauce*

RECIPE TO PRODUCE 6 PORTIONS	U.S.A.	IMPERIAL	METRIC
Ox tongue, **fresh,** not pickled	3 lb.	3 lb.	1.5 kilo
Butter	¼ cup	2 oz.	60 grams
Flour	½ cup	2 oz.	60 grams
Beef stock (p. 26, rec. 15)	1½ cups	12 fl. oz.	345 milliliters
Dry white wine	½ cup	4 fl. oz.	115 milliliters
Raisins	7½ tbsp.	2½ oz.	70 grams
Currants	7½ tbsp.	2½ oz.	70 grams
Lemon peel	1 tsp.	1 tsp.	1 tsp.
Malt vinegar	1 tsp.	1 tsp.	5 milliliters
Superfine granulated sugar	To taste	To taste	To taste
Lemon juice	To taste	To taste	To taste
Almonds	1 tbsp.	1 tbsp.	5 grams

METHOD OF PREPARATION

1. Sift flour.
2. Measure stock, butter, wine, raisins, and currants.
3. Finely slice lemon peel.
4. Juice 1 lemon.
5. Peel and chop almonds roughly; extra for garnish if required.

METHOD OF COOKERY

1. Place tongue in cold water, bring to boil—pour off water. Fill again with cold water; simmer gently for 3 hours. Add a good bunch of herbs to the water and as many vegetable trimmings as you can find. When cooked, remove skin and cool.
2. Make a roux with butter and flour and cook until fawn colored. Add stock, wine, currants, raisins, vinegar and lemon peel.
3. Simmer until fruit is soft. Adjust flavor balance of sweet and sour with lemon and sugar to suit your taste. If necessary add more wine.
4. Cut tongue in thin slices and lay it in overlapping slices in a shallow casserole dish. Pour sauce over and heat through in the oven.

*This is a typical German-style dish with a light fawn sauce.

SERVING

Serve with Ngauruhoe Potatoes (p. 222, rec. 172), green peas, and broiled tomato halves. I would choose a chilled rosé wine for this dish.

RECIPE TO PRODUCE 1 PORTION	U.S.A.	IMPERIAL	METRIC
Porterhouse steak	8 oz.	8 oz.	.25 kilo
Salt	To season	To season	To season
Ground black peppercorns	To season	To season	To season
Garlic	1 clove	1 clove	1 clove
Clarified butter	To cover pan	To cover pan	To cover pan

Step 1
Porterhouse is my favorite steak. It has the advantage of always being cut across the grain and is therefore relatively tender, especially if hung for ten days after killing. It also has an excellent flavor. One way in which it is spoiled is by failing to remove the sinew that lies beneath the fat at the backbone end. Always cut this out, as it stops the steak from "bunching."

Step 2
Especially where steak has been hung, it is essential to wipe it with a clean damp cloth and to dry the surface thoroughly.

COMMENT ON METHOD

Have you ever stopped to consider how interesting is the choice of titles for food, for example, the word "broiled" when applied to steak. It is so much more appetizing than the word "fried," and yet I'm certain that in seven out of ten cases where "broiled" steak is served, it is in fact "fried." I believe that unless you have a really excellent broiler, it is better to shallow fry a steak. If you are careful with the fat, it need not be fattening and the method allows for numerous variations.

METHOD OF PREPARATION

1. Heat frying pan to 400° F.
2. Melt butter.
3. Peel garlic.

Step 3
Before you add the seasoning, place the clarified butter in the pan to heat. Now season with salt and roughly ground black peppercorns. Garlic can be added by using a cheese knife (with the barbed end); jam the garlic onto the points and cut the clove. This is an easy nonmessy way of adding a "sigh of garlic." Then fry immediately. Never keep a steak hanging around when seasoned.

Step 4
Always handle the steak with a blunt pair of tongs. Sear the meat first on both sides and then cook to the stage you prefer. I have weaned my assistant from a well-cooked steak to a definitely "bloody" one—she is delighted and so am I. Why don't you risk it too?

111 Porterhouse Steak Whakatane
(Shallow-fried Meat)

RECIPE TO PRODUCE 4 PORTIONS

	U.S.A.	IMPERIAL	METRIC
Porterhouse steaks	4 8-oz.	4 8-oz.	4 230-gram
Clarified butter	¼ cup	2 oz.	60 grams
Salt	To season	To season	To season
Black peppercorns	To season	To season	To season
Garlic cloves	2	2	2
Spring onions	Small bunch	Small bunch	Small bunch
Sweet tomatoes—small	2 cups	10 oz.	285 grams
Parsley	Small bunch	Small bunch	Small bunch
Sweet green pepper	1 large	1 large	1 large
Cultivated mushrooms	2 cups	4 oz.	115 grams

METHOD OF PREPARATION

1. Remove gristle beneath fat.
2. Roughly grind peppercorns.
3. Peel and roughly chop spring onions.
4. Cut tomatoes in quarters.
5. Chop parsley roughly.
6. Slice green pepper and mushrooms finely.
7. Dry steaks well.

METHOD OF COOKERY

1. Heat a little clarified butter in a large frying pan.
2. Season steaks and rub all over with a cut clove of garlic.
3. Seal the meat at a high heat, reduce temperature, and turn to create an even color.
4. In another pot, melt remaining butter, add spring onions and garlic. Fry for 2 minutes. Add green pepper, mushrooms, and tomato. Reduce heat and allow tomato to soften.
5. When steaks are cooked, lay on an oval dish, cover with vegetables, and dust with parsley.

SERVING

Serve with Bennett Potatoes (p. 223, rec. 173) and Sesame Crust Parsnips (p. 242, rec. 200). Select a dry vigorous red wine.

112 Pork Chops Ngauruhoe

RECIPE TO PRODUCE 4 PORTIONS	U.S.A.	IMPERIAL	METRIC
Single rib pork chops (1½ inch thick)	4	4	4
Large raisins	6 tbsp.	2 oz.	60 grams
Apple	1	1	1
Root ginger (fresh)	¼ tsp.	¼ oz.	5 grams
Orange	1	1	1
Cloves	To season	To season	To season
White peppercorns	To season	To season	To season
Salt	To season	To season	To season
Matches or cocktail sticks	16	16	16
Fine string			
Clarified butter	6 tbsp.	3 oz.	85 grams

METHOD OF PREPARATION

1. Remove rind, make an incision into eye meat through fat to bone.
2. Peel, core, and slice finely the apple.
3. Peel and cut ginger in fine slivers.
4. Cut off thin slices of orange peel and slice into very fine strips like cotton.
5. Grind cloves, peppercorns.
6. Cut off heads of matches, sharpen to a point.
7. Heat frying pan to 300° F.

METHOD OF COOKERY

1. Use 12 raisins, ¼ apple, 1 sliver ginger, ¼ teaspoon zest of orange per chop, mix, and stuff into incision.
2. Spear fat edges with match sticks (about 4 per chop). Intertwine with string and tie up.*
3. This may be done the day before, the chops being wrapped in waxed paper and put in the refrigerator.
4. Melt butter in a frying pan, season chops, and shallow fry 20 minutes for 1–1½-inch chops—35 minutes for 2-inch chops.
5. Turn from time to time.

*See method used for poultry (p. 93, ill. 8)

SERVING

Serve with Ngauruhoe Potatoes (p. 222, rec. 172) and a tossed salad. Serve a cold beer or chilled sake and soda—an acquired taste!

Ⓖ For Veal Cutlets Yerex see page 208.

113 BROILED MEAT

RECIPE TO PRODUCE 4 PORTIONS

	U.S.A.	IMPERIAL	METRIC
Lamb cutlets	8	8	8
Clarified butter	To brush	To brush	To brush
Black peppercorns	To season	To season	To season
Garlic	To season	To season	To season
Salt	To season	To season	To season

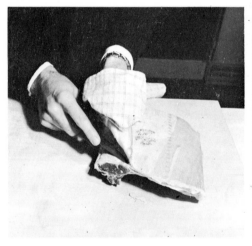
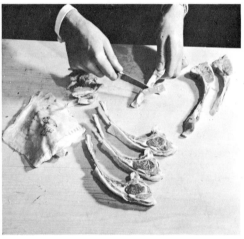

Step 1
In the case of lamb (and this is why I have chosen it for the basic method) you must first remove the "fell" or outer skin. If this is not done, then the skin contracts, pulling the cutlet out of shape and making it go brittle. At least ask your butcher to see that it is done!

Step 2
Cutlets look so much more attractive when the bones are trimmed as shown above. The trimmings make an excellent addition to an Irish stew. A further refinement in trimming can be made by getting the butcher to remove the backbone completely, leaving only the rib.

COMMENT ON METHOD

I hope you will forgive the obvious plug for New Zealand Lamb in the Step 1 photograph below. I have no reservations in this direction because I am confident, having tasted lamb from many countries, that New Zealand leads the world in over-all quality. My favorite lamb comes from the coastline stations where up to one ton of sea salt falls to the acre. This adds a tang to the meat which places it beyond international competition. Here endeth the commercial—now on with the method!

METHOD OF PREPARATION

1. Peel garlic.
2. Prepare seasoning.
3. Brush broiler rack with clarified butter.
4. Heat broiler medium hot.

 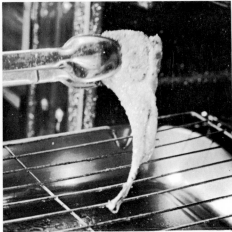

Step 3
Dry the cutlets and then season immediately before placing under the broiler. Brush with clarified butter and cook for 5 minutes either side. Turn only once.

Step 4
When turning the meat use a blunt pair of tongs. If you use a fork or knife, you release the natural juices and spoil the supreme succulence.

114 Fillet Steak Paddy

RECIPE TO PRODUCE 4 PORTIONS	U.S.A.	IMPERIAL	METRIC
Tenderloin steaks	4 8-oz.	4 8-oz.	4 225-grams
Garlic clove	1	1	1
Salt	To season	To season	To season
Black peppercorns	To season	To season	To season
Clarified butter	4 tbsp.	2 oz.	60 grams
Liver sausage	6 tbsp.	3 oz.	85 grams
Capers	4 tsp.	4 tsp.	10 grams
Dry red wine	½ cup	4 fl. oz.	115 milliliters

METHOD OF PREPARATION

1. Dry steaks well, season with garlic, salt, freshly ground peppercorns.
2. Weigh liver sausage, capers, and wine.
3. Warm serving plate.

METHOD OF COOKERY

1. Melt butter and fry steaks until cooked to suit your taste.
2. Remove to plate, pour off fats from pan.
3. Pour in the red wine and scrape up the meat residues.
4. Spread liver sausage on steaks and sprinkle with capers.
5. Pour wine sauce over steaks and serve.

SERVING

Unless you happen to be a potato addict, may I suggest that only a tossed green salad should be served. As a wine, you would do well to buy a smooth full-bodied red.

115 Apple Gammon: Ham

RECIPE TO PRODUCE 4 PORTIONS	U.S.A.	IMPERIAL	METRIC
Ham steaks	4 7-oz.	4 7-oz.	4 200-grams
Black peppercorns	To season	To season	To season
Clarified butter	To brush	To brush	To brush
Sliced apples	2	2	2
Soft brown sugar	6 tbsp.	2 oz.	60 grams
Lemon parsley butter (pp. 260-61, rec. 222)	4 tbsp.	4 tbsp.	60 grams

METHOD OF PREPARATION

1. Soak $\frac{1}{2}$-inch-thick gammon steaks for 12 hours in cold water. Rinse. Snip rind every inch. Dry. Season with ground black peppercorns (no salt).
2. Slice apple ($\frac{1}{2}$ apple per steak).
3. Measure sugar.
4. Heat broiler to medium.

METHOD OF COOKERY

1. Brush steaks with clarified butter.
2. Place under medium broiler and cook 5 minutes, turn and broil 3 minutes.
3. Remove from heat, cover with sliced apples, and dust with brown sugar.
4. Replace under hot broiler for 2-3 minutes to glaze.
5. Serve topped with a large pat of lemon parsley butter.

SERVING

Glazed whole carrots and perfectly cooked asparagus tips go well as vegetables. Green Pepper Potatoes (p. 224, rec. 175) also help to set the meal going. Very cold cider then makes it all worthwhile.

Ⓖ **For Pork and Mushroom Teko Teko see page 209.**

RECIPE TO PRODUCE 4 PORTIONS

	U.S.A.	IMPERIAL	METRIC
White veal boned neck	1½ lb.	1½ lb.	.75 kilo
Carrots	2 medium	8 oz.	.25 kilo
Parsnips	1 medium	3 oz.	85 grams
Onion	1 large	6 oz.	170 grams
Chicken stock	2¼ cups	1 pint	570 milliliters
Parsley	2 stalks	2 stalks	2 stalks
Thyme	2 sprigs	2 sprigs	2 sprigs
White peppercorns and salt	To season	To season	To season
Cloves of garlic	1	1	1
Bay leaf	1	1	1
Egg yolks	2	2	2
Cream	4 tbsp.	4 tbsp.	70 milliliters

Step 1

It is essential to use cuts of meat from the neck and shoulder for a white stew. The connective tissue melts during cookery and adds flavor and texture. As much fat as possible should be trimmed from the meat before cutting.

Step 2

Season the meat well and then place all the ingredients in a saucepan. Add the cold stock and squeeze in the garlic clove; stir and bring to a simmer. Skim the surface from time to time during cookery.

COMMENT ON METHOD

The French have a method of preparing light pigment meats in a stewed form called "blanquette." This is one of my favorite dishes. The meat used in this basic recipe is milk-fed white veal. The quality and quantity of the milk produces an excellent product, and modern farming techniques avoid the unpleasant methods used in Europe. If you cannot get local supplies, then try young lamb or pork in lieu.

METHOD OF PREPARATION

1. Cut meat into 1-inch cubes.
2. Peel and slice vegetables into 1-inch-thick pieces.
3. Peel garlic.
4. Prepare chicken stock.
5. Ready the herbs.
6. Separate yolks from whites of egg.
7. Measure cream.

Step 3
After 50-60 minutes, strain off the liquid. You should then have 1¼ cups. Combine the cream and egg yolks in a small bowl and add the stock by degrees—it will start to thicken.

Step 4
Pour the egg- and cream-enriched stock back over the meat and stir over a very gentle heat until thick and glossy. Do not allow to boil; otherwise the eggs will curdle.

117 Pork Stew Waikato

RECIPE TO PRODUCE 4 PORTIONS	U.S.A.	IMPERIAL	METRIC
Pork shoulder or neck meat	1½ lb.	1½ lb.	.75 kilo
Parsley	1 bunch	1 bunch	1 bunch
Bay leaf	1	1	1
Celery leaves	2 tbsp.	½ oz.	15 grams
Salt and white pepper	To season	To season	To season
Carrot	1 cup	4 oz.	115 grams
Onion	½ cup	2 oz.	60 grams
Tomatoes	4 medium	4 medium	4 medium
Butter	3 tbsp.	1½ oz.	45 grams
Flour	7 tbsp.	1¾ oz.	50 grams
Stock	2 cups	16 fl. oz.	455 milliliters
Dry white wine	¼ cup	2 fl. oz.	60 milliliters
Parsley	To garnish	To garnish	To garnish

METHOD OF PREPARATION

1. Dice meat and soak for 1 hour in cold water.
2. Finely dice carrot.
3. Slice onion in ½-inch pieces.
4. Peel, pip, and dice tomatoes.
5. Make a white sauce with butter, flour, add stock from pork (after 30 minutes' cookery) and wine.
6. Chop parsley for garnish.

METHOD OF COOKERY

1. Add parsley, bay leaf, celery leaves, onion, and seasoning to soaked pork.
2. Bring to boil, skim, reduce to simmer, cover, and cook for 1 hour.
3. After 30 minutes, add carrot and remove 1 cup stock to make white sauce.
4. Season white sauce.
5. Remove celery leaves and herbs from meat; add further 1 cup stock to sauce. Strain off remaining stock (if any) and add sauce to meat.
6. Serve garnished with diced tomato and chopped parsley.

SERVING

Serve with Cheddar Baked potatoes (p. 220, rec. 169) and Brussels sprouts. A full-bodied white wine is a good match.

118 Veal Shoulder Downstage

RECIPE TO PRODUCE 4 PORTIONS	U.S.A.	IMPERIAL	METRIC
Veal shoulder	2 lb.	2 lb.	1 kilo
White stock (chicken, veal, or vegetable)	To cover	To cover	To cover
Salt	½ tsp.	½ tsp.	2 grams
Carrot	1 small	1 small	1 small
Onion	1 medium	1 medium	1 medium
Cloves	6	6	6
Leek	1	1	1
Parsley stalks	2	2	2
Thyme	1	1	1
Bay leaf	1	1	1
Butter	3 tbsp.	1½ oz.	45 grams
Flour	6 tbsp.	1½ oz.	45 grams
Veal cooking liquor	2½ cups	1 pint	570 milliliters
Small onions	12	12	12
Button mushrooms	15	15	15
Egg yolks	2	2	2
Cream	¼ cup	2 fl. oz.	60 milliliters
Lemon juice	½ lemon	½ lemon	½ lemon
Parsley	To garnish	To garnish	To garnish

METHOD OF PREPARATION

1. Cut veal into 1-inch cubes.
2. Peel carrots, onion (stick with cloves).
3. Tie leek, parsley, bay leaf, and thyme together.
4. Remove and keep stalks from mushrooms.
5. Peel small onions and cook in white stock.
6. Mix yolks with cream.
7. Measure butter, flour.
8. Chop parsley.

METHOD OF COOKERY

1. Place cubed veal in saucepan, cover with stock, add salt, and bring to boil—skim.
2. Add carrot, onion, and herbs. Simmer for 1½ hours.
3. Prepare a roux with butter and flour after 1 hour's cookery.
4. Measure ½ pint veal cooking liquor and add the mushrooms and their stalks. Cook for 15 minutes. Remove mushrooms, throw away stalks.
5. Remove vegetables and herbs from meat and add cooked mushrooms and onions.
6. Finish sauce by adding yolks and cream and a few drops of lemon juice. Strain over veal, mushrooms and onions.
7. Heat (DO NOT BOIL). Serve sprinkled with chopped parsley.

SERVING

Serve with plain Boiled Rice (pp. 226-27, rec. 177) mixed with chopped parsley and skinned, pipped, and diced red tomatoes. Serve a very good, full-bodied, white wine.

Ⓖ **For Shoulder of Lamb Wellington see page 210.**

RECIPE TO PRODUCE 4 PORTIONS	U.S.A.	IMPERIAL	METRIC
Blade steak	1½ lb.	1½ lb.	.75 kilo
Flour	To coat steaks	To coat steaks	To coat steaks
Clarified butter	¼ cup	2 oz.	60 grams
Black peppercorns and salt	To season	To season	To season
Carrot	2 medium	8 oz.	.25 kilo
Onion	1 large	6 oz.	170 grams
Parsnip	1 medium	3 oz.	85 grams
Beef stock (p. 26, rec. 15 for quick-method)	2¼ cups	1 pt.	570 milliliters
Bay leaf	1	1	1
Thyme	2 sprigs	2 sprigs	2 sprigs
Parsley stalks	2 stalks	2 stalks	2 stalks
Cloves of garlic	1	1	1
Parsley, chopped	To garnish	To garnish	To garnish
Arrowroot	2 tbsp.	2 tbsp.	20 grams

Step 1
It has been my experience that meat cooks better by this method when cut into large pieces. The meat is first dried thoroughly, coated with seasoned flour, and then fried really brown in the butter. Remove the meat and add the vegetables. Fry these until well colored.

Step 2
Place cooked meat back in the casserole and add the stock and herbs. Scrape the meat residues from the casserole pan up into the liquid. Cover and simmer for 1½-2 hours or place in an oven set at 325° F. for the same duration.

COMMENT ON METHOD

You could just as easily call this a "casserole," and most people do because it sounds better. The method is identical and is a great favorite of mine because, as a vehicle for variety, it is unsurpassed. There is virtually no limit to your attempts at improvisation and they will be basically successful if you apply this simple method.

METHOD OF PREPARATION

1. Slice vegetables into ¼-inch-thick slices.
2. Tie herbs in bundle.
3. Peel clove of garlic.
4. Cut steak into 1- by 2-inch pieces.
5. Measure stock.
6. Mix arrowroot with 3 tablespoons water to a smooth paste.

Step 3
If you can plan far enough ahead, place the casserole in the refrigerator to cool overnight. The next day the fats will have set on the surface and they can be easily removed. If you are in a rush, then skim off the fats and remove the herbs.

Step 4
Bring the casserole to the boil and pour in the paste of arrowroot, stirring all the time until it thickens and clears. Taste for seasoning and dust with parsley before serving. Fresh vegetables can replace those cooked from the beginning if added 30 minutes before cookery is completed.

120 Kare Poaka No. 1: Pork Curry

RECIPE TO PRODUCE 4 PORTIONS	U.S.A.	IMPERIAL	METRIC
Pork collar or neck and shoulder	2 lb.	2 lb.	1 kilo
Salt and ground peppercorns	To season	To season	To season
Clarified butter	4 tbsp.	2 oz.	60 grams
Onion, medium	1	1	1
Curry powder, mild	2 tbsp.	½ oz.	15 grams
Sweet green pepper	1 medium	4 oz.	115 grams
Bay leaf	1	1	1
Garlic clove	1	1	1
Mustard seeds	¼ tsp.	¼ tsp.	2 grams
Lemon juice	½ lemon	½ lemon	½ lemon
Red currant jelly	1 tbsp.	1 tbsp.	20 grams
Coconut stock (p. 264, rec. 229)	1¼ cup	10 fl. oz.	285 milliliters
Tomato sauce	¼ cup	2 fl. oz.	60 milliliters
Coconut cream	1 cup	8 fl. oz.	230 milliliters
Chili powder	1 large tsp.	1 large tsp.	5 grams

METHOD OF PREPARATION

1. Remove skin from pork and cut into 1-inch cubes.
2. Season with salt and peppercorns.
3. Slice onion into ¼-inch rings.
4. Cut green peppers into 1-inch squares.
5. Crush or squeeze garlic.
6. Squeeze lemon.
7. Make coconut stock and coconut cream.
8. Combine tomato sauce with stock.

METHOD OF COOKERY

1. Heat butter in large saucepan.
2. Add seasoned meat and stir.
3. Add onion and curry powder—stir well.
4. Add mustard seeds, green peppers, bay leaf, garlic, and blend.
5. Pour in lemon juice, red currant jelly, combined stock, and sauce.
6. Simmer in an open pot for 1½ hours. If possible, cook the day before and leave in refrigerator overnight.
7. Skim off all fats and add ⅝ cup coconut cream; reheat and pour off ¾ cup of cooking liquid (add more coconut cream if needed). Blend liquor with the chili powder and pour into a small sauceboat. This extra hot sauce can be added by those who prefer an "undemocratic curry"!

SERVING

Serve with plenty of plain Boiled Rice (p. 226-27, rec. 177). Side dishes may be prepared—some of these are given (p. 265, rec. 230). Never serve wine—only lime juice and soda, or beer.

121 Pork Chops Parramatta

RECIPE TO PRODUCE 4 PORTIONS	U.S.A.	IMPERIAL	METRIC
Pork chops	4 6-oz.	4 6-oz.	4 170-gram
Clarified butter	4 tbsp.	2 oz.	60 grams
Salt	To season	To season	To season
Black peppercorns	To season	To season	To season
Onion	1 medium	3 oz.	85 grams
Garlic clove	1	1	1
New Zealand Sauce (p. 258, rec. 220)	1½ cups	12 fl. oz.	340 milliliters
Bay leaves	2	2	2
Water	1½ cups	12 fl. oz.	340 milliliters
Mushrooms	3 cups	6 oz.	170 grams
Butter	4 tbsp.	2 oz.	60 grams
Arrowroot	2 tbsp.	2 tbsp.	20 grams
Parsley	To garnish	To garnish	To garnish

METHOD OF PREPARATION

1. Trim rind from chops—dry well.
2. Slice onion.
3. Crush garlic.
4. Grind peppercorns.
5. Make New Zealand sauce and reduce by boiling to 1¼ cups. Add an equal amount of water to the sauce.
6. Peel mushrooms and remove stalks.
7. Make a paste with arrowroot and 2 tablespoons water.

METHOD OF COOKERY

1. Season chops and fry in clarified butter.
2. Add sliced onion and crushed garlic. Brown.
3. Add watered down sauce and bay leaves.
4. Bake in uncovered casserole for 1 hour at 325° F.
5. Add mushrooms shallow fried in butter.
6. Thicken with arrowroot paste and continue to simmer on stove until tender.

SERVING

This is a very spicy dish and needs bland accompaniments. I suggest plain Boiled Rice (pp. 226-27, rec. 177) and plain cooked peas. Serve a really extrovert dry red wine.

Ⓖ **For Back Sticks Venison Stew see page 211.**

122 LAMBROLL

COMMENT ON METHOD

I have devoted two pages to the Lambroll because it should become a speciality meat cut. It is quite simply a double lamb chop without the bone, and it is the absence of bone that makes it a fitting dish for such excellent meat. A chop or cutlet is an easy, quick, pleasant dish, but the remaining bones give the finished plate a messy appearance. Lambroll makes the ultimate best of the cutlet.

Step 1
As with all loin of lamb dishes, the outer membrane must be removed first. Cut lightly in 4-inch-wide strips, loosen the skin at the neck end—grip and tear off.

Step 2
Cut the meat away from the bone, starting at the backbone. Keep the knife close to the bone all the way.

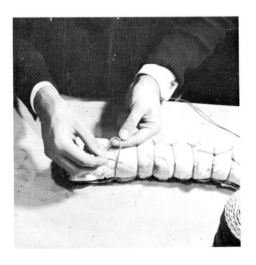

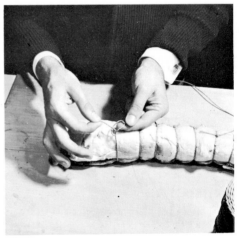

Step 5
Short end under long end, then over itself.

Step 6
Pull short end through loop and pull tight.

Step 3
Trim the fillet from the leg end and place this on the boned loin so that it makes it appear even. Season the open loin with salt and freshly ground black peppercorns. You can also add a filling at this stage. Roll up and cut off excess breast.

Step 4
Tie the joint every 1½ inches—long end toward you.

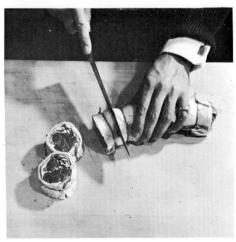

Step 7
With long end make a lasso and throw it over the short end. Pull tight again and cut off excess string.

Step 8
Cut between the strings just before they are cooked.

123 Lambroll Arneb

RECIPE TO PRODUCE 6 PORTIONS	U.S.A.	IMPERIAL	METRIC
Whole loin of lamb	1	1	1
Garlic salt	To season	To season	To season
Black peppercorns	To season	To season	To season
Clarified butter	½ cup	4 oz.	115 grams
Fresh mint	1 small bunch	1 small bunch	1 small bunch
Potatoes	1 lb.	1 lb.	.5 kilo
Mint jelly	8 tsp.	2 oz.	60 grams

METHOD OF PREPARATION

1. Prepare loin as shown in basic method. Season inside with garlic salt.

2. Heat pan.

3. Finely chop mint.

4. Peel, boil, and mash potatoes.

5. Preheat oven to 325° F.

METHOD OF COOKERY

1. Season lambrolls again with a little garlic salt and freshly ground black peppercorns.

2. Place in hot pan with a little butter and sear both sides quickly.

3. Transfer to small roasting pan, brush with butter and sprinkle with mint. Place in oven for 10 minutes. Turn. Give another 10-15 minutes. Brush again with mint and butter.

4. When cooked, cut strings and place in rows on serving dish. Decorate around their base with creamed potatoes. On top of each, place a spoonful of mint jelly. Parsley and quartered tomatoes may also be used as garnishes.

SERVING

Traditionally these miniature roasts should be served with Bennett Potatoes (p. 223, rec. 173) and a tossed Salad (pp. 246-47, rec. 207). Serve a light dry red wine.

124 Lambaty

RECIPE TO PRODUCE 4 PORTIONS	U.S.A.	IMPERIAL	METRIC
Loin of lamb	1	1	1
Garlic salt	To season	To season	To season
Black peppercorns	To season	To season	To season
Clarified butter	6 tbsp.	3 oz.	85 grams
Tomato sauce	¾ cup	6 fl. oz.	170 milliliters
Dry white wine	¾ cup	6 fl. oz.	170 milliliters
Garlic cloves	2	2	2
Bread	8 rounds	8 rounds	8 rounds
Pâté or good liver sausage	8 rounds	8 rounds	8 rounds
Parsley stalks	2	2	2
Parsley head	1 tbsp.	1 tbsp.	10 grams

METHOD OF PREPARATION

1. Cut loin into 1½-inch lambrolls.
2. Roughly chop or grind peppercorns.
3. Measure sauce and wine—warm wine.
4. Crush or squeeze garlic.
5. Cut bread to same size as lambrolls and fry.
6. Slice pâté thinly to cover bread rounds (or use liver sausage sliced).
7. Finely chop parsley stalks and head.
8. Heat serving dish.

METHOD OF COOKERY

1. Season lambrolls before cookery with garlic salt and ground peppercorns.
2. Melt butter in heavy based frying pan. Add lambrolls. Brown quickly on both sides, turn down heat, and cook for 15-20 minutes, turning if one side becomes overcrisp.
3. When cooked, pour off excess butter; pour sauce over lambrolls. Turn meat in this sauce and add garlic. Now add wine (warmed), stir well. Simmer gently to reduce volume.
4. Place fried bread on hot serving dish; spread with pâté.
5. Remove lambrolls from sauce, cut off string. Place on bread rounds.
6. Add stalks to sauce and pour over lambrolls, dust with parsley and serve.

SERVING

Asparagus tips, broiled tomatoes, and the good old chips make a delightful combination. Serve a powerful red wine.

Ⓖ **For Lambroll Ruakura see page 212.**

125 SWEETBREADS AND BRAINS

COMMENT ON METHOD

Sweetbreads are glands. They come from either the pancreas (stomach sweetbread) or the thymus (neck or breast sweetbread). We eat sweetbreads from either lambs or calves. The lamb sweetbreads are small and as you can see from these photographs, those from the calf

Step 1
Soak sweetbreads for at least 1 hour in plenty of cold water. Rinse well and place in a saucepan of cold unsalted water.

Step 2
Slowly bring the water to a boil and when the water boils, remove the sweetbreads and place immediately into cold water.

126 Pickled Pork Sweetbreads

RECIPE TO PRODUCE 2 PORTIONS

	U.S.A.	IMPERIAL	METRIC
Lean pickled pork cooked	4 oz.	4 oz.	115 grams
White Sauce (pp. 256-57, rec. 216)	1¼ cups	10 fl. oz.	285 milliliters
Lamb sweetbreads	8 oz.	8 oz.	230 grams
Capers	1 tbsp.	1 tbsp.	10 grams
Salt	To season	To season	To season
White peppercorns	To season	To season	To season
Parsley	1 tbsp.	1 tbsp.	5 grams

METHOD OF PREPARATION

Cut pickled pork into 1-inch cubes—make up white sauce—cook sweetbreads as per basic method—chop capers—grind peppercorns—chop parsley.

METHOD OF COOKERY

1. Stir sweetbreads into sauce.
2. Cook for 5 minutes at a "Rotorua mud pool bubble"!
3. Add pickled pork, capers, and seasoning—heat.
4. Lastly add chopped parsley and serve.

SERVING

Serve in a nest of plain Boiled Rice (pp. 226-27, rec. 177)—add 1 ounce blanched sliced almonds—with a good tossed Red and Green Cabbage Salad (p. 246, rec. 208). Beer is best in my opinion.

are large. It doesn't matter how you prepare them later on, the basic preparation remains the same. You can also apply the same method to brains, leaving out Step 4.

Step 3
When cooled, strip off the surrounding skin and pieces of fat.

Step 4
Place the stripped sweetbreads between two plates; wrap in a cloth and place them under one leg of your dining table. (This is the best improvised press I know). Leave it for 30 minutes, then dry the flattened sweetbreads. They can now be used far a wide variety of dishes.

127 Kuku Schnitzel

RECIPE TO PRODUCE 4 PORTIONS	U.S.A.	IMPERIAL	METRIC
Calves' sweetbreads (thymus)	4	4	4
Flour	½ cup	2 oz.	60 grams
Egg	1	1	1
Breadcrumbs	½ cup	2 oz.	60 grams
Tomato sauce	¾ cup	6 fl. oz.	170 milliliters
Dry white wine	¾ cup	6 fl. oz.	170 milliliters
Parsley stalks	1 tbsp.	1 tbsp.	5 grams
Garlic cloves	1	1	1
Butter	1 tbsp.	1 tbsp.	15 grams

METHOD OF PREPARATION

Soak sweetbreads—blanch—peel off skin—press—season and flour—mix egg—place breadcrumbs on a dish—measure sauce and wine—peel garlic—chop parsley stalks—measure butter.

METHOD OF COOKERY

1. Dip sweetbreads in flour, egg, then breadcrumbs, and shallow fry in butter, melted in pan set at 300° F.
2. Make sauce: Heat butter, add crushed garlic, then tomato sauce and wine. Reduce by ⅓ at the boil.
3. Add parsley stalks—pour into sauceboat.
4. Serve with sweetbreads.
5. Garnish with chilled watercress and lemon wedges.

SERVING

My good old Ngauruhoe Potatoes are a must with this dish (p. 222, rec. 172) and I would prefer a salad to a cooked vegetable. A dry white wine, even one that sparkles, balances well.

171

128 LIVER

COMMENT ON METHOD

A well-known television personality admitted to me that he was a keen consumer of lamb's fry. A little later on he described as one of his pet hates—lamb's liver. Digging deeper into this curious contradiction, I (and he) discovered that his mother had used the title "lamb's fry" to overcome his aversion to liver. This proves, to me at least, that you should never reject a food without giving it a reasonable chance.

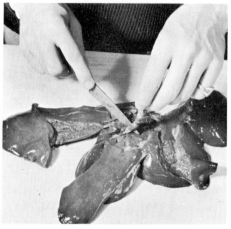

Step 1
This liver is obviously too large for a lamb. It is in fact pork liver and I consider it to be second only to calves' liver in quality. Remove the heavy sinews with a sharp knife and then wipe the liver with a clean damp cloth.

Step 2
Cut into slices about ¼ to ½ inch thick. Allow 4 ounces per portion.

129 Braised Lamb's Liver Henderson

RECIPE TO PRODUCE 4 PORTIONS	U.S.A.	IMPERIAL	METRIC
Lamb's liver	1 lb.	1 lb.	.5 kilo
Onions	2	2	2
Clarified butter	½ cup	4 oz.	115 grams
Dry red wine	½ cup	4 fl. oz.	115 milliliters
Chopped parsley	¼ cup	¼ cup	15 grams
Bay leaf	1	1	1
Thyme	1 sprig	1 sprig	1 sprig
Flour	½ cup	2 oz.	60 grams
Salt	1 tsp.	1 tsp.	2 grams
Ground black peppercorns	To season	To season	To season
Garlic cloves	1	1	1
Water	½ cup	4 fl. oz.	115 milliliters

METHOD OF PREPARATION

Slice liver finely and coat with flour—slice onions ½-inch thick—chop parsley—preheat oven to 350° F.—crush garlic.

METHOD OF COOKERY

1. Brown onion in clarified butter in casserole with crushed garlic.
2. Dot with butter, add wine, parsley, bay leaf, thyme, salt, pepper, and water. Cover and bake at 350° F. in oven for 30 minutes.
3. Shallow fry floured liver slices quickly—to color only—lay them on top, cover, and bake 10 minutes at same heat, basting two or three times with red wine mixture.
4. Remove cover, bake further 5 minutes, then serve.

SERVING

Serve from a clean shallow casserole with Ngauruhoe Potatoes (p. 222, rec. 172) and asparagus tips.

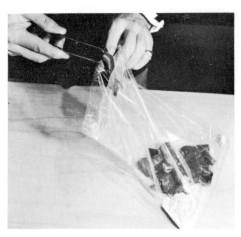

Step 3
Place 3 ounces of well-seasoned (pepper and salt) flour into a plastic or paper bag and add the liver. Shake vigorously in order to coat the slices.

Step 4
Melt some clarified butter in a pan set at 300° F. and cook until small drops of meat juices percolate through the flour (see above); turn and cook for 2 minutes. Maximum time for 1/2-inch-thick slices—5 minutes. NEVER (please) overcook.

130 Bell Block Chicken Livers

RECIPE TO PRODUCE 4 PORTIONS	U.S.A.	IMPERIAL	METRIC
Chicken livers	8 oz.	8 oz.	230 grams
Mushrooms	1 cup	2 oz.	60 grams
Whole-meal flour	7/8 cup	4 oz.	115 grams
Onion	1 small	2 oz.	60 grams
Lemon	1	1	1
Parsley	1 tbsp.	1 tbsp.	10 grams
Whole-meal bread	2 slices	2 slices	2 slices
Clarified butter	4 tbsp.	2 oz.	60 grams
Salt	To season	To season	To season
White peppercorns freshly ground	To season	To season	To season
Red wine	1/4 cup	2 fl. oz.	60 milliliters

METHOD OF PREPARATION

Season chicken livers and roll in whole-meal flour—slice onions finely—juice the lemon—slice mushrooms—chop parsley—fry bread or toast and butter it.

METHOD OF COOKERY

1. Fry livers in clarified butter with onions (5 minutes maximum).
2. Add mushrooms, lemon juice, and seasonings.
3. Stir in the wine, heat, and pile onto toast. Sprinkle with chopped parsley.

SERVING

I would recommend this dish as either a first course for 4 or as a Sunday night snack for 2. I have it for brunch—delicious at 11 A.M. with champagne!

173

131 KIDNEYS

Step 1
Grasp your kidney in the left hand and run a knife lightly over the skin—peel back the skin and detach. *Note:* On looking back over this instruction it looks odd. By "your kidney," of course I mean the lamb's.

Step 2
Cut out the heavy white ligament by cutting through the kidney from the dimpled side—do not cut right through.

132 Lambs' Kidneys Otaki

RECIPE TO PRODUCE 4 PORTIONS

	U.S.A.	IMPERIAL	METRIC
Lambs' kidneys	4	4	4
Tomatoes	4 large firm	4 large firm	4 large firm
Black peppercorns	To season	To season	To season
Garlic salt	To season	To season	To season
Parsley butter	4 tbsp.	4 tbsp.	60 grams
Bacon slices	4	4	4
Clarified butter	To brush	To brush	To brush

METHOD OF PREPARATION

Prepare kidneys as per basic method—use skewers—cut tomatoes in half—grind peppercorns—prepare and chill parsley butter—preheat broiler to medium hot.

METHOD OF COOKERY

1. Broil kidneys on cut side only for 3 minutes.
2. Season tomato halves with pepper, garlic salt.
3. Place on rack with kidneys round side uppermost, on top of tomatoes. Brush with butter and finish broiling for 3 minutes.
4. Fry bacon slices or broil on same rack as kidneys.
5. Take skewers out of kidneys, top them with parsley butter, and serve with fried bacon.

SERVING

This is a snack suitable for Sunday night around the fire. Serve with potato chips and Ngauruhoe Potatoes (p. 222, rec. 172) if you have a hearty appetite.

Step 3
When you broil kidneys (a perfect technique) you should push wooden spikes through each "wing" to keep them flat.

Step 4
Season the kidneys with salt and freshly ground black peppercorns, then spread with melted clarified butter. Position underneath the kidneys pieces of lightly cooked toast. The meat juices and butter drip down and are soaked up—fabulous! I recommend you slightly undercook the kidneys—medium hot broiler—3 minutes on either side—3 inches from heat.

133 Tom Muir's Kidney

RECIPE TO PRODUCE 4 PORTIONS

	U.S.A.	IMPERIAL	METRIC
Lambs' kidneys (or 1¼ lb. veal kidneys)	12	12	12
Shallots	2 tbsp.	2 tbsp.	60 grams
Mushrooms	1¾ cup	4 oz.	115 grams
Sweet green pepper	1	5 oz.	140 grams
Clarified butter	½ cup	4 oz.	115 grams
Whisky	¼ cup	2 fl. oz.	60 milliliters
Chicken stock	1 cup	8 fl. oz.	230 milliliters
Arrowroot	3 tbsp.	1 oz.	30 grams
Salt	To season	To season	To season
Black peppercorns	To season	To season	To season
Rice	1⅛ cup	8 oz.	230 grams
Parsley	¾ cup	1 oz.	30 grams
Water	¼ cup	2 fl. oz.	60 milliliters

METHOD OF PREPARATION

Split kidneys, skin, and cut into quarters—dice shallots—peel and slice mushrooms—dice green pepper—cook rice (pp. 226-27, rec. 177)—chop parsley—mix flour with salt, ground peppercorns, and water.

METHOD OF COOKERY

1. Shallow fry shallots and green pepper in clarified butter for 5 minutes; add mushrooms.
2. Add kidneys, simmer 5 minutes stirring once or twice.
3. Heat whisky—pour into spoon—light and add to kidneys. When flames are out add chicken stock.
4. Cover, simmer 10 minutes.
5. Stir in arrowroot with salt, pepper, water. Cook until thickened, stirring constantly.
6. Serve over hot rice mixed with parsley.

SERVING

This is a pleasant dish that is self-contained. A light rosé wine and crusty garlic bread balance well.

134 HEARTS

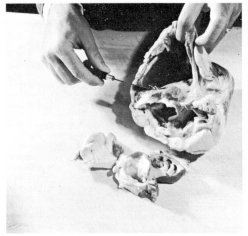 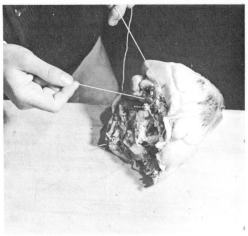

Step 1
Make quite sure that the heart is really fresh. Cut away the heavy fatty gristle that forms the entry to the heart pockets.

Step 2
Stuff the heart with the stuffing given on page 98. Using stainless steel wire, make up pins and secure the outer flaps, then lace up the wires with fine string and tie securely.

135 Ox Heart Wine Casserole

RECIPE TO PRODUCE 4 PORTIONS	U.S.A.	IMPERIAL	METRIC
Ox heart (weight after trimming)	3 cups	1½ lbs.	.75 kilo
Marinade:			
Olive oil	¼ cup	2 fl. oz.	60 milliliters
Dry red wine	¾ cup	6 fl. oz.	170 milliliters
Bay leaf	1	1	1
Thyme	1 tsp.	1 tsp.	1 tsp.
Parsley stalk	1	1	1
Peppercorns	6	6	6
Onion	1 medium	1 medium	1 medium
Garlic clove	1	1	1
Carrots	2 medium	8 oz.	230 grams
Onion	1 large	6 oz.	170 grams
Parsnip	1 medium	3 oz.	85 grams
Beef stock (p. 26, rec. 15)	2½ cups	1 pint	570 milliliters
Garlic clove	1	1	1
Bay leaf	1	1	1
Thyme, parsley stalks, each	2	2	2
Peppercorns	6	6	6

METHOD OF PREPARATION

Remove fat and vessels from heart—cut into 1-inch cubes—marinate 12 hours—slice carrots, onion, and parsnip—crush garlic—tie herbs in small bag—make and measure stock.

METHOD OF COOKERY

1. Remove meat from marinade, dry and brown casserole dish. Remove and brown vegetables.
2. Replace meat, pour in stock, add herbs in bags and cover. Simmer 2 hours until tender.
3. Skim off fat, add strained marinade—thicken with arrowroot and boil for 5 minutes.

SERVING

Dust with parsley. Serve with Sesame Crust Parsnips (p. 242, rec. 200), glazed whole carrots, and Creamed Potatoes (p. 222, rec. 171). Serve a full-bodied red wine or beer.

Step 3
Peel and slice 1½ pounds of mixed root vegetables and onions and fry these in a little clarified butter in a large pot until light brown. Season the heart and brown this on all sides to develop a deep crusty appearance.

Step 4
Add sufficient stock or broth to cover, together with 2 bay leaves, 1 large spray of thyme, and 2 sprays of parsley. Cover and simmer for 45 minutes per pound until tender. Cool in the stock in a cold place and slice cold. The stock can be reduced and thickened as a sauce in which the heart can be reheated for winter eating.

136   Queensland Lambs' Hearts

RECIPE TO PRODUCE 4 PORTIONS	U.S.A.	IMPERIAL	METRIC
Lambs' hearts	4	4	2 kilos
Salt	1 tbsp.	1 tbsp.	15 grams
Clarified butter, melted	½ cup	4 fl. oz.	115 milliliters
Pineapple pieces	1 x 30 oz.	1 x 30 oz.	1 x 850 grams
Sweet green peppers	2	2	2
Fresh ginger, grated	1 tsp.	1 tsp.	3.5 grams
Pineapple juice	1 cup	8 fl. oz.	230 milliliters
Soya bean sauce	2 tbsp.	2 tbsp.	30 milliliters
Arrowroot	2 tbsp.	2 tbsp.	20 grams
Black whole peppercorns	1 tsp.	1 tsp.	5 grams
Long grain rice	1½ cups	10 oz.	285 grams

METHOD OF PREPARATION

Remove vessels and excess fat from hearts—strain juice from pineapple and keep—mix juice with arrowroot, peppercorns (ground), and soya sauce—grate ginger—skin, peel, and pip green peppers, cut to same size as pineapple. Cook rice as per basic method on pages 226-27.

METHOD OF COOKERY

1. Place hearts in large saucepan with 5 pints of water.
2. Cook at the simmer, covered, for 2 hours.
3. Remove hearts, dry well, and cut into thin slices.
4. Strain cooking liquid, removing fat from surface.
5. Shallow fry hearts in butter 15 minutes, until golden brown.
6. Return to saucepan with sufficient strained liquid to cover. Add green peppers, pineapple, and ginger. Cover—simmer 1 hour.
7. Skim fat from surface, bring to boil. Pour in the pineapple juice, soya sauce, and arrowroot mixture. Stir until thickened and clear.

SERVING

Serve with the rice and plenty of very green buttered peas. Beer, light and cold, goes best with this dish.

Hand Raised Pork Pies (Basic Method), recipe page 190

Veal Steak, Kidney, and Mushroom Pudding, recipe page 185

Parramatta Chicken Pie, recipe page 204

About Pastry

Terry Thomas, the English comedian, won a sweepstakes on the nearest date and time of my birth. This has no particular significance—but it helps to fill up space. Actually he does tell a good story about New Zealand.

...I was in my club when Fotheringill told me about a fabulous dish you can get in New Zealand called a poi; I expressed interest and he told me where you could get it. Straightaway I booked my passage to New Zealand. I thought you had to go by canoe for the last couple of thousand miles, but to my surprise we flew *all* the way. They cleared the sheep off the runway and we landed. I went by a train aptly called the "Limited" and then on a charming vessel called—well, it's awfully difficult to spell—to Christchurch—a sort of Cecil B. de Mille re-creation of an English country town. By but I went to a small airstrip and took off in a delightful little plane which flew—yes, it's true—slap into the Alps. We landed in the snow. Of course my appetite was reaching fever pitch at this point. We trekked over snow and ice to a small hotel called the Hermitage on Mount Cook, a place that plays Swiss music until you go mad. I crawled across the carpet and asked for Bill the maître d'hôtel (I feel his name should be William—but there you are—when in Rome—) and through cracked lips breathed the magic word "Poi—have you a poi." "Certainly, mate" he replied. "Which do you want, meat poi or apple poi?" I expired.

Terry thinks this a great laugh but in fact he has unwittingly stumbled upon what must be regarded as Australia's greatest delicacy—it takes the place of Swiss fondue, American hamburgers, English fish and chips, French quiche, Italian pizza, and Turkish kebabs. It is a take-away food par excellence, and judging by its vast production, every man, woman, and child consumes at least three each per year!

My modest feelings come to the fore—how can I compete? I can but list my poor competition to this altar of the South Pacific gourmet.

CONTENTS OF SECTION

137 SUET PUDDING

RECIPE TO PRODUCE 6 PORTIONS	U.S.A.	IMPERIAL	METRIC
Pastry:			
Flour	1 lb.	1 lb.	.5 kilo
Baking powder	1 heaping teaspoon	1 heaping teaspoon	4 grams
Salt	Pinch	Pinch	Pinch
Suet	9 oz.	9 oz.	255 grams
Water	1⅛ cups	10 fl. oz.	285 milliliters
Filling:			
Blade steak of beef	1½ lb.	1½ lb.	.75 kilo
Ox kidney	8 oz.	8 oz.	.25 kilo
Fresh thyme leaves	1½ tsp.	1½ tsp.	1½ tsp.
Parsley stalks	1 tbsp.	1 tbsp.	1 tbsp.
Salt and pepper	To season	To season	To season
Flour	To dust	To dust	To dust
Water (approximately 10 fl. oz.)	To cover ¾	To cover ¾	To cover ¾

Step 1
Sift flour with salt and baking powder. Rub in suet or mix together in beater. Add the water and mix to a smooth dough. Take ⅔ of paste and roll out ½-inch thick. Line the pudding basin (7 inches diameter).

Step 2
Combine the meat, kidney with seasonings, herbs, and a little flour. Pack the mixture into the basin until it comes level with the rim. Add sufficient water to three quarters fill the basin.

COMMENT ON METHOD

"My mother makes a wonderful steak and kidney pudding." This is the kind of statement that usually leads to music hall comments being made about mothers-in-law. As I am the cook in our home, I face a curiously psychological problem when my wife says, "Yes—it's good. But not as good as your mother's!" What would you do?

METHOD OF PREPARATION

1. Measure flour, baking powder, salt, suet, and water for pastry.
2. Grease pudding bowl with butter.
3. Chop parsley stalks.
4. Cut meat and kidney into 1-inch cubes.
5. Measure thyme leaves, parsley stalks, and water.

Step 3
Roll out the remaining paste, dampen the top of the crust in the basin, and lay on the top. Press the top on well and tie on a well-floured cloth, knotting the ends in the center.

Step 4
Place in a large saucepan. Add cold water until it comes halfway up the basin. Fix a lid on top and boil gently for 3 hours. It is a good plan to put 2 marbles in the saucepan. When the water level gets very low they make a fearful din! When cooked, strip off cloth and serve from the basin.

138 Chicken Pudding

RECIPE TO PRODUCE 4-6 PORTIONS	U.S.A.	IMPERIAL	METRIC
Suet pudding crust (pp. 182-83, rec. 137)	1 batch	1 batch	1 batch
Chicken flesh (cut from 3½ lb. fowl)	1 lb.	1 lb.	.5 kilo
Chicken livers	8 oz.	8 oz.	230 grams
Onion	1 cup	4 oz.	115 grams
Flour	To dust	To dust	To dust
Celery	1 cup	4 oz.	115 grams
Lemon thyme leaves	1 sprig	1 sprig	1 sprig
Parsley stalks	1 tbsp.	1 tbsp.	5 grams
Salt	To season	To season	To season
Freshly ground black peppercorns	To season	To season	To season
Water	1 cup 2 tbsp.	7 fl. oz.	200 milliliters

METHOD OF PREPARATION

1. Strip raw flesh from a 3½-pound boiling fowl and weigh.

2. Cube meat and chicken livers—flour and season.

3. Slice onion and celery.

4. Chop parsley stalks finely.

5. Measure fresh lemon thyme leaves.

6. Prepare pan of boiling water for pudding.

7. Grease basin.

8. Scald cloth.

METHOD OF COOKERY

1. Prepare suet crust and roll out to fit 7-inch basin. Roll out top ½-inch thick.

2. Mix parsley stalks, thyme leaves, chicken flesh, and livers. Coat with flour.

3. Place in pastry-lined basin. Pour in water.

4. Seal on pastry top. Tie over scalded floured cloth. Set in boiling water, cover, and boil for 3 hours.

5. Remove from boiling water when cooked, take off cloth, and serve.

SERVING

Serve with plenty of buttered peas and glazed baby carrots. I don't think that wine is suitable—perhaps a light chilled beer?

139 Veal Steak, Kidney, and Mushroom Pudding

RECIPE TO PRODUCE 4-6 PORTIONS	U.S.A.	IMPERIAL	METRIC
Veal topside	1½ lb.	1½ lb.	.75 kilo
Veal kidney	8 oz.	8 oz.	230 grams
Flour	½ cup	2 oz.	60 grams
Zest of lemon	½ tbsp.	½ tbsp.	5 grams
Shallots	½ cup	2 oz.	60 grams
Mushrooms	2 cups	4 oz.	115 grams
Salt	To season	To season	To season
Ground black peppercorns	To season	To season	To season
Dried wild marjoram	1 tsp.	1 tsp.	1 tsp.
Tomato purée	½ cup	4 fl. oz.	115 milliliters
Water	6 tbsp.	3 fl. oz.	85 milliliters
Bay leaf	1	1	1
Suet pastry (pp. 182-83, rec. 137)	1 batch	1 batch	1 batch

METHOD OF PREPARATION

1. Make pastry as shown on pages 182-83.
2. Cube meat and dust with flour.
3. Grate lemon zest.
4. Chop shallots.
5. Finely slice mushrooms.
6. Mix water and tomato purée.
7. Place large saucepan with 4 inches of hot water on stove ready to receive pudding.
8. Scald cloth.

METHOD OF COOKERY

1. Season meat with zest of lemon, pepper, and salt.
2. Stir in mushrooms, shallots, herbs.
3. Place paste bag in greased bowl.
4. Fill up with meat and pour in diluted tomato purée.
5. Cover with paste top and tie on the cloth.
6. Cover saucepan and boil for 3 hours—keep a watch on the water level. If it boils dry it makes a shocking mess—I know!

SERVING

This is a delightful winter dish—you won't need potatoes because of the suet crust, but long sliced glazed carrots and Brussels sprouts with a tankard of strong beer make quite an experience.

Ⓖ **For Cullers Bluff Pudding see page 213.**

RECIPE TO PRODUCE 4 PORTIONS	U.S.A.	IMPERIAL	METRIC
Five-minute pie pastry:			
Butter	¾ cup	6 oz.	170 grams
Flour	2 cups	8 oz.	230 grams
Salt	To season	To season	To season
Water	½ cup	4 fl. oz.	115 milliliters
Filling:			
Onion	1 medium	3 oz.	85 grams
Carrot	1 medium	3 oz.	85 grams
Clarified butter	1 oz.	1 oz.	30 grams
Neck of lamb	1½ lb.	1½ lb.	.75 kilo
Flour	To dust	To dust	To dust
Salt	To season	To season	To season
Black peppercorns, freshly ground	To season	To season	To season
Water	¾ cup	6 fl. oz.	170 milliliters
Meat stock	Half fill pan	Half fill pan	Half fill pan

Step 1
Sieve flour and salt together and add the butter pieces. Pinch these pieces flat with thumb and forefinger. Add the water gradually, mixing with a wooden spoon.

Step 2
Fry the vegetables in the pan with a little clarified butter. Dust the meat with flour and season with salt and pepper. Add this to the vegetables. Brown the meat well. Take the pan off the heat and allow to cool.

COMMENT ON METHOD

I have found from experience that an old heavy-based frying pan makes the best pie dish—that is, for a top-crust pie like this one. The handle has to be taken off but this doesn't prove too difficult when once you make the decision, and the end results are worth the trouble. The finished pie is on color page 180.

METHOD OF PREPARATION

1. Measure flour; cut butter into 1-inch squares, each ¼ inch thick.
2. Measure water.
3. Peel and cut vegetables into ¼-inch-thick slices.
4. Cube meat from neck of lamb.
5. Prepare "stock."
6. Preheat oven to 375° F.

Step 3
Roll out the pastry, using plenty of dusting flour—fold several times—roll ⅛-inch thick and allow to stand for 5 minutes to relax. Cut a round piece the size of the rim of the pan and another about 1 inch oversize. Place the outer ring onto the **cooled** pan rim—brush the top with water.

Step 4
Add the diluted extract to half fill the pan and then roll the pastry top onto a pin and lay it over the meat. The pie filling should always rise in a dome slightly higher in the center than the outer rim. (I added some extra filling after this shot was taken.) Brush the pastry top with beaten egg, decorate (pp. 178-79), and bake at 375° F. for 1 hour 20 minutes. Cover with damp brown paper if top browns too quickly.

141 Veal Sweetbread and Bacon Pie

RECIPE TO PRODUCE 4 PORTIONS	U.S.A.	IMPERIAL	METRIC
Five-minute pastry (pp. 186-87, rec. 140)	1 batch	1 batch	1 batch
Veal sweetbreads (pp. 170-71, rec. 125)	¾ cup	11 oz.	310 grams
Tomatoes	1 medium	5 oz.	140 grams
Bacon	½ lb.	8 oz.	230 grams
Salt	To season	To season	To season
Black peppercorns	To season	To season	To season
Parsley	2 tbsp.	2 tbsp.	5 grams
Wild marjoram (also called oregano)	1 tsp.	1 tsp.	5 grams
Lemon juice	1 tbsp.	1 tbsp.	15 milliliters
Egg	1	1	1

METHOD OF PREPARATION

1. Soak sweetbreads, rinse well, blanch, skin, and press. Dry.
2. Slice tomatoes into ¼-inch slices.
3. Grind black peppercorns.
4. Cut rind from bacon.
5. Beat egg.
6. Make pastry—roll out top and bottom for pie.
7. Fry bacon.
8. Chop parsley.
9. Preheat oven to 375° F.

METHOD OF COOKERY

1. Line pie tin with pastry.
2. Lay half lightly fried bacon slices in bottom of tin, cover with pressed dried sweetbreads, then remainder of bacon.
3. Cover with sliced tomatoes, season, pour on lemon juice, and sprinkle with herbs.
4. Put top on pie and seal edges.
5. Gild with egg and place in oven set at 375° F. for 25-30 minutes until pastry is cooked.

SERVING

Serve with a Red and Green Cabbage Salad (p. 246, rec. 208) and Otaki Potatoes (p. 219, rec. 167). Strange as it may seem, a dry red wine is the best partner.

142 Porterhouse Pie

RECIPE TO PRODUCE 4 PORTIONS	U.S.A.	IMPERIAL	METRIC
Porterhouse steaks	2 8-oz.	2 8-oz.	2 .25-kilos
Mushrooms	4 large	4 large	4 large
Five-minute Pastry (pp. 186-87, rec. 140)	1 batch	1 batch	1 batch
Salt	To season	To season	To season
Freshly ground black peppercorns	To season	To season	To season
Clarified butter	¼ cup	2 oz.	60 grams
Lemon juice	1 tbsp	1 tbsp.	15 milliliters

METHOD OF PREPARATION
1. Trim fat off steaks, dry well, and season.
2. Peel mushrooms and leave whole.
3. Make pastry and divide into 2 portions for steaks.
4. Beat egg to brush edges.
5. Preheat oven to 350° F.

METHOD OF COOKERY
1. Melt clarified butter in **very** hot pan and sear steaks rapidly on both sides to seal in juices.
2. Remove and dry well.
3. Add mushrooms and lemon juice to pan. Fry lightly.
4. Remove and pat-dry.
5. Place mushrooms, round side down on pastry, steak on top. Make up 2 pies, one for each steak.
6. Fold over pastry, brush egg on edges, and crimp firmly together. Brush with egg wash.
7. Place on baking sheet in oven for 25-30 minutes.

SERVING
Serve on an oval platter surrounded with broiled half tomatoes and chilled watercress Cut pies in half to make 4 portions. Serve with a rich red wine.

ⓖ **For Parramatta Chicken Pie see page 204.**

143 RAISED PIES

COMMENT ON METHOD

This is another one of those methods that needs ample illustration. In order to cover it adequately, I have placed the recipe items before each step-by-step shot. The finished pies can be seen on color pages 178–79. The method of molding took me three days of testing to develop. I hope it works as well for you—first time!

Step 1
Boil 5 ounces lard with ¾ cup water. Place 1 pound of sifted flour and ½ teaspoon salt into a basin. Stand the basin in warm water.

Step 2
Add the boiling lard and water to the flour, mixing in well. Note that the bowl is still in the hot water.

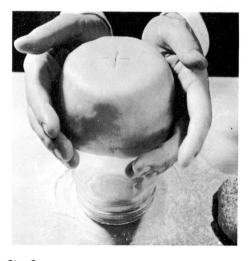

Step 5
Upend a 2-pound bottling jar and dust it well with flour. Also dust the piece of dough.

Step 6
Place the dough onto the jar and mold it carefully, so that it is roughly ¼-inch thick—no less. Cut a cross on top. This helps to release the paste.

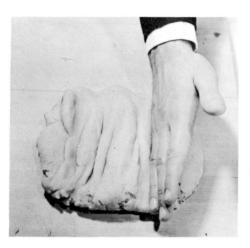

Step 3
Blend the dough on the board by using "poor man's karate" technique! When it is smooth and pliable (and still hot), roll it into a loaf shape.

Step 4
Cut off a quarter of the paste and put it into a plastic bag to keep it moist. This will be used for the tops.

Step 7
Clip a piece of double folded paper around the paste and then up end and pour hot water into the jar. The paste will slide off easily.

Step 8
Fill the pie with 1-inch cubes of meat. Season well and half fill with water or stock. Seal the top paste securely. Make a steam hole on top and bake at 350° F. for 1½ hours. Brush the top with egg before baking. After 1 hour remove the paper. When cooked, remove and pour in some jelly stock through the steam hole. Cool and then serve.

191

144 Fillet Steak Washington

RECIPE TO PRODUCE 4 PORTIONS	U.S.A.	IMPERIAL	METRIC
Fillet steaks	2 lbs.	2 lbs.	1 kilo
Clarified butter	¼ cup	2 oz.	60 grams
Black peppercorns and salt	To season	To season	To season
Mushrooms	4 large	4 large	4 large
Puff pastry	1 lb.	1 lb.	.5 kilo
Lemon	1	1	1
Cayenne pepper	To season	To season	To season
Egg	1	1	1
Clarified butter for deep fryer (or oil)	To deep fry	To deep fry	To deep fry
For garnish:			
Small potatoes	2 lb.	2 lb.	1 kilo
Parsley	Several sprays	Several sprays	Several sprays
Mint	2 small heads	2 small heads	2 small heads
Butter	¼ cup	2 oz.	60 grams
Salt and white pepper	To season	To season	To season

METHOD OF PREPARATION

1. Trim steaks of all fat and sinew and season.
2. Roll pastry ⅛-inch thick.
3. Beat egg well.
4. Parboil potatoes 10-12 minutes and skin.
5. Finely chop mint.
6. Wash mushrooms and remove stalks.

METHOD OF COOKERY

1. Heat shallow pan and add clarified butter.
2. Place steaks in pan, sear both sides and edges.
3. Remove steaks, place on wire cake stand, reduce heat of pan, add mushrooms (vein side uppermost). Season with a few drops of lemon juice, a dusting of salt, and a sprinkle of cayenne pepper. Turn mushrooms and cook to just darken seasoned side. Remove mushrooms and place on top of steaks to cool.
4. Take a cup that fits over steak and use to mark out a circle on pastry. Repeat four times, cutting ½-inch wider than the cup. Take a saucer and check that the impression created by the inverted saucer rim is a good inch wider than the cup size. Repeat four times and cut out.
5. Pat steaks and mushrooms dry with a clean cloth. Place the small round of pastry on the table—brush lightly with beaten egg; place steak in center and put mushrooms on steak. Brush the large round of pastry with egg. Place pastry (egg-washed side down) on top of the mushroom and steak. Press the edges of pastry and crimp together to seal completely.
6. Place sealed steaks in paper bag and put in refrigerator. If they are kept overnight, they must be removed from the refrigerator 30 minutes before cookery.
7. **To cook:** Heat clarified butter to 375° F. and place the pastries in very gently with a perforated spoon. They may now be left for 7 minutes.

SERVING

Cover the serving dish with paper doilies and remove the cooked steaks to the dish. Arrange neatly and surround with the boiled potatoes, mint, and sprigs of parsley. Serve with a colorful "all in salad" and a full-bodied Hermitage.

145 Eltham Cheesecake*

RECIPE TO PRODUCE 4 PORTIONS	U.S.A.	IMPERIAL	METRIC
Flour	1 cup	4 oz.	115 grams
Butter	¼ cup	2 oz.	60 grams
Egg yolk	1	1	1
Chilled water	1½ tbsp.	1½ tbsp.	25 milliliters
Filling:			
Cream cheese	¼ cup	2 oz.	60 grams
Blue vein cheese	2 tbsp.	1 oz.	30 grams
Butter	1½ tbsp.	¾ oz.	25 grams
Sugar	3 tbsp.	1½ oz.	45 grams
Cream	1 tbsp.	1 tbsp.	15 milliliters
Flour	2 tbsp.	½ oz.	15 grams
Large raisins	¼ cup	2 oz.	60 grams
Eggs	2	2	2

METHOD OF PREPARATION

1. Weigh or measure all ingredients.
2. Sieve cheeses.
3. Separate eggs and whip whites with 1 teaspoon water, ¼ teaspoon salt.
4. Grease 7-inch sponge tin.
5. Preheat oven to 400° F.
6. Sieve flour.

METHOD OF COOKERY

1. Prepare pastry by rubbing butter and flour together. Add yolk and water.
2. Roll out ⅛-inch thick. Line greased sponge tin.
3. For filling, cream butter and sugar well. Add flour, fruit, egg yolks, and cream.
4. Add cheeses and mix well.
5. Fold in whipped whites.
6. Fill pastry case, smooth surface, and bake 20 minutes at 400° F. If the top browns too rapidly, cover with a piece of brown paper dampened with water. Remove and cool.

*This is a cheat—it isn't a raised pie, but, frankly, it is so good that I felt it should fit in somewhere! Serve it with coffee. It's delightful.

SERVING

An acquired taste, so test it first on yourself. I use it in place of a cheeseboard—makes a good change.

About Graduate Recipes

If you are about to embark upon this section then I have to assume that you have either used a simpler extension of the basic methods, or you are an excellent cook, or that you can afford to run the risk of failure.

So be it!

Each of the recipes in this GRADUATE section is relatively complicated. It helps if you read, once again, the "basic method" indicated by page number under each recipe title.

Once you have successfully mastered each (or any one) of the graduate recipes, you can assume that you have passed out (not literally, I trust).

You can now join the ranks of creative cooks who prefer to cook without a book.

When once the basic method is understood and applied, cooking is reduced to a list of ingredients assembled in such balance as to appeal to your own sense of taste.

Good luck to you and yours—may you give great pleasure for years to come.

CONTENTS OF SECTION

146 Oyster Soup
(Thin Soup—Basic Method, pages 26-27)

RECIPE TO PRODUCE 4 PORTIONS	U.S.A.	IMPERIAL	METRIC
Fish stock:			
Fish bones	1 cup	8 oz.	230 grams
Onion, finely chopped	3 tbsp.	1 oz.	30 grams
Carrot, finely chopped	3 tbsp.	1 oz.	30 grams
Parsley stalks	2	2	2
Black peppercorns	3	3	3
Salt	½ tsp.	½ tsp.	1 milliliter
Lemon zest	Small piece	Small piece	Small piece
Dry white wine	2 tbsp.	1 fl. oz.	30 milliliters
Water	2½ cups	1 pint	570 milliliters
Garnish:			
Oysters, fresh	16	16	16
Fillets of sole	½ cup	4 oz.	115 grams
Dry white wine	¼ cup	2 fl. oz.	60 milliliters
Kneaded butter (1 oz. each flour and butter, rubbed together)	¼ cup	1-2 oz.	60 grams

METHOD OF PREPARATION

Prepare stock:

1. Place chopped vegetables with parsley stalks, peppercorns, salt, lemon zest, wine, and water in sauce-pan—bring to boil, skim, and simmer 30 minutes. Strain off liquid.

Fillet sole:

2. Remove both skins and slice fillets into very thin strips 1 by ¼ inch.
3. Prepare kneaded butter for thickening.
4. Clarify stock if necessary.

METHOD OF COOKERY

1. Add wine to stock and then the strips of sole.
2. Poach sole for 6 minutes, then thicken with kneaded butter. Do not boil after addition.
3. Put oysters into warmed soup plates and cover with the hot soup.

SERVING

The soup should be only just thickened—not sufficient to make it suited to thick soup service. Thin crisp cracker biscuits go well as an accompaniment.

147 Fairfield Flounder Fillets

(Deep-fried Fish—Basic Method, pages 38-39)

RECIPE TO PRODUCE
4 FIRST-COURSE PORTIONS

	U.S.A.	IMPERIAL	METRIC
Button mushrooms	1 cup	4 oz.	115 grams
Lemon juice	1 tbsp.	1 tbsp.	15 milliliters
Parsley stalks	1 tbsp.	1 tbsp.	5 grams
Salt	¼ tsp.	¼ tsp.	¼ tsp.
Cayenne pepper	½ tbsp.	½ tbsp.	7.5 grams
Dry white wine	¼ cup	2 fl. oz.	60 milliliters
Egg yolks	2	2	2
Flounder fillets	4	4	4
Breadcrumbs	1½ cups	6 oz.	170 grams
Cheese	½ cup	2 oz.	60 grams
Flour	½ cup	2 oz.	60 grams
Oil	To deep fry	To deep fry	To deep fry

METHOD OF PREPARATION

1. Peel and dice mushrooms finely.
2. Chop parsley stalks.
3. Measure wine.
4. Skin fillets and season.
5. Grate cheese and mix with breadcrumbs.
6. Heat oil in deep fryer to 350° F.

METHOD OF COOKERY

1. Poach mushrooms in lemon juice with wine, parsley stalks, salt, cayenne pepper for 5 minutes. Put in a blender and add egg yolks to make a smooth paste.
2. Dip seasoned fillets in plain flour, then mushroom mixture,* then into crumbs and cheese.
3. Deep fry for 2½ minutes at 350° F. Drain well and serve.

*Or spread with a spatula.

SERVING

Providing they are kept on waxed paper in the refrigerator, the fillets can be pre-prepared up to and including step 2. Garnish with lemon wedges. A full-bodied medium dry white wine is recommended.

148 Potts Point Fish Pot
(Shallow-fried Fish—Basic Method, pages 42-43)

RECIPE TO PRODUCE 6 PORTIONS	U.S.A.	IMPERIAL	METRIC
White Sauce (pp. 256-57, rec. 216)	3¾ cups	1½ pints	850 milliliters
Dry white wine	½ cup	4 fl. oz.	115 milliliters
Flounder or sole fillets	1½ lb.	1½ lb.	.75 kilo
Clarified butter	4 tbsp.	2 oz.	60 grams
Oysters	1 doz.	1 doz.	1 doz.
Crayfish (or lobster)	1 small	1 small	1 small
Brandy	¼ cup	2 fl. oz.	60 milliliters
Seasoned flour	¾ cup	3 oz.	85 grams
Button mushrooms	2 cups	4 oz.	115 grams
Tomatoes	1 large	8 oz.	230 grams
Shrimp (or 24 fresh)	1 tin	1 tin	1 tin
Dry matured grated Cheddar	¼ cup	1 oz.	30 grams
Lemons	2	2	2
Chopped parsley	1 tbsp.	1 tbsp.	5 grams
Cayenne pepper	To garnish	To garnish	To garnish

METHOD OF PREPARATION

1. Make sauce.
2. Measure wine.
3. Fillet flounder, skin completely, and cut into 2- by 1-inch fish fingers.
4. Cut crayfish into 1-inch pieces.
5. Warm brandy.
6. Season flour.
7. Slice mushrooms finely.
8. Blanch, peel, pip, and chop tomatoes.
9. Drain shrimp.
10. Grate cheese.
11. Chop parsley.

METHOD OF COOKERY

1. Heat white sauce gently, add wine.
2. Place flounder in seasoned flour and shake off excess.
3. Melt butter in large frying pan, add floured fish.
4. Add crayfish, tomatoes, and lastly oysters.
5. Toss gently and move all foods to one side. Pour brandy onto cleared pan base, set alight with a match. Stir seafoods into these flames.
6. Pour over sufficient sauce to douse flames and bind the seafoods.
7. Stir in shrimp carefully.
8. In another pan, toss mushrooms in butter with lemon juice and a touch of cayenne. Spoon over the main dish. Dust all with parsley and cayenne pepper and serve.

SERVING

Serve in a nest of plain Boiled Rice (pp. 226-27, rec. 177). I like a Red and Green Cabbage Salad (p. 246, rec. 208) with this, but you may enjoy some spears of asparagus served quite plain. A full-bodied medium dry white wine goes well.

198

149 Taupo Trout Steaks with Herb Butter
(Broiled Fish—Basic Method, pages 46-47)

RECIPE TO PRODUCE 4 PORTIONS	U.S.A.	IMPERIAL	METRIC
Trout	1½ lb.	1½ lb.	.75 kilo
Clarified butter	4 tbsp.	2 oz.	60 grams
Salt, white peppercorns	To season	To season	To season
Butter:			
Butter	4 tbsp.	2 oz.	60 grams
Lemon juice	1 tbsp.	1 tbsp.	15 milliliters
Garlic cloves	½	½	½
Fennel	¼ tsp.	¼ tsp.	¼ tsp.
Cayenne pepper	¼ tsp.	¼ tsp.	¼ tsp.

METHOD OF PREPARATION
1. Remove scales and wash trout—cut into steaks 1-inch thick crosswise.
2. Heat broiler to moderate.
Butter:
3. Soften butter, measure pepper and lemon juice, and crush garlic.
4. Add all ingredients to softened butter.

METHOD OF COOKERY
1. Season trout on both sides, brush with clarified butter.
2. Brush broiler rack with butter. Begin cooking 3 inches away from flame.
3. Cook 5 minutes on one side, turn, and brush with butter again. Cook 4 minutes longer.
4. Roll butter in greaseproof paper to form long roll 1 inch in diameter. Put in refrigerator until firm.
5. Cut in thin slices and place on fish just before serving.

SERVING
Serve with wedges of lemon and asparagus. A full-bodied white Burgundy goes well.

150　Tarakihi Tauranga
(Poached Fish—Basic Method, pages 50-51)

RECIPE TO PRODUCE 4-6 PORTIONS	U.S.A.	IMPERIAL	METRIC
Whole pompano	2 lb.	2 lb.	1 kilo
Pompano fillets	1 lb.	1 lb.	.5 kilo
Chinese gooseberries	½ lb.	½ lb.	.25 kilo
(Kiwi fruit)	10 tbsp.	5 fl. oz.	140 milliliters
Milk	4 tbsp.	2 oz.	60 grams
Butter	9 tbsp.	2¼ oz.	65 grams
Flour	1¼ cups	10 fl. oz.	285 milliliters
Milk	10 tbsp.	5 fl. oz.	140 milliliters
Fish stock:			
Water	1¼ cups	10 fl. oz.	285 milliliters
Onion	1 small	2 oz.	60 grams
Bay leaf	1	1	1
Parsley	1 sprig	1 sprig	1 sprig
Salt, white pepper	To season	To season	To season
Dry white wine	¼ cup	2 fl. oz.	60 milliliters
Grated Cheddar cheese	½ cup	2 oz.	60 grams

METHOD OF PREPARATION

1. Detach head and tail of whole fish and keep on one side.
2. Remove skin and fillet fish.
3. Make stock with center bones, adding water, bay leaf, onion, and parsley.
4. Butter a shallow casserole dish.
5. Measure Chinese gooseberries, peel, and slice.
6. Measure butter, flour, milk, wine, and cheese.

METHOD OF COOKERY

1. Simmer bones with water, onion, and herbs for 30 minutes.
2. Lay fillets in casserole dish, cover with milk (10 tbsp.) and fish stock. Seal with lid. Simmer gently for 8 minutes.
3. Start sauce; make a roux with butter and flour. Add remainder of milk (1¼ cups), stirring all the time.
4. When fish is cooked, strain poaching liquor into sauce and beat.
5. Season sauce and stir in wine.

SERVING

Place head and tail on oval dish. Place fillets in a pile between to resemble shape of whole fish. Coat with sauce—dust with cheese and place under grill to brown. Garnish with finely sliced Chinese gooseberries until fish is completely coated. Serve with Otaki Potatoes (p. 219, rec. 167). A heavy white wine goes well.

151 Baked Trout with Taupo Stuffing
(Baked Fish—Basic Method, pages 54-55)

RECIPE TO PRODUCE 6 PORTIONS	U.S.A.	IMPERIAL	METRIC
Stuffing:			
Cooked crayfish (lobster)	⅔ cup	5 oz.	140 grams
Mushrooms, finely sliced	1 cup	2 oz.	60 grams
Onion, finely sliced	¼ cup	1 oz.	30 grams
Chopped parsley	1 tbsp.	1 tbsp.	2 grams
Lemon thyme leaves	1 spray	1 spray	1 spray
Celery leaves	⅜ cup	½ oz.	15 grams
Butter	2 tbsp.	1 oz.	30 grams
Lemon juice	1 tsp.	1 tsp.	1 tsp.
Salt	To season	To season	To season
Cayenne pepper	To season	To season	To season
Black peppercorns	To season	To season	To season
Trout, dressed weight—head off	4 lb.	4 lb.	2 kilos

METHOD OF PREPARATION
1. Cut cooked crayfish into ½-inch dice.
2. Remove leaves from thyme.
3. Finely chop celery leaves.
4. Grind peppercorns.
5. Clean trout inside and out.
6. Preheat oven 350° F.

METHOD OF COOKERY
1. Melt butter, fry onion lightly.
2. Add mushrooms, lemon juice, salt, cayenne pepper.
3. Stir in diced crayfish and herbs.
4. Take off heat and stuff into trout.
5. Lace up as per chicken (pp. 92-93).
6. Score sides, brush with clarified butter, season with salt and pepper.
7. Weigh and cook for 10 minutes per pound.
8. Remove string and pins to serve; strip off skin.

SERVING
Present the trout at the table on a large oval dish. Be very careful how you carve it—try to take the fillets off the bones. Do not cut through like cutlets. Serve with plain boiled herb potatoes (pp. 218-19, rec. 165) and Green Beans (p. 236, rec. 190). A light dry red wine will balance well with this game fish.

152 Roast Wild Duck: Cream and White Sauce
(Roast Poultry—Basic Method, pages 96-97)

RECIPE TO PRODUCE 2 PORTIONS	U.S.A.	IMPERIAL	METRIC
Wild duck	1	1	1
Clarified butter	To brush	To brush	To brush
Salt	To season	To season	To season
Black peppercorns	To season	To season	To season
Marinade:			
Olive oil	¼ cup	2 fl. oz	60 milliliters
Dry red wine	¾ cup	6 fl. oz.	170 milliliters
Garlic cloves	1	1	1
Onion	1 medium	1 medium	1 medium
Thyme	1 tsp.	1 tsp.	3.75 grams
Parsley stalk	1	1	1
Black peppercorns	6	6	6
Bay leaf	1	1	1
Egg yolks	2	2	2
Cream	4 tbsp.	4 tbsp.	60 milliliters
Parsley, chopped	1 tbsp.	1 tbsp.	7.5 grams

METHOD OF PREPARATION

1. Prepare marinade—mix all ingredients and marinate duck in mixture for at least 4 hours.*
2. Preheat oven to 450° F.
3. Mix egg yolks and cream.
4. Chop parsley.

*Overnight for preference.

METHOD OF COOKERY

1. Remove duck from marinade, dry well, season with salt and freshly ground peppercorns.
2. Tie up as for roast chicken, brush with melted clarified butter, and place in oven on rack with small tray underneath.
3. After 20 minutes, remove, pour off residue from pan, replace duck in pan, and put back in oven at 450° F. for a further 10 minutes.
4. Meanwhile add residue to strained marinade and boil down to a syrup. Skim off all surface fats.
5. When duck is cooked, pour juices from inside into reduced syrup.
6. Over a low heat stir the yolks and cream into the sauce. Add chopped parsley.
7. Serve over the duck which is cut in half down the center.

SERVING

Serve plain boiled and buttered potatoes (pp. 218-19, rec. 165) and an orange, celery, walnut, and cucumber salad. A good full-bodied red wine blends well.

153 Oriental Bay Pancakes
(Boiled Poultry—Basic Method, pages 100-1)

RECIPE TO PRODUCE 8-9 PORTIONS	U.S.A.	IMPERIAL	METRIC
Boiling fowl, cooked	3½ lb.	3½ lb.	1.75 kilos
Butter	½ cup	4 oz.	115 grams
Flour	1 cup	4 oz.	115 grams
Milk	2½ cups	1 pint	570 milliliters
Salt	To season	To season	To season
White peppercorns	To season	To season	To season
Dry matured Cheddar cheese	½ cup	2 oz.	60 grams
Celery	4 large stalks	8 oz.	230 grams
Pancakes (pp. 88-89, rec. 75)	8-9	8-9	8-9
Dry white wine	½ cup	4 fl. oz.	115 milliliters
Cayenne pepper	To garnish	To garnish	To garnish
Parsley	To garnish	To garnish	To garnish

METHOD OF PREPARATION

1. Prepare fowl as shown in basic method on pp. 100-1.
2. Strain and clarify chicken stock.
3. Grate cheese.
4. Slice celery into ¼-inch pieces.
5. Make pancakes.
6. Chop parsley.
7. Strip all flesh from chicken and dice into ½-inch pieces.

METHOD OF COOKERY

1. Make sauce with flour and butter roux. Add milk gradually. Reduce strained cooking liquor from chicken to 2½ cups.
2. Add chicken stock to sauce—beat well.
3. Poach celery until just tender.
4. Add celery to chicken pieces and cover with 1⅞ cups sauce.
5. Add cheese to remaining sauce—beat well until dissolved.
6. Add ¼ cup wine to chicken and celery and ¼ cup to cheese sauce—reheat both mixtures.
7. Place spoonful of chicken mixture onto pancake—roll up—place on serving dish, and coat with the cheese sauce completely. Dust with cheese and place in hot broiler to brown.

SERVING

Makes a good buffet-style dish when served with crusty bread and a good tossed salad. Serve a good "fruity" white wine—chilled.

154 Buttered Breast of Chicken
(Deep-fried Poultry—Basic Method, pages 112-13)

RECIPE TO PRODUCE 2 PORTIONS	U.S.A.	IMPERIAL	METRIC
Chicken breasts (from 2-lb. bird)	2	2	2
Parsley butter (p. 48, rec. 28)	1/4 cup	2 oz.	60 grams
Eggs	2	2	2
Breadcrumbs	1/2 cup	2 oz.	60 grams
Flour	1/2 cup	2 oz.	60 grams
Oil	To deep fry	To deep fry	To deep fry

METHOD OF PREPARATION
Cut and remove bones from breast (pp. 112-13, rec. 91)—beat breast with rolling pin to flatten to about 1/8-inch. Prepare parsley butter and place in freezer to harden—beat egg—place breadcrumbs and flour on separate plates—heat oil in deep fryer to 325° F.

METHOD OF COOKERY
1. Place 1 oz. of frozen parsley butter inside each halved breast, fold in ends, and roll up, sealing with beaten egg.
2. Flour each breast, dip in egg, then breadcrumbs.
3. Place carefully in hot oil and deep fry until golden brown—6 minutes at 325° F.
4. Drain and serve.

SERVING
This dish is excellent when served with a simple tossed green salad and Moreland Potatoes (p. 218, rec. 166), Golden Coast Sauce (p. 68, rec. 52). Serve a full-bodied, slightly chilled white wine.

155 Parramatta Chicken Pie
(Pastry Pies—Basic Method, pages 186-87)

RECIPE TO PRODUCE 6 PORTIONS	U.S.A.	IMPERIAL	METRIC
Chicken meat (from 3 lb. chicken)	2 cups	1 lb.	.5 kilo
Water	1 cup	8 fl. oz.	230 milliliters
Lemon juice	1 tbsp.	1 tbsp.	15 milliliters
Sliced ham, diced	1/2 cup	4 oz.	115 grams
Mushrooms, small	1 cup	2 oz.	60 grams
Five-Minute Pastry (pp. 186-87, rec. 140)	1/2 batch	1/2 batch	1/2 batch
Bay leaf	1	1	1
Thyme	1 spray	1 spray	1 spray
Parsley	1 spray	1 spray	1 spray
Celery	1 large stalk	2 oz.	60 grams
Onions	1 small	2 oz.	60 grams
Salt	To season	To season	To season
White peppercorns	To season	To season	To season
Flour	5 tbsp.	1 1/4 oz.	40 grams
Butter	2 tbsp.	1 oz.	30 grams
Cream	1/4 cup	2 fl. oz.	60 milliliters
White wine	1/4 cup	2 fl. oz.	60 milliliters
Egg	1	1	1

METHOD OF PREPARATION
Cut chicken into 1-inch cubes—leave mushrooms whole—finely slice onions and celery—grind peppercorns—measure flour, butter, cream, and wine—prepare five-minute pastry using only half quantity—roll out a top only for the pie.

METHOD OF COOKERY
1. Place chicken in only suffecent water to cover. Add herbs, cover, and simmer for 25 minutes.
2. Make a roux with butter and flour. Strain off 5 fluid ounces chicken stock to make a stiff sauce.
3. Season the sauce, add the wine and cream. Stir well.
4. Lay half chicken meat with onions and celery in pie dish, cover with ham, then place very lightly fried whole mushrooms, black side down, on ham. Sprinkle with lemon juice and top with remaining chicken. Pour over sauce. Cover with pastry top. Gild pastry with beaten egg.
5. Bake at 375° F. for 40 minutes. Cover pie top with foil if it colors too soon.

SERVING
Serve with Bell Block Rice Bake (p. 229, rec. 182) and a tossed "all in salad." A chilled white wine goes very well.

156 Broiled Chicken Carson

(Broiled Poultry—Basic Method, pages 116-17)

RECIPE TO PRODUCE 2 PORTIONS	U.S.A.	IMPERIAL	METRIC
Chicken	2 lb.	2 lb.	1 kilo
Marinade:			
White wine	½ cup	4 fl. oz.	115 grams
Onion	1 small	2 oz.	60 grams
Bay leaf	1	1	1
Thyme sprig	1	1	1
Black peppercorns	6	6	6
Grated green ginger	½ tsp.	½ tsp.	1 gram
Mushrooms, sliced	1 cup	2 oz.	60 grams
Cream	6 tbsp.	3 fl. oz.	85 milliliters
Lemon juice	½ tsp.	½ tsp.	5 milliliters
Parsley stalks	1 tsp.	1 tsp.	1 gram
Cayenne pepper	To sprinkle	To sprinkle	To sprinkle
Parsley	To garnish	To garnish	To garnish

METHOD OF PREPARATION

Cut up chicken as shown in basic method—marinade in wine, chopped onion, bay leaf, thyme, pepper-corns, and green ginger for 1 hour—strain off solids from wine and reserve wine. Dry chicken pieces well and flour—chop parsley stalks and parsley for garnish—preheat broiler to medium hot.

METHOD OF COOKERY

1. Broil chicken pieces in manner indicated in basic method. Place in warming oven to keep hot.
2. Pour fat from broiler tray into frying pan—heat—add mushrooms, lemon juice, parsley stalks, and cayenne and fry lightly.
3. In broiler tray, add wine from strained marinade and boil down to a syrup, scraping up residue from chicken. Add cream.
4. Place mushrooms over chicken, then pour over cream and wine. Serve sprinkled with chopped parsley.

SERVING

Buttered broccoli and glazed carrots are suitable vegetables. I like Queensland Rice as a starch accompaniment (p. 226, rec. 178). A full-bodied dry white wine goes well.

157 Stuffed Saddle of Lamb Roxdale

(Roast Meat—Basic Method, pages 132-33)

RECIPE TO PRODUCE 6-10 PORTIONS	U.S.A.	IMPERIAL	METRIC
Boned saddle of lamb	5½ lb.	5½ lb.	2.5 kilo
Garlic	To season	To season	To season
Salt	To season	To season	To season
Black peppercorns	To season	To season	To season
Stuffing:			
Canned apricots	16 oz. can	16 oz. can	5 kilo
Brandy	2 tbsp.	1 fl. oz.	30 milliliters
Long grain rice	1 cup	8 oz.	225 milliliters
Grated cinnamon	1 tsp.	1 tsp.	5 grams
Black peppercorns		To season well	
Glaze:			
Juice from can	⅞ cup	7 fl. oz.	200 milliliters
Use half the can of apricots listed under stuffing			

METHOD OF PREPARATION

1. Drain apricots—use half for filling and dice.
2. Measure brandy.
3. Cook rice 5 minutes and drain.
4. Roughly grind peppercorns.
5. Measure remainder of apricots and juice for glaze.

METHOD OF COOKERY

1. Season the inside of the saddle well with garlic, roughly ground peppercorns, and salt.
2. Spread the cooked rice over the surface of the meat and cover this with the apricots. Sprinkle the apricots with the brandy.
3. Season very well with salt, black peppercorns, and the fresh-grated cinnamon.
4. Roll up and tie (pp. 166-67, rec. 122).
5. Weigh and cook for 30 minutes per pound at 325° F.
6. Purée items for glaze in blender. When lamb is cooked, remove the strings and place onto a serving dish—coat with the glaze. Put back into the broiler, moderate to hot, to just brown the surface.

SERVING

Serve with a large dish of Green Beans (p. 236, rec. 190) and a few Green Pepper Potatoes (p. 224, rec. 175). A good red Hermitage wine goes well.

158   Bluff Bolar: Beef

(Braised Meat—Basic Method, pages 140-41)

RECIPE TO PRODUCE 4 PORTIONS	U.S.A.	IMPERIAL	METRIC
Blade steaks	4 6-oz.	4 6-oz.	4 170-grams
Flour	½ cup	2 oz.	60 grams
Onion	1 medium	4 oz.	115 grams
Carrot	1 large	4 oz.	115 grams
Bay leaf	1	1	1
Parsley stalks	2	2	2
Thyme	1 sprig	1 sprig	1 sprig
Clarified butter	¼ cup	2 oz.	60 grams
Salt	To season	To season	To season
Black peppercorns	To season	To season	To season
Garlic	1 clove	1 clove	1 clove
Beef stock (pp. 26-27, rec. 15)	2½ cups	1 pint	570 milliliters
Mushrooms, small	2 cups	4 oz.	115 grams
Oysters	2 doz.	2 doz.	2 doz.

METHOD OF PREPARATION

1. Dry steaks well—flour and season them.
2. Melt butter.
3. Slice onion and carrot.
4. Tie up herbs.
5. Measure stock.
6. Crush garlic.
7. Peel mushrooms.
8. Heat frying pan to 400° F.

METHOD OF COOKERY

1. Brown steaks thoroughly on both sides in butter.
2. Remove from pan.
3. Add onions and carrots. Brown these.
4. Add garlic and steak, stock and herbs.
5. Stir well to scrape off the meat residue. Replace lid and cook for 2½ hours at 220° F. Add mushrooms 20 minutes before serving.
6. Remove fat from surface, take out herbs, thicken at the boil with arrowroot, add oysters, correct seasoning, and serve.

SERVING

Dust steaks with parsley. Serve with Ngauruhoe Potatoes (p. 222, rec. 172) and Brussels sprouts or Green Beans (p. 236, rec. 190). A good quality full-bodied red wine should blend well.

159 Veal Cutlets Yerex

(Shallow-fried Meat—Basic Method, pages 150-51)

RECIPE TO PRODUCE 4 PORTIONS	U.S.A.	IMPERIAL	METRIC
Veal loin chops	4	4	4
Salt, white peppercorns	To season	To season	To season
Clarified butter	2 tbsp.	2 tbsp.	30 grams
Heavy cream	10 tbsp.	5 fl. oz.	150 milliliters
Egg yolks	2	2	2
Chinese gooseberries	3	3	3
Cauliflower	1 small	1 small	1 small
Broccoli	1 bunch	1 bunch	1 bunch
Dry white wine	¼ cup	2 fl. oz.	60 milliliters
Lemon peel	1 lemon	1 lemon	1 lemon
Black grapes	20	20	20
Lemon juice	1 lemon	1 lemon	1 lemon
Butter	2 tbsp.	2 tbsp.	30 grams
Mint	To garnish	To garnish	To garnish
Paprika	To garnish	To garnish	To garnish

METHOD OF PREPARATION

1. Trim chops.
2. Combine cream with egg yolks.
3. Peel and slice Chinese gooseberries ¼-inch thick.
4. Chop mint.
5. Finely slice lemon peel.
6. Break up cauliflower and broccoli into small pieces.
7. Measure dry white wine.

METHOD OF COOKERY

1. Place broccoli and cauliflower in salted boiling water and cook 10 minutes. Drain and place the vegetables in an ovenproof dish. Place small pieces of butter on top and add a squeeze of lemon juice. Place under the broiler unit.
2. Season chops and gently fry in clarified butter for about 6 minutes either side. Remove and keep warm.
3. Place the Chinese gooseberries in a small saucepan (don't add butter) and add squeeze of lemon juice and the grapes. Add lemon peel and cream and egg yolks—stir over a gentle heat until thickened.
4. Deglaze pan (in which veal chops were cooked) with wine and add a little of the pan juices to the fruit in the cream.
5. Pour sauce over chops and serve garnished with very finely chopped mint and a dusting of paprika. Pour a little of the pan juices over the vegetables and arrange around the chops.
6. Serve accompanied by small new potatoes garnished with chopped mint.

SERVING

Accompany with a full flowery Moselle.

160 Pork and Mushroom Teko Teko
(Broiled Meat—Basic Method, pages 154-55)

RECIPE TO PRODUCE 4 PORTIONS	U.S.A.	IMPERIAL	METRIC
Pork fillets	4 6-oz.	4 6-oz.	4 170 grams
Bacon slices	4	4	4
Mushrooms, sliced	1 cup	4 oz.	115 grams
Dry white wine	¼ cup	2 fl. oz.	60 milliliters
Lemon juice	1 tbsp.	1 tbsp.	15 milliliters
Cayenne pepper	½ tsp.	½ tsp.	1.5 grams
Parsley stalks	1 tbsp.	1 tbsp.	5 grams
Salt	¼ tsp.	¼ tsp.	1 gram
Clarified butter	To brush	To brush	To brush
Salt	To season	To season	To season
Black peppercorns	To season	To season	To season

METHOD OF PREPARATION

1. Cut fillets almost in half lengthways—beat out flat.
2. Finely chop parsley stalks.
3. Heat broiler to medium.

METHOD OF COOKERY

1. Poach mushrooms with wine, lemon juice, salt, cayenne, and parsley stalks for 5 minutes.
2. Purée in blender or rub through a sieve.
3. Fill pork fillets with the paste and bind the two sides together by wrapping a bacon slice around each one.
4. Season and brush with clarified butter.
5. Grill for 4 minutes either side.
6. Drive a kebob stick into the top end and serve.

SERVING

Serve with plain Baked Potatoes in their jackets (pp. 220-21, rec. 168) and a tossed Red and Green Cabbage Salad (p. 246, rec. 208). A good rosé wine that has a "crackle," served lightly chilled, balances well.

161 Shoulder of Lamb Wellington
(Light Stews—Basic Method, pages 158-59)

RECIPE TO PRODUCE 4 PORTIONS	U.S.A.	IMPERIAL	METRIC
Lamb shoulder meat	2 lb.	2 lb.	1 kilo
Light veal or chicken stock (pp. 26-27, rec. 15)	1½ cups	12 fl. oz.	340 milliliters
Carrots	2 medium	2 medium	2 medium
Onions	2 medium	2 medium	2 medium
Parsley	1 sprig	1 sprig	1 sprig
Celery stalk	1 small	1 oz.	30 grams
Leek	1	1	1
Thyme	¼ tsp.	¼ tsp.	¼ tsp.
Bay leaf	1	1	1
White peppercorns	To season	To season	To season
Natural clove essence	2 drops	2 drops	2 drops
Onions	8 small	8 small	8 small
Asparagus	8 spears	8 spears	8 spears
Butter	6 tbsp.	3 oz.	85 grams
Flour	⅞ cup	3½ oz.	100 grams
Milk	1¼ cups	10 fl. oz.	285 milliliters
Paprika	To dust	To dust	To dust
Egg yolks	2	2	2
Cream	2 tbsp.	2 tbsp.	30 milliliters
Dry white wine	½ cup	4 fl. oz.	115 milliliters

METHOD OF PREPARATION
1. Cut meat in 1-inch cubes, place in cold water for 1 hour.
2. Slice carrots and 2 onions thickly.
3. Place parsley, celery, chopped leek, thyme, and bay leaf in muslin bag.
4. Peel and lightly cook in water 8 small onions.
5. Use fresh asparagus if possible.
6. Measure butter, flour, milk, wine.
7. Blend yolks and cream.

METHOD OF COOKERY
1. Drain water from lamb, cover with stock and add sliced vegetables, herbs, and seasoning.
2. Bring to boil, skim off foam, and reduce to simmer. Cover and cook for 1 hour.
3. Strain off cooking liquor (10 fluid ounces). Add an equal quantity of milk.
4. Make a roux with butter and flour, and stock and milk to make a thick creamy sauce.
5. Remove herbs and vegetables from meat. Pour sauce over meat, add onions, wine, asparagus, bring to serving heat. Stir in eggs and cream at end (DO NOT BOIL). Garnish with paprika and parsley.

SERVING
Serve in a piped nest of creamed potatoes, and surround this with peas cooked in butter with ¼-inch cubes of ham. Serve a light dry white wine.

162 Back Sticks Venison Stew
(Dark Stews—Basic Method, pages 162-63)

RECIPE TO PRODUCE 4 PORTIONS	U.S.A.	IMPERIAL	METRIC
Venison neck, flap, or shoulder	2 lb.	2 lb.	1 kilo
Marinade:			
Olive oil	¼ cup	2 fl. oz.	60 milliliters
Dry red wine	¾ cup	6 fl. oz.	170 milliliters
Bay leaf	1	1	1
Thyme	1 tsp.	1 tsp.	3 grams
Parsley stalks	1 spray	1 spray	1 spray
Peppercorns	6	6	6
Onion	1 medium	1 medium	1 medium
Garlic clove	1	1	1
Gin	2 tbsp.	1 fl. oz.	30 milliliters
Parsnip	1 medium	3 oz.	85 grams
Mushrooms, quartered	1 cup	2 oz.	60 grams
Onion	1 large	6 oz.	170 grams
Carrots	2 large	8 oz.	230 grams
Beef stock (pp. 26-27, rec. 15)	2½ cups	1 pint	570 milliliters
Garlic clove	1	1	1
Herbs: 2 parsley stalks, 1 sprig thyme,			
1 bay leaf, 6 crushed juniper berries	1 bunch	1 bunch	1 bunch

METHOD OF PREPARATION

1. Cut meat into 1-inch cubes.
2. Mix all ingredients for marinade—marinate 24 hours.
3. Dice onion finely.
4. Crush garlic well.
5. Slice vegetables ½-inch thick.
6. Tie up herbs in muslin bag.
7. Measure stock.
8. Make an arrowroot thickening paste with 2 tablespoons each of arrowroot and water.

METHOD OF COOKERY

1. Strain off marinade and keep to one side for later use.
2. Dry meat **well.**
3. Fry to brown all over; add onion, carrots, and parsnips and brown these.
4. Add herbs and stock.
5. Cook for 1 hour until tender.
6. Skim off fat and add strained marinade.
7. Add mushrooms and thicken with arrowroot paste. Simmer for 10 minutes and serve.

SERVING

Moreland Potatoes (p. 218, rec. 166), Sweet Potato Cakes (p. 242, rec. 199) and Swiss chard or spinach leaves (pp. 236-37, rec. 189) go well. Serve a full-bodied red wine.

163 Lambroll Ruakura

(Lambroll—Basic Method, pages 166-67)

RECIPE TO PRODUCE 5-6 PORTIONS	U.S.A.	IMPERIAL	METRIC
Loin of lean lamb	5½ lb.	5½ lb.	2.5 kilos
Mushrooms, sliced	2 cups	4 oz.	115 grams
Lemons	2	2	2
Parsley	1 tbsp.	1 tbsp.	5 grams
Butter	6 tbsp.	3 oz.	85 grams
Garlic salt	To season	To season	To season
Black peppercorns	To season	To season	To season
Lemon Parsley Butter (p. 48, rec. 28)	5 tbsp.	5 tbsp.	5 tbsp.
Tomatoes	5	5	5
Parsley	To garnish	To garnish	To garnish

METHOD OF PREPARATION

1. Prepare loin as shown in basic method, but do not tie up.
2. Steep mushrooms and finely chopped parsley in lemon juice for 30 minutes.
3. Cut tomatoes in fancy shapes.
4. Cut parsley for garnishing in small sprays.
5. Heat pan to 300° F.

METHOD OF COOKERY

1. Season inside of loin with garlic salt and freshly ground peppercorns; add drained and dried mushrooms.
2. Roll up loin as shown in basic method. Cut into "steaks."
3. Melt butter in pan set at 300° F. and cook lambrolls for 8 minutes both sides, turning often.
4. Remove from pan, cut strings, top each with lemon parsley butter. Garnish with tomatoes and parsley sprays.

SERVING

Serve with Ngauruhoe Potatoes (p. 222, rec. 172) and sprouting broccoli. This dish deserves a very good dry red wine!

164 Cullers Bluff Pudding
(Suet Pudding—Basic Method, pages 182–83)

RECIPE TO PRODUCE 4 PORTIONS	U.S.A.	IMPERIAL	METRIC
Pastry:			
Flour	1 lb.	1 lb.	5 kilo
Baking powder	1 heaping tsp.	1 heaping tsp.	1 heaping tsp.
Salt	Pinch	Pinch	Pinch
Suet	9 oz.	9 oz.	255 grams
Water	1¼ cup	10 fl. oz.	285 milliliters
Filling:			
Venison neck	1½ lb.	1½ lb.	.75 kilo
Ox kidney	8 oz.	8 oz.	230 grams
Fresh thyme leaves	1½ tsp.	1½ tsp.	5 grams
Parsley stalks	1 tbsp.	1 tbsp.	5 grams
Mushrooms, sliced	2 cups	4 oz.	115 grams
Oysters	1 doz.	1 doz.	1 doz.
Juice from oysters			

METHOD OF PREPARATION

1. Sift flour well with salt and baking powder.
2. Measure suet and water.
3. Cube meat and flour.
4. Measure thyme leaves.
5. Chop parsley stalks finely and measure.
6. Drain juice from oysters.
7. Put water in large saucepan to heat.
8. Grease basin.
9. Prepare scalded floured cloth and cut string to tie.

METHOD OF COOKERY

1. Add suet to flour and place in mixer to rub together. Gradually mix in water.
2. Roll out ⅔ of paste and shape it over greased basin. Place inside bowl.
3. Add herbs and mushrooms to floured meat. Season well with salt and pepper and put in paste-lined basin. Add oyster juice and water to ¾ fill.
4. Roll out remaining paste to ½-inch thickness. Press down well on top. Tie over cloth and boil 3 hours. Cut out wedge—add oysters, stir in, replace wedge, and serve.

SERVING

My mind cannot extend past plain cooked peas and glazed whole carrots, and, frankly, a glass of heavy "stout type" beer is better than any wine in this case.

Fattening but nice

About Starch Foods

The foods covered in this section are responsible for a multimillion-dollar industry. In themselves they are cheap—but. Listen to this conversation.

"I've got nothing to wear."

"Nonsense, darling, you have some beautiful clothes."

"What does this look like?"

"Lovely."

"Do I look fat?"

"...No."

"Are you telling me the truth—look at me sideways—isn't it thick—you must tell the truth!"

"I am, you look lovely—I said so—I mean it."

"I don't, you must be blind—how can I rely on you?"

"...Ummph."

"Can't you say anything?"

"What do you expect me to say?"

"Tell the truth—I'm fat!"

"All right, you look a little plump. But I like you that way."

"So I look plump, do I? (shouting) . . . well, for that I'm going to buy a new dress."

"Where does the money come from?"

"You criticized it—you pay."

"But I said you looked lovely—didn't I?"

"You lied—you admitted it."

"We're getting late—let's go."

"I'm not going—I haven't a thing to wear."

"Women!"

That this sort of thing goes on all over the world shows how much starch foods are enjoyed.

CONTENTS OF SECTION

165 BOILED POTATOES

COMMENT ON METHOD

Surprising as it may seem, the leading chefs in London test their potential cooks by asking them to cook either a plain omelet or boil potatoes. It isn't as easy as some people think to boil the humble spud, and this probably accounts for the fact that it is, in my opinion, the perfect way of cooking potatoes.

Step 1
Select potatoes of even size and scrub well. Place in a saucepan and, in the case of new potatoes, cover them with boiling water. Old potatoes should still be boiled with skins on unless very badly marked, but they should be put in cold water.

Step 2
Add salt and a sprig each of parsley and mint. Make sure that the water level well covers the potatoes and then cover with a close-fitting lid. Boil for 20-25 minutes according to size.

166 Moreland Potatoes

RECIPE TO PRODUCE 4 PORTIONS	U.S.A.	IMPERIAL	METRIC
Potatoes	8 medium	8 medium	8 medium
Chives	2 tbsp.	2 tbsp.	15 grams
Butter	4 tbsp.	2 oz.	60 grams
Whole-meal flour	7 tbsp.	2 oz.	60 grams

METHOD OF PREPARATION

1. Peel potatoes.
2. Chop chives finely.
3. Melt butter.
4. Measure flour onto plate.

METHOD OF COOKERY

1. Cook potatoes in boiling water and salt—remove skins.
2. Dry over low heat as shown above.
3. Brush with melted butter and chopped chives.
4. Dust with flour and serve at once.

218

Step 3
When the potatoes are **just** cooked, test by driving a thin knife or skewer into the potato. When lifted, it should slide off. With old potatoes, place under cold running water and peel off the skin with a knife. Put back into the dry saucepan—cover with a clean cloth and "steam" for 3 minutes on a low heat.

Step 4
After the potatoes have dried out they will be floury on the outside. Add butter and a small handful of mixed chopped mint and parsley. Turn gently until coated with buttered herbs and then serve immediately.

167 Otaki Potatoes

RECIPE TO PRODUCE 4 PORTIONS	U.S.A.	IMPERIAL	METRIC
Large potatoes	4	4	4
Onion	1 medium	1 medium	1 medium
Clarified butter	4 tbsp.	4 tbsp.	60 grams
Tomato sauce	1¼ cups	10 fl. oz.	285 milliliters
Salt	To season	To season	To season
Pepper	To season	To season	To season
Water	¾ cup	5 fl. oz.	140 milliliters
Chopped parsley	To garnish	To garnish	To garnish

METHOD OF PREPARATION

1. Peel and slice potatoes ½ inch thick.
2. Peel and chop onion.

METHOD OF COOKERY

1. Heat butter in saucepan. Cook chopped onion until golden brown.
2. Add potato slices, tomato sauce, and water. Cover and cook gently until potatoes are tender and liquid has reduced, approximately 30 minutes.

168 BAKED POTATOES

COMMENT ON METHOD

Having lived among the Sassenachs most of my life before I went to live "down under," I had the choice of many fine restaurants in which to eat. But the meal that had the most impact was at Lyons Cornerhouse in Leicester Square, London. I had just received all my inoculations for the trip across and hadn't been told not to drink any alcohol. We had a thick slice of underdone roast beef, baked potatoes in their jackets, and a tossed salad, and washed it down with cold draughts of Carlsberg beer—the last thing I remember was the baked potato—it was magnificent!

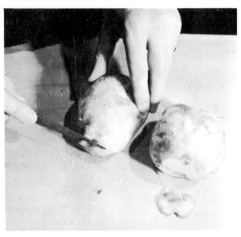 

Step 1
Choose large, even-size, good-quality potatoes; scrub well and dust thoroughly with salt. This saves the outer skin from being scorched. Trim off a thin slice from one end. If you have ever experienced an exploded potato you will understand the reason why!

Step 2
Place the potatoes in an oven set at 350° F. and bake for 1½ hours for size used in these photographs. It is only economical to use this method when some other food requires the oven to be operated, as in this case.

169 Cheddar Baked

RECIPE TO PRODUCE 4 PORTIONS	U.S.A.	IMPERIAL	METRIC
Potatoes	4 large	4 large	4 large
Cheddar cheese	4 oz.	4 oz.	115 grams
Salt	To season	To season	To season
White peppercorns	To season	To season	To season

METHOD OF PREPARATION

Bake potatoes as shown in basic method—slice cheese into 4 even slices—preheat broiler to medium hot.

METHOD OF COOKERY

1. Slice potatoes in two lengthwise when cooked.
2. Cut into potato flesh with a small knife—do not cut through the skin. Season this cut surface with the salt and freshly ground white peppercorns.
3. Lay sices of cheese onto potatoes and place under the hot broiler. Cook until nicely browned.
4. Dust with chopped parsley and serve.

Step 3
Fold a cloth so that it can be slipped like a noose around the potato and cut deeply into the center to form a cross.

Step 4
Squeeze the cloth, gently at first and then harder. The object is to fracture the potato flesh without damaging the skin. Gradually the cut will open out as shown above. A dab of butter, a touch of cream, and a sprinkle of chives and you can eat.

170   Mushroom and Bacon Baked

RECIPE TO PRODUCE 4 PORTIONS	U.S.A.	IMPERIAL	METRIC
Potatoes	4 large	4 large	4 large
Bacon slices	4	4	4
Butter	4 tbsp.	2 oz.	60 grams
Milk	¾ cup	6 fl. oz.	170 milliliters
Salt	To season	To season	To season
Pepper	To season	To season	To season
Parsley	2 tbsp.	2 tbsp.	10 grams
Mushrooms	4	4	4
Butter	To fry	To fry	To fry
Lemon juice	1 tbsp.	1 tbsp.	15 milliliters

METHOD OF PREPARATION

Bake potatoes—cut in half lengthwise and spoon out filling—chop parsley—squeeze lemon.

METHOD OF COOKERY

1. Fry bacon crisp and then chop finely.
2. Add butter and milk to potato and cream well. Season highly. Add chopped parsley and bacon.
3. Fit pastry bag with a star nozzle and pipe mixture into potato "jackets."
4. Top each serving with 1 mushroom fried in butter and lemon.

171 CREAMED POTATOES

COMMENT ON METHOD

My grandmother used to live in Broadstairs, near Margate, in a house called "Greenshutters." The things I remember most about her are her stories about my grandfather, The Gold and Silver Waltz and her creamed potatoes. My grandfather, a typical Scot, used to creep downstairs in the middle of the night for a drop of whisky. But the cupboard door used to squeak, so he oiled the hinges when Grandmother was out and she dried off the oil when he was out! She also taught my Treena and me to do the quick waltz—and her creamed potatoes were a meteorologist's delight.

Step 1
Creamed potatoes can be made from either well-boiled (and dried) potatoes (pp. 218-19, rec. 165) or from baked potatoes. I prefer the latter for quality, and there is very little waste.

Step 2
Scoop out the potato but do not throw away the skins. We butter these and slip them under the grill to get crisp and golden. They are always eaten with great relish—especially by our children.

172 Ngauruhoe Potatoes

RECIPE TO PRODUCE 4 PORTIONS	U.S.A.	IMPERIAL	METRIC
Large potatoes	3 lb.	3 lb.	1.5 kilos
Cream	¼ cup	2 fl. oz.	60 milliliters
Spring onions	4	4	4
Tomatoes	2	2	2
Salt	To season	To season	To season
White peppercorns	To season	To season	To season
Parsley	1 sprig	1 sprig	1 sprig

METHOD OF PREPARATION

Wash potatoes well, dust with salt, bake in 350° F. oven for 1-1¼ hours until cooked—roughly chop onions—dice tomatoes—grind peppercorns—measure cream.

METHOD OF COOKERY

1. Remove potatoes from oven, cut in half, scoop out centers into large saucepan.
2. Blend with cream, season, add spring onions and tomato. Heat through, stirring gently.

Step 3
When you mash the potato you will see the reason for the improved quality obtained from baking. The flesh isn't waterlogged, but dry and floury.

Step 4
Add butter, salt, freshly ground white peppercorns, and just a touch of grated nutmeg. Beat well with a wooden spoon over the heat and add very little cream.

173 Bennet Potatoes

RECIPE TO PRODUCE 4 PORTIONS	U.S.A.	IMPERIAL	METRIC
Potatoes	1½ lb.	1½ lb.	.75 kilo
Egg whites	3	3	3
Chives or spring onions (tops)	3 tbsp.	3 tbsp.	25 grams
Parsley	To garnish	To garnish	To garnish
Salt	To season	To season	To season
White peppercorns	To season	To season	To season
Oil or fat	To deep fry	To deep fry	To deep fry

METHOD OF PREPARATION

Bake potatoes in their jackets (pp. 220-21, rec. 168) or boil them carefully (pp. 218-19, rec. 165)—separate egg whites and whip until stiff—chop spring oinon tops and parsley to garnish—heat oil or deep fat to 400° F.—prepare pastry bag with ½-inch plain nozzle.

METHOD OF COOKERY

1. Mash potatoes well—add seasoning to taste.
2. Add chopped chives or spring onion tops.
3. Fold in whipped egg whites.
4. Place mixture in pastry bag.
5. Squeeze into deep fat set at 400° F. and cook until crisp and golden brown (2 minutes).
6. Drain and serve dusted with parsley.

174 FRIED POTATOES

COMMENT ON METHOD

Surely "chips" must be the most popular form of potato throughout the world and yet, when you look at it, they are seldom made in the private home. I am a "chip fanatic." My chips have to be crisp and stay crisp until I get them down. This requires a very special process.

Step 1
Part of my fanaticism for chips is that all chips should be the same size and shape. This obviously involves cutting loss, but as you will see, I keep the peelings and trimmings in a plastic bag and use them up as flavor thickeners in soups.

Step 2
I find that chips are wonderful when they get an hour's soaking in warm water with a piece of lemon to keep their color. The warming oven is a good place to keep the water at the right temperature.

175 Green Pepper Potatoes

RECIPE TO PRODUCE 4 PORTIONS	U.S.A.	IMPERIAL	METRIC
Potatoes	1½ lb.	1½ lb.	.75 kilo
Clarified butter	3 tbsp.	1½ oz.	45 grams
Sweet green pepper	1 cup	4 oz.	115 grams
Onion	1 small	2 oz.	60 grams
Salt	To season	To season	To season
Black peppercorns	To season	To season	To season
Parsley	To garnish	To garnish	To garnish

METHOD OF PREPARATION

Boil and dry potatoes—slice ½-inch thick—very finely slice green pepper and onion—chop parsley.

METHOD OF COOKERY

1. Shallow fry potato slices in clarified butter.
2. After first turn, add sliced green pepper and onion rings.
3. When browned lightly, turn out, dust with salt, freshly ground pepper, and chopped parsley.

Step 3
Warm water helps to create a gradual conversion of some surface starches to a sugar and this, when fried, goes crisp and stays crisp. After the hour, re-move and dry thoroughly.

Step 4
Lower into fat or oil set at 350° F. for 10 minutes. This cooks the potatoes but doesn't brown them. Increase the heat to 450° F. and return the chips. Cook for a further 3 minutes or until a crisp golden brown.

176 Nobop* Potatoes

RECIPE TO PRODUCE 4 PORTIONS	U.S.A.	IMPERIAL	METRIC
Large potatoes	4	4	4
Deep fat or oil	To deep fry	To deep fry	To deep fry
Salt	To season	To season	To season

METHOD OF PREPARATION

Peel and trim potatoes exactly square—cut into slices ⅛-inch thick—preheat oil to 350° F. Reserve potato trimmings for use as a soup thickener.

METHOD OF COOKERY

1. Dry potato slices well. Drop in hot deep fat or oil and fry at 350° F. until they rise to the surface (2 minutes). Remove.
2. Raise heat immediately to 450° F.–500° F.
3. Return potatoes to heat until they puff up like small balloons and become golden brown.
4. Drain, sprinkle with salt, and serve immediately.

*I am almost ashamed to say that the title "Nobop" is derived from the fact that they are square!

177 BOILED RICE

COMMENT ON METHOD

When my first book came out it created a good deal of favorable comment from people who wanted to cook rice dishes and succeed. The traditionalists, however, reacted against some of my techniques, saying, "He has taken too many short cuts. People who like cooking are prepared to spend all day doing so." Unfortunately, these people are few and far between and the number is getting fewer every day. This method of boiling rice was criticized, but I have yet to find a better method. Even my Chinese greengrocer uses it now!

Step 1
The best rice for boiling is long grain—the short grain being the finest in the world for rice puddings. You need ⅝ cup rice for 4 reasonable portions. Wash the rice under cold running water until not a trace of white is left in the water.

Step 2
For ⅝ cup rice you need 3 pints of water and 1 tablespoon of salt. Bring the water to a vigorous boil and rain in the rice. Boil for exactly 10 minutes.

178 Queensland Rice

RECIPE TO PRODUCE 4 PORTIONS	U.S.A.	IMPERIAL	METRIC
Water	7½ cups	3 pints	1.7 litre
Salt	1 tbsp.	½ oz.	15 grams
Long grain rice	⅝ cup	6 oz.	170 grams
Large raisins (after soaking)	6 tbsp.	2 oz.	60 grams
Pineapple pieces	2 oz.	2 oz.	60 grams
Almonds	¼ cup	1 oz.	30 grams

METHOD OF PREPARATION

Soak large raisins and weigh—finely dice pineapple—wash rice thoroughly—skin and slice almonds.

METHOD OF COOKERY

1. Boil 3 pints of water with salt.
2. Add rice, stir to boil and leave to boil for 5 minutes.
3. Drain rice into colander and place over saucepan of boiling water.
4. Add raisins (drained), pineapple, and almonds. Mix through thoroughly.
5. Place lid on top and steam for 10 minutes.

Step 3
Pour rice into a colander and set it on top of the saucepan in which a small amount of water has been added. Put a lid on top of the rice and steam for 8 minutes.

Step 4
The rice, as you can see, is separate, fluffy, and, I can promise, delicious. It will also keep well without going like clods of sticky Turkish delight.

179 Anchovy Rice

RECIPE TO PRODUCE 4 PORTIONS	U.S.A.	IMPERIAL	METRIC
Long grain rice	1 cup	8 oz.	230 grams
Onion	1 small	1 small	1 small
Anchovy fillets	6	6	6
Milk	½ cup	4 fl. oz.	115 milliliters
Clarified butter	2 tbsp.	2 tbsp.	30 grams
Parsley, finely chopped	2 tsp.	2 tsp.	5 grams
Tomato sauce	¼ cup	2 fl. oz.	60 milliliters

METHOD OF PREPARATION
Cook rice 5 minutes, **add no salt**—chop onion finely—soak anchovy fillets in milk for 30 minutes—chop anchovies.

METHOD OF COOKERY
1. Cook onion until transparent in clarified butter.
2. Stir in parsley and anchovies. Heat through.
3. Stir in tomato sauce, bring to boil, and mix with rice.
4. Serve.

180 SAVORY RICE BAKE

COMMENT ON METHOD
This is my favorite rice dish—favorite because it always works and because it is as versatile as an omelet for a quick, cheap meal. It can also be done in bulk. We served it to the cast of

Step 1
Finely slice 1 small onion and shallow fry in a flameproof dish in 4 tablespoons clarified butter, until softened but not colored. Wash 1¼ cups rice well under cold running water and dry thoroughly.

Step 2
Add rice to onions and fry for 3 minutes. Add a bunch of herbs consisting of 1 sprig thyme and parsley and 1 bay leaf. Pour in 1 pint of stock. The type of stock depends on whether you have fish, chicken, beef, lamb, vegetables, etc.

181 Boston Rice Bake

RECIPE TO PRODUCE 4 PORTIONS	U.S.A.	IMPERIAL	METRIC
Long grain rice	1⅛ cup	8 oz.	230 grams
Crayfish (lobster)	1½ lb.	1½ lb.	.75 kilo
Mushrooms, thinly sliced	1 cup	2 oz.	60 grams
Lemon juice	1 tbsp.	1 tbsp.	15 milliliters
Chives, chopped	2 tbsp.	2 tbsp.	30 milliliters
Onion	1 small	2 oz.	60 grams
Clarified butter	3 tbsp.	1½ oz.	45 milliliters
Bay leaf	1	1	1
Crayfish or lobster stock	2½ cups	1 pint	570 milliliters
Parsley	1 sprig	1 sprig	1 sprig
Salt	To season	To season	To season
White pepper	To season	To season	To season

METHOD OF PREPARATION
Buy a crayfish or lobster which is slightly undercooked—slice the whole body in two lengthways, remove the tail and body flesh (take out the thin blackish tube that runs down the middle of the back)—cut the flesh into ½-inch pieces—make stock from crushed shell—wash rice and dry—slice onion, measure stock, and chop chives—preheat oven to 450° F.

METHOD OF COOKERY
1. Shallow fry onion and rice in clarified butter. Add seasoning and stock.
2. Combine crayfish with lemon juice and add to rice mixture. Add mushrooms.
3. Place in oven and bake at 450° F. for 20 minutes.
4. Dust with chives and serve.

Who's Afraid of Virginia Woolf after their opening night in Wellington. The particular recipe we used is called Boston Rice Bake (see below).

Step 3
Add salt and freshly ground peppercorns and set in an oven preheated to 450° F. Do not cover. You can add special fillings at this stage or cook them separately and mix in at Step 4.

Step 4
Bake for 20 minutes, remove herbs. You will see that all the liquid has been absorbed by the rice. This is the most wonderful rice dish I know.

182 Bell Block Rice Bake

RECIPE TO PRODUCE 4 PORTIONS

	U.S.A.	IMPERIAL	METRIC
Long grain rice	1⅛ cup	8 oz.	230 grams
Onion	1 small	2 oz.	60 grams
Butter	4 tbsp.	2 oz.	60 grams
Parsley	1 sprig	1 sprig	1 sprig
Thyme	1 sprig	1 sprig	1 sprig
Bay leaf	1	1	1
Chicken stock	2½ cups	1 pint	570 milliliters
Salt	To season	To season	To season
White pepper	To season	To season	To season
Parsley	To garnish	To garnish	To garnish
Cayenne pepper	¼ tsp.	¼ tsp.	¼ tsp.
Chicken livers	1 cup	8 oz.	230 grams
Mushrooms, small	1 cup	2 oz.	60 grams
Clarified butter	3 tbsp.	1½ oz.	45 grams
Lemon juice	1 tbsp.	1 tbsp.	15 milliliters
Flour	To coat	To coat	To coat

METHOD OF PREPARATION

Wash rice and dry—slice onion—tie parsley, thyme, bay leaf up together—measure stock (chicken if possible)—chop parsley for garnish—dice chicken livers and toss in flour—slice mushrooms finely—preheat oven 450° F.

METHOD OF COOKERY

1. Shallow fry onion and rice in butter. Add herbs, seasoning, and stock.
2. Toss chicken livers in clarified butter for 1 minute, then add mushrooms.
3. Toss 30 seconds, add lemon juice and cayenne pepper.
4. Turn into rice mixture.
5. Place in oven and bake at 450° F. for 20 minutes.
6. Remove herbs, dust with parsley, and serve.

183 PASTA

COMMENT ON METHOD

Pasta is wonderful when used for variety, but it should never rule the roost in famous meat producing nations.

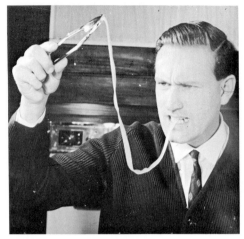

Step 1
For 1 pound of pasta you need 1 gallon of water and 1 tablespoon of salt. Bring the water to the boil and place the ends into the pot, bending the strips around as they soften. When all are covered, make sure that the pieces are separate by prodding around gently with a fork.

Step 2
Boil until when you bite a piece, there is resistance to the teeth. Al dente this is called. It should not be so soft that it melts in the mouth. Spaghetti needs 8-12 minutes; vermicelli 6-10 minutes; macaroni 10-12 minutes; noodles (egg-made) 6-9 minutes.

184 Bacon and Egg Spaghetti

RECIPE TO PRODUCE 4 PORTIONS	U.S.A.	IMPERIAL	METRIC
Spaghetti (per portion)	¼ lb.	4 oz.	115 grams
Bacon slices	4	4	4
Onions	2 medium	2 medium	2 medium
Eggs	4	4	4
Parsley	To garnish	To garnish	To garnish
Dry matured Cheddar, grated	1 cup	4 oz.	115 grams
Clarified butter	4 tbsp.	2 oz.	60 grams

METHOD OF PREPARATION

Chop parsley—chop onions finely—cut bacon into small pieces.

METHOD OF COOKERY

1. Cook spaghetti for 6-8 minutes in boiling salted water. Pour in iced water. Drain.
2. Meanwhile fry chopped onions in butter until a pale gold.
3. Add chopped bacon. When cooked stir in drained spaghetti.
4. Break in eggs and stir rapidly with a wooden spoon.
5. Serve immediately eggs begin to thicken. Dust thickly with cheese and parsley.

Step 3
When once the right texture has been achieved, pour into the saucepan a pint of iced water, stir rapidly, and pour into a colander. DO NOT RINSE UNDER RUNNING WATER.

Step 4
You can serve the plain pasta straight from the colander or you can drain it well and then put it back into a pot with some clarified butter and toss it well over the heat before you serve. (I prefer butter to oil and so do a great many Italians.)

185   Spaghetti with Meat Sauce

RECIPE TO PRODUCE 4 PORTIONS	U.S.A.	IMPERIAL	METRIC
Spaghetti	1 lb.	1 lb.	.5 kilo
Butter	2 tbsp.	1 oz.	30 grams
Olive oil	¼ cup	2 fl. oz.	60 milliliters
Onions	2	2	2
Leek leaves	4	4	4
Beef topside	2 cups	1 lb.	.5 kilo
Beef stock (pp. 26-27, rec. 15)	2½ cups	1 pint	570 milliliters
Bay leaf	1	1	1
Thyme	1 tsp.	1 tsp.	3 grams
Oregano (wild marjoram)	½ tsp.	½ tsp.	½ tsp.
Black peppercorns	6	6	6
Parsley stalks	6	6	6
Garlic cloves	4	4	4
Large tomatoes	4	4	4
Tomato paste	½ cup	4 fl. oz.	115 milliliters
Dry matured Cheddar cheese,* grated	½ cup	2 oz.	60 grams

METHOD OF PREPARATION
Prepare sauce first—chop onions—chop leek leaves finely—chop or mince beef—prepare stock—place herbs and spices in muslin bag—skin and pip tomatoes—measure tomato paste.

METHOD OF COOKERY
Sauce:
1. Melt butter in small saucepan. Add oil, shallow fry onion and leeks, add minced beef.
2. Cook until golden brown adding squeezed or chopped garlic.
3. Add stock and herb bag. Bring to simmer and cook uncovered for 30 minutes.
4. Remove herbs, add tomatoes and paste. Stir and keep hot.
5. Cook spaghetti as shown (rec. 183) above.

*My preference to Parmesan, but **please** please yourself.

186 Reheating Meats

..."Leftovers"—a revolting word, and yet why should the result be a hash?—a rather sub-standard concoction used to help stretch the budget.

This sort of attitude is based on a totally incorrect premise—believing that leftover roasted meats cost nothing! In actual fact they frequently cost more than ham and certainly as much as fillet steak—work it out and see.

Meat obtained from roasts must, therefore, be looked upon as a luxury—to be treated with a little more care in their reheating. If they are relegated to such uses as cottage pie, then what you are doing is using meat that can cost *four times as much* as a cheap cut that can be purchased to produce exactly the same result.

One tip, if you are left with a partly carved roast—brush the cut surface with a little of the dripping; this will seal the area and prevent the meat from becoming dry and unpleasant.

Most important of all—*always* place the joint in the refrigerator as soon as possible after carving. Meat left to cool slowly is prone to develop a charming bug called *Clostridium welchii* that gives you a tummy ache for at least a day. What is serious is that it puts you off your food!

187   Hawke's Bay Lamb

RECIPE TO PRODUCE 4 PORTIONS	U.S.A.	IMPERIAL	METRIC
Cold roast lamb (or hogget)	1 lb.	1 lb.	.5 kilo
Onion Sauce:			
Medium onions	2	2	2
Clarified butter	6 tbsp.	3 oz.	85 grams
Flour	10 tbsp.	2½ oz.	75 grams
Cold milk	2 cups	16 fl. oz.	455 milliliters
Dry white wine	¼ cup	2 fl. oz.	60 milliliters
Salt	To season	To season	To season
White peppercorns	To season	To season	To season
Potatoes	2 lb.	2 lb.	1 kilo
Butter, salt, nutmeg	To season	To season	To season
Parsley	1 tbsp.	1 tbsp.	5 grams
Paprika	To sprinkle	To sprinkle	To sprinkle

METHOD OF PREPARATION

Cut lamb into 1-inch pieces—finely slice onions—sift flour—grind white peppercorns—boil and mash potatoes and mix with butter, salt, and nutmeg until very smooth—chop parsley finely—measure milk and wine.

METHOD OF COOKERY

1. Shallow fry onion in clarified butter without coloring. When softened, add flour and mix with wooden spoon over a low heat.
2. Add milk gradually, drawing pan off heat each time.*
3. Simmer sauce in double boiler for 10 minutes.
4. Add cubed lamb. Heat through; add wine and season to taste—do not season before.

*See method of making White Sauce (pp. 256-57, rec. 216).

SERVING

Serve in a nest of piped creamed potatoes (squeezed straight on the dinner plate). Dust surface with parsley and paprika. Serve also a good quantity of Buttered Green Beans (p. 110, rec. 190). A light dry white wine goes well.

188   Beef Gherkins

RECIPE TO PRODUCE 4 PORTIONS	U.S.A.	IMPERIAL	METRIC
Cold roast beef	1 lb.	1 lb.	.5 kilo
Gherkins	4	4	4
New Zealand Sauce (p. 258, rec. 220)	¾ cup	6 fl. oz.	170 milliliters

METHOD OF PREPARATION

Slice beef thinly into 8 slices—halve gherkins lengthwise—prepare New Zealand sauce—preheat oven to 350° F.

METHOD OF COOKERY

1. Wrap beef slices around half gherkins.
2. Lay in a shallow casserole.
3. Cover with New Zealand sauce and place in oven for 30 minutes.

SERVING

Serve with plain Boiled Rice (pp. 226-27, rec. 177) and, if available, beansprouts tossed in hot butter for 3 minutes only. Best with beer.

About Vegetables
and Salads

Are vegetarians food faddists? I sometimes wonder. I dislike excess in any direction, on any subject, I also like my food—and this includes a great hunk of fork-tender, succulent, flavorsome beef, a sweet, aromatic lamb chop, or even a plump, sexy sausage. Try as I may I cannot get as worked up over a leaf of crisp, cool green lettuce, crunchy stick of celery, or even a rich, red-hot radish.

I am the first to admit that a diet of vegetables, fruit, and nuts is very good for you. I have tried to set aside one month of the year as a kind of "annual decoke." A month in which I have nothing but a vegetarian diet. I choose February because there are fewer days than in any other month—I avoid a decoke in leap years!

Apart from a feeling that I'm on a cure, I feel fine; in a curious way I feel refreshed and clean inside—toward the end of the month (largely because I know I have only another four or five days to go!) I start to develop the symptoms of fanaticism. A kind of self-righteous justification for hardships undertaken. On the first of March I sink my teeth into that steak—and it never tasted better.

The important thing about this annual diet has, however, been my further education on how to cook vegetables. You have to go on a meat-free diet to appreciate properly how we normally mutilate these poor defenseless plants. To the vegetarian it is essential to preserve the maximum goodness and to gain the maximum flavor. To the meat eater they are a garnish that we feel should be eaten for some obscure health reason—scurvy, or something like that.

I don't suggest you follow the annual decoke idea but *please* I beg of you—cook your vegetables with great care. Never pre-prepare and always just undercook.

234

CONTENTS OF SECTION

189 GREEN VEGETABLES

COMMENT ON METHOD

I have quite a "thing" about green vegetables, largely, I think, because my mother had more rows with our chefs over this point than any other. Why—if something is so beautifully colored by nature—does it have to be boiled into a gray pulpy mess? We should respect our vegetables.

Step 1
I have chosen Swiss chard because it contains a trap. The heavy white stalks take twice as long as the green to cook, therefore either the stalks are undercooked or the green is overcooked. Obviously the best way is to strip off the green and cook each separately.

Step 2
Leave the leaves whole whenever possible; shredding only releases the natural vitamins. Season with salt and freshly ground black peppercorns, having first washed the leaves very well—don't dry them (use same technique for all green leaf vegetables).

190 Green Beans

RECIPE TO PRODUCE 4 PORTIONS

	U.S.A.	IMPERIAL	METRIC
Thin stringless beans	1 lb.	1 lb.	.5 kilo
Garlic clove	1	1	1
Butter	2 tbsp.	1 oz.	30 grams
Salt	To season	To season	To season
Black peppercorns	To season	To season	To season
Lemon	½	½	½
Parsley	1 tbsp.	1 tbsp.	10 grams
Nutmeg	To dust	To dust	To dust

METHOD OF PREPARATION

If beans are thin, young, and tender, leave whole: if larger, then cut into 3-inch lengths. Squash garlic with knife (do not chop or crush)—squeeze ½ lemon—chop parsley—measure butter.

METHOD OF COOKERY

1. Place butter in pan, add garlic, then beans.
2. Season, cover, and cook approximately 10 minutes on medium heat until tender.
3. Toss from time to time with lid on.
4. Just before serving, add juice of ½ lemon, parsley, and light dusting of nutmeg. Remove the garlic piece.

236

Step 3
Melt 4 tablespoons of butter to each 1½ pounds of leaf vegetable in a saucepan and add the leaves. Place a lid on top. *Add no water.*

Step 4
Shake the pot, holding the lid on firmly. This coats the leaves in butter. Allow 5 minutes at a low heat and then remove leaves direct to table. They should not be left to "stew in their own juice"! The stalks are cooked in lemon-flavored water for 10 minutes.

191 Spiced Red Cabbage

RECIPE TO PRODUCE 6 PORTIONS

	U.S.A.	IMPERIAL	METRIC
Red cabbage	1½ lbs.	1½ lbs.	.75 kilo
Cooking apple	1	1	1
Onion, chopped	1 tbsp.	1 tbsp.	15 grams
Butter	2 tbsp.	1 oz.	30 grams
Salt	½ tsp.	½ tsp.	3 grams
Cayenne pepper	Pinch	Pinch	Pinch
Nutmeg	Pinch	Pinch	Pinch
Brown sugar	1 tbsp.	1 tbsp.	5 grams
Vinegar	1 tbsp.	1 tbsp.	15 milliliters
Powdered cloves	Pinch	Pinch	Pinch
Powdered cinnamon	Pinch	Pinch	Pinch
Dry white wine	¼ cup	2 fl. oz.	60 milliliters
Parsley, chopped	Good bunch	Good bunch	Good bunch

METHOD OF PREPARATION
Slice cabbage finely—remove hard veins—soak shreds in cold water for 30 minutes—peel, core, and slice apple—measure wine.

METHOD OF COOKERY
1. Place cabbage straight into pot from cold water.
2. Add apple, onion, butter, salt, pepper, nutmeg.
3. Cover tightly, cook very slowly for 1 hour.
4. Stir in sugar, vinegar, cloves, cinnamon, wine, parsley. Cook all together another 5 minutes uncovered.
5. Serve hot.

192   Asparagus with Herb Butter

RECIPE TO PRODUCE 4 PORTIONS	U.S.A.	IMPERIAL	METRIC
Asparagus	1 bunch	1 bunch	1 bunch
Butter	½ cup	4 oz.	120 grams
Parsley	1 tbsp.	1 tbsp.	10 grams
Chives	1 tbsp.	1 tbsp.	10 grams
Lemon juice	To season	To season	To season
Salt, black pepper	To season	To season	To season

METHOD OF PREPARATION

1. Break off woody end of asparagus—shave off lower "bird" formations—tie asparagus together.
2. Chop parsley and chives finely.
3. Melt butter gently.

METHOD OF COOKERY

1. Place asparagus in boiling salted water, allowing the tender heads to steam above the level of the water. Cover and cook 20-25 minutes. Drain.
2. Mix herbs with the melted butter and season with salt, pepper, and lemon juice.
3. Place asparagus on a serving dish and dot with herb butter.

193   Chicory Meunière

RECIPE TO PRODUCE 5 PORTIONS	U.S.A.	IMPERIAL	METRIC
Chicory	6	6	6
Butter	¼ cup	1 oz.	30 grams
Salt, black pepper	To season	To season	To season
Butter	¼ cup	. 1 oz.	30 grams
Basil	To garnish	To garnish	To garnish

METHOD OF PREPARATION

1. Wash and dry chicory.
2. Measure butter.

METHOD OF COOKERY

1. Bring a small amount of salted water to the boil and add chicory and 1 ounce of butter. Cook gently 15 minutes. Drain.
2. Place chicory on a heated serving dish, garnish with flecks of butter, and sprinkle with basil.

238

194   Peas à l'Etouffée

RECIPE TO PRODUCE 4 PORTIONS	U.S.A.	IMPERIAL	METRIC
Peas	1 lb.	1 lb.	500 grams
Onions	2 small	2 small	2 small
Parsley	1 spray	1 spray	1 spray
Chervil	1 spray	1 spray	1 spray
Mint	1 spray	1 spray	1 spray
Butter	1 tbsp.	1 tbsp.	15 grams
Salt, black pepper	To season	To season	To season
Sugar	1 tsp.	1 tsp.	5 grams
Water	½ cup	4 fl. oz.	112 milliliters

METHOD OF PREPARATION
1. Shell peas.
2. Cut onions into quarters.
3. Tie parsley, chervil, and mint together.

METHOD OF COOKERY
1. Place peas with onions, herbs, butter, sugar, and water into a saucepan. Season with salt and pepper. Bring to the boil—cover and boil quickly, shaking the pan from time to time until the peas are soft (15 minutes).
2. If necessary add a little hot water to peas during cookery.

195   Broad Beans with Bacon

RECIPE TO PRODUCE 4 PORTIONS	U.S.A.	IMPERIAL	METRIC
Broad beans	1 lb.	1 lb.	500 grams
Salt, black pepper, nutmeg	To season	To season	To season
Bacon slices	4	4	4
Cream	3 tbsp.	3 tbsp.	45 milliliters

METHOD OF PREPARATION
1. Cut bacon into ¼-inch dice—fry until crisp.
2. Measure the cream.

METHOD OF COOKERY
1. Place broad beans into salted boiling water and cook until tender. Drain.
2. Place the beans in dry saucepan—add the cream—bring to boil, and season with salt, pepper, and nutmeg. Add the crisp bacon and combine.

196 Creamed Spinach

RECIPE TO PRODUCE 4 PORTIONS	U.S.A.	IMPERIAL	METRIC
Spinach	2 lbs.	2 lbs.	1 kilo
Water	2 tbsp.	1 fl. oz.	30 milliliters
Butter	2 tbsp.	1 oz.	30 grams
Salt, black pepper	To season	To season	To season
Sugar	1 tbsp.	1 tbsp.	15 grams
Cream	¼ cup	2 fl. oz.	60 milliliters

METHOD OF PREPARATION

1. Wash spinach well and remove stalks.
2. Measure cream and sugar.

METHOD OF COOKERY

1. Place spinach in saucepan with water and butter. Season with salt and pepper. Cover and cook over low heat 5 minutes. Drain and purée in blender.
2. Heat purée and add the sugar and then the cream. Season again if necessary.

197 Buttered Spinach

RECIPE TO PRODUCE 4 PORTIONS	U.S.A.	IMPERIAL	METRIC
Spinach	2 lbs.	2 lbs.	1 kilo
Butter	1 tbsp.	1 tbsp.	15 grams
Salt, black pepper, nutmeg	To season	To season	To season
Butter	¼ cup	2 oz.	60 grams

METHOD OF PREPARATION

1. Wash spinach thoroughly.
2. Measure butter.

METHOD OF COOKERY

1. Place spinach in large pot—do not add any water except that remaining on the leaves after washing—cover and cook slowly with 1 tablespoon of butter for 8 minutes. Drain and press moisture out of leaves with hands.
2. Slice spinach finely—place back in a dry saucepan—add the ¼ cup butter—season with salt, pepper, and nutmeg. Heat through and serve.

COMMENT ON METHOD

I am basically against the use of water with vegetables but I do appreciate that, for strict diet reasons, there may be no alternative. I have given below two methods of cooking root vegetables. The main thing to remember with all vegetable cookery is to "keep it short and eat it crisp." There is such an abundance of vitamins in our vegetables that it appears ridiculous to compensate for bad cooking by buying pills.

Step 1
One pound of root vegetables, if carefully peeled, usually serves 4 people. I like to mix roots. My favorite combination is kumera (the Maori sweet potato), parsnip (with center core removed—see above), and tender juicy carrots. If you have space *always* keep them in the refrigerator and cut them immediately before cookery. *Don't* cut and leave in cold water. Keep the peelings for soups.

Step 2
Add just enough cold water to cover and some salt. Cover and boil until just tender.

Step 3
The water should boil away almost completely. Strain off the excess (if any). Add butter (I use the foam and sediment from the making of clarified butter—pp. 264-65, rec. 228) just before you serve. Taste for seasoning. A little sugar can also be added if you want a high gloss finish.

Step 4
Root vegetables can also be shallow fried very gently in butter in a frying pan with a close-fitting lid. Stir from time to time to keep from scorching.

199 Sweet Potato Cakes

RECIPE TO PRODUCE 4 PORTIONS	U.S.A.	IMPERIAL	METRIC
Sweet potatoes—peeled weight	1 lb.	1 lb.	.5 kilo
Butter	2 tbsp.	1 oz.	30 grams
Flour	¼ cup	1 oz.	30 grams
Egg	1	1	1
Onion, finely chopped	¼ cup	1 oz.	30 grams
Parsley, finely chopped	1 tbsp.	1 tbsp.	10 grams
Lemon	1	1	1
Salt	To season	To season	To season
Pepper	To season	To season	To season
Butter	To fry	To fry	To fry

METHOD OF PREPARATION

1. Peel sweet potatoes and boil until tender—mash well.
2. Measure butter, flour, onion, parsley.
3. Slice lemon into wedges, not rings.

METHOD OF COOKERY

1. Add butter and flour to well-mashed potatoes.
2. Beat in egg and seasonings, onion and parsley.
3. Drop like pancakes onto a lightly buttered frying pan and fry 4 minutes; flip and brown other side.
4. Serve dusted with parsley, position lemon so that your guests can use it if they wish.

200 Sesame Crust Parsnips

RECIPE TO PRODUCE 6 PORTIONS	U.S.A.	IMPERIAL	METRIC
Parsnips	2 lb.	2 lb.	1 kilo
Salt	To taste	To taste	To taste
Butter	¼ cup	2 oz.	60 grams
Ground cardamom	¼ tsp.	¼ tsp.	¼ tsp.
Sesame seeds	1 tbsp.	1 tbsp.	10 grams
Fresh white breadcrumbs	½ cup	2 oz.	60 grams

METHOD OF PREPARATION

1. Place sesame seeds on tray and put under grill to toast lightly.
2. Scrub and peel parsnips—if old, remove hard center core (allow an extra ½ pound in recipe if cores are removed).
3. Preheat oven to 400° F.
4. Butter casserole.
5. Mix crumbs and sesame seeds together.

METHOD OF COOKERY

1. Boil parsnips in slightly salted water. When tender, pass through a sieve or purée in a blender.
2. Add butter and ground cardamom. Add salt if necessary.
3. Place in buttered casserole. Sprinkle with breadcrumbs and sesame seeds.
4. Dot with thin slices of butter. Place in oven to brown top well, 20-23 minutes.
5. Serve from casserole at table.

201 Glazed Rum Carrots

RECIPE TO PRODUCE 4 PORTIONS	U.S.A.	IMPERIAL	METRIC
Baby carrots	1 lb.	1 lb.	500 grams
Salt, pepper, coriander	To season	To season	To season
Rum	1 tbsp.	1 tbsp.	15 milliliters
Sugar	2 tbsp.	1 oz.	30 grams
Butter	2 tbsp.	1 oz.	30 grams

METHOD OF PREPARATION
1. Peel carrots and cut into 2-inch pieces—trim to small barrel shape.
2. Measure sugar and butter.

METHOD OF COOKERY
1. Place carrots in a very little water—add sugar, rum, and butter. Season with salt, pepper, and ground coriander. Cook, boiling gently, until the water has evaporated, leaving the carrots glazed.

202 Carrots Chantilly

RECIPE TO PRODUCE 6 PORTIONS	U.S.A.	IMPERIAL	METRIC
Carrots	2 lb.	2 lb.	1 kilo
Peas	1 lb.	1 lb.	500 grams
Cream	½ cup	4 fl. oz.	112 milliliters
Salt, white pepper	To season	To season	To season
Butter	2 tbsp.	1 oz.	30 grams

METHOD OF PREPARATION
1. Peel carrots and slice across into ¼-inch pieces.
2. Shell the peas.
3. Measure cream and butter.

METHOD OF COOKERY
1. Place carrots into cold salted water—bring to the boil and simmer 15 minutes. Drain. (If baby carrots, cook whole.) Place the peas into salted boiling water and cook 12 minutes. Drain.
2. Place the peas and carrots together in a saucepan with the butter—heat and combine—season with salt and pepper and then stir in the cream. When the cream starts to come to the boil, serve.

203 Fried Cauliflower

RECIPE TO PRODUCE 4 PORTIONS	U.S.A.	IMPERIAL	METRIC
Cauliflower	1 medium	1 medium	1 medium
Clarified butter	¼ cup	2 oz.	60 grams
Salt, black pepper	To season	To season	To season
Parsley	2 tbsp.	2 tbsp.	20 grams
Cheddar cheese	1 tbsp.	1 tbsp.	15 grams

METHOD OF PREPARATION

1. Break cauliflower into small flowerets.
2. Finely grate cheese.
3. Finely chop parsley.

METHOD OF COOKERY

1. Heat the butter in a frying pan—add the cauliflower and fry gently until browned. Season with salt and pepper.
2. Place onto a heated serving dish and sprinkle with parsley and cheese. Garnish with a few small cubes of butter.

204 Cauliflower with Black Butter

RECIPE TO PRODUCE 4 PORTIONS	U.S.A.	IMPERIAL	METRIC
Cauliflower	1	1	1
Butter	½ cup	4 oz.	112 grams
Fresh breadcrumbs	1 cup	5 oz.	140 grams
Vinegar	1 tbsp.	1 tbsp.	15 milliliters
Salt, black pepper	To season	To season	To season

METHOD OF PREPARATION

1. Divide cauliflower into flowerets and boil in salted boiling water for 8 minutes—drain.
2. Fry breadcrumbs in 2 tablespoons of clarified butter until crisp and golden.

METHOD OF COOKERY

1. Place butter in a pan and allow to brown—remove the pan from the heat.
2. Place the cauliflower on a heated serving dish—sprinkle with vinegar—brush with the browned butter, and sprinkle with breadcrumbs.

205 Tomatoes Filled with Creamed Corn Maître d'Hôtel Butter

RECIPE TO PRODUCE 4 PORTIONS	U.S.A.	IMPERIAL	METRIC
Tomatoes	2 large	2 large	2 large
Creamed corn	4 tbsp.	4 tbsp.	60 grams
Butter	¼ cup	2 oz.	60 grams
Parsley	1 tbsp.	1 tbsp.	10 grams
Salt, pepper	To season	To season	To season
Lemon juice	To season	To season	To season

METHOD OF PREPARATION

1. Cut tomatoes in half and scoop out seeds.
2. Make maître d'hôtel butter by combining softened butter with finely chopped parsley and seasoning with salt, pepper, and lemon juice.
3. Preheat broiler unit.

METHOD OF COOKERY

1. Place 1 tablespoon of creamed corn in each hollowed out tomato half. Place under the broiler for 4 minutes.
2. Garnish with maître d'hôtel butter.

206 Braised Heart of Celery with Basil Butter

RECIPE TO PRODUCE 4 PORTIONS	U.S.A.	IMPERIAL	METRIC
Celery heart	1 large	1 large	1 large
Butter	2 tbsp.	1 oz.	30 grams
Dried basil	To garnish	To garnish	To garnish
Salt, black pepper	To season	To season	To season

METHOD OF PREPARATION

1. Place celery heart in seasoned boiling water and cook gently for 23 minutes.
2. Measure butter.
3. Drain celery.

METHOD OF COOKERY

1. Cut celery heart into quarters and place on a heated serving dish.
2. Garnish with thin slices of butter and sprinkle with basil.

207 SALADS

COMMENT ON METHOD

I eat salads with practically anything. My favorite combination is a plain broiled (or fried) steak, a baked potato, and a tossed green salad. We are "all in" salad eaters. Substantially we keep to one technique but literally bung in anything that is crisp and edible. On this page I have highlighted what I believe to be the most important elements in salad preparation.

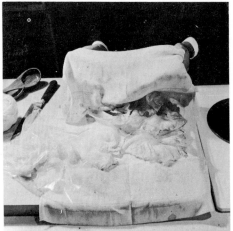

Step 1
Salads, if they must be kept, are best protected by peeling off the leaves, washing them gently, and then either drying with a cloth or spinning in one of those wire salad baskets. The leaves can then be put into polythene bags and kept in the crisper.

Step 2
Garlic is a delightful flavor for salad. I add it in three ways:
1. Rub the bowl around with a cut clove—finest flavor, very light.
2. Cook small bread pieces with cut cloves—slightly stronger.
3. Rub bread pieces with cut clove—stronger still—usually the bread is not eaten.

208 Red and Green Cabbage Salad

RECIPE TO PRODUCE 4 PORTIONS

	U.S.A.	IMPERIAL	METRIC
Crisp green cabbage heart	¼ small head	4 oz.	115 grams
Crisp red cabbage heart	¼ small head	4 oz.	115 grams
Sweet green pepper	½ cup	2 oz.	60 grams
Tomatoes, quartered	4 medium	4 medium	4 medium
G.K. Salad Dressing (p. 263, rec. 227)			

METHOD OF PREPARATION

Measure salad dressing ingredients—make dressing and, if possible, soak tomatoes overnight in the dressing.

METHOD OF COOKERY

1. Drain tomatoes just before service. Slice both cabbage and green pepper finely—place in salad bowl with tomatoes.
2. Serve dressing at table.

Step 3
Lettuce and other leaf salads should be torn apart, never sliced with a knife. Knife cuts create greater loss of vitamin C. An exception can be made with cabbage for fine-shredded salads.

Step 4
If a dressing is used, add it to the salad at the last possible moment. In this photograph a little sugar, mustard, and cayenne pepper are mixed with oil, and then twice the quantity of good vinegar is added. It is then mixed well and scattered over the salad at the table. This is a very good piece of showmanship for the man of the house!

209 Downstage Cucumber Salad

RECIPE TO PRODUCE 4 PORTIONS	U.S.A.	IMPERIAL	METRIC
Cucumber	1 slim	8 oz.	230 grams
Apple	1	1	1
Spring onions	¾ cup	3 oz.	85 grams
Cream	6 tbsp.	3 fl. oz.	85 milliliters
Lemon juice	1 tbsp.	½ fl. oz.	15 milliliters
Lettuce leaves	4 large	4 large	4 large

METHOD OF PREPARATION

Peel cucumber—finely dice—soak in salt water at least 2 hours—chop spring onions finely—add lemon juice to cream and beat slightly—wash lettuce leaves well—use a Granny Smith apple in preference to others.

METHOD OF COOKERY

1. Drain cucumber. Combine with spring onions and soured cream.
2. Peel, core, and finely slice apple; add to salad immediately before serving.
3. Place mixture in crisp lettuce leaves and serve.

210 Mushroom Salad

RECIPE TO PRODUCE 4 PORTIONS	U.S.A.	IMPERIAL	METRIC
Mushrooms (button)	1 lb.	1 lb.	500 grams
Salt, black pepper, nutmeg	To season	To season	To season
Lemon juice	To flavor	To flavor	To flavor
French dressing	½ cup	4 fl. oz.	112 milliliters
Chives	1 tbsp.	1 tbsp.	10 grams
Parsley	1 tbsp.	1 tbsp.	10 grams
Lemon thyme	1 sprig	1 sprig	1 sprig
French dressing:			
Olive oil	⅜ cup	3 fl. oz.	90 milliliters
White wine vinegar	⅛ cup	1 fl. oz.	30 milliliters
Salt, black pepper	To season	To season	To season

METHOD OF PREPARATION

1. Mix all ingredients together for dressing until combined.

2. Wash mushrooms and slice thinly.

3. Finely chop parsley, thyme, and chives.

METHOD OF COOKERY

1. Season mushrooms with salt, pepper, and nutmeg.

2. Toss mushrooms in the dressing, adding lemon juice to taste. Allow to stand for 15 minutes.

3. Garnish with finely chopped parsley, chives, and thyme.

211   Zucchini Salad

RECIPE TO PRODUCE 4 PORTIONS	U.S.A.	IMPERIAL	METRIC
Zucchini (baby marrows)	4	4	4
Tomatoes	2 medium	2 medium	2 medium
Green pepper	1	1	1
Parsley, chives	To garnish	To garnish	To garnish
Marjoram	Small sprig	Small sprig	Small sprig
French dressing	¼ cup	2 fl. oz.	60 milliliters

METHOD OF PREPARATION

1. Cook zucchini in salted boiling water for 10 minutes—drain and cut into ½-inch slices—place in a salad bowl with the tomatoes cut into quarters.
2. Chop green pepper finely and add to tomatoes and zucchini.

METHOD OF COOKERY

Combine ingredients with French dressing and garnish with chopped herbs. Serve chilled.

212   Tanunda Salad

RECIPE TO PRODUCE 4 PORTIONS	U.S.A.	IMPERIAL	METRIC
Sultana grapes	½ lb.	½ lb.	250 grams
Sour cream	3 tbsp.	1½ fl. oz.	45 milliliters
Red currant jelly	2 tsp.	2 tsp.	15 grams
Walnuts	¼ cup	1½ oz.	45 grams

METHOD OF PREPARATION

1. Roughly chop walnuts.
2. Measure sour cream.

METHOD OF COOKERY

1. Place the grapes in a bowl and dribble with sour cream dressing.
2. **Dressing:** Combine the sour cream with the red currant jelly. Carefully stir in the walnuts.

"Literally bung in anything that is crisp and edible," recipe page 246

About Kitchen Aids

This is a loose section. It covers such wonders as sauces, clarified butter, coconut stock, herbs, spices, coffee, and some side dishes for a curry. What on earth can one say about this odd heap of culinary bric-a-brac?

It is possibly enough to say that the best things in life depend on attention to the most minute detail. It is the little things that make or break a really fine dish.

Sauces are placed with a dish to enhance the flavor of the basic food—not drown it—as mint sauce does with lamb. A sauce made with flour should be left to "cook out" the raw flour taste—otherwise it may well ruin a perfectly good chicken or fish.

Cooking fats can fill the house with an odious pong. The drippings jar that has been built up in incredible layers of lamb, beef, pork, chicken, bacon, and veal fats does nothing for a tender cutlet or a good steak. Butter, for all its cost, when clarified adds a bloom to all foods. Its cost difference in cookery can be measured in cents—its effect—beyond comparison.

The cook who grows herbs, in garden or window box, always wins. He who buys spices wisely keeps them tightly sealed and grates or mills them just before use is not only an economist but a splendid host.

Coffee, in my humble opinion, is the great test of modern man. In the face of stiff "instant" opposition, it becomes more and more difficult to tell the few who "do it themselves" from the pretenders to this gastronomic throne. Coffee goes with discussion and this is the real reason why we learn—struggle—develop—and finally entertain.

CONTENTS OF SECTION

213 BATTER

COMMENT ON METHOD

I have broken a rule in this case. This is not a basic batter—recipe 214 will serve that purpose. This is a beer batter and is, in my humble opinion, the only batter to use with fish—it is fantastic. This recipe was supposed to have originated at Madame Prunier's restaurant in London.

Step 1
First warm the mixing bowl. Now add 1 cup flour sifted with ¼ teaspoon salt. Make a well in the center.

Step 2
Place 1 teaspoon active dry yeast in the well and add 5 tablespoons warmed fish stock made from fish bones (or water if you are in a rush, which you shouldn't be if you are making this gastronomic batter!). Dissolve the yeast and incorporate the flour. Add 5 tablespoons flat beer and 1 tablespoon olive oil.

214 Egg Batter

RECIPE TO PRODUCE ¾ PINT	U.S.A.	IMPERIAL	METRIC
Plain flour	1 cup	4 oz.	115 grams
Salt	1 pinch	1 pinch	1 pinch
White pepper	1 pinch	1 pinch	1 pinch
Eggs	1 + 1 yolk	1 + 1 yolk	1 + 1 yolk
Milk	1¼ cups	10 fl. oz.	285 milliliters
Butter	1 tbsp.	1 tbsp.	15 grams

METHOD OF PREPARATION

Sift flour, salt, and pepper—measure milk—separate yolk of 1 egg and add to 1 whole egg—melt butter and cool slightly.

METHOD OF COOKERY

1. Combine dry ingredients, make a well in center, and add eggs and milk gradually, beating all the time.
2. Add cooled melted butter, beat well, and leave covered for at least 4 hours to allow starch cells to swell and absorb liquid.
3. This batter can be used for frying fish, pancakes, or fritters.

Step 3
Put the mixture in the warming oven for at least 2 hours, preferably 4. Cover with a clean cloth.

Step 4
Add the whipped white of egg—half an egg white is enough—immediately before you use the batter. See pages 38-39, recipe 21 for fish frying method.

215 Yorkshire Pudding

RECIPE TO PRODUCE 4 PORTIONS	U.S.A.	IMPERIAL	METRIC
Flour	2 cups	8 oz.	230 grams
Eggs	4	4	4
Milk	2½ cups	1 pint	570 milliliters
Salt	1 tsp.	1 tsp.	2½ grams
Beef dripping			

METHOD OF PREPARATION

Sift flour with salt—raise oven heat to 400° F. and place pudding in oven when your roast beef has only 25 minutes left to cook*—in this way the joint will have the necessary 20 minutes to set before carving and be ready at the same time as the pudding.

METHOD OF COOKERY

1. Combine all ingredients (other than dripping), slowly mixing in eggs and milk.
2. Cover and allow to stand for at least 1 hour in a warm place. Beat well.
3. Heat dripping from roast beef in the oven. There should be sufficient to cover an 8-inch-round cake tin by ¼-inch.
4. When blue haze leaves the surface, pour in batter. Place on top rung of oven for 45 minutes. Serve immediately.

*If you have the space, it is a good idea to place the pudding under the joint. In this way the juices from the beef fall into the pudding—result—absolutely fantastic—a culinary masterpiece.

216 WHITE SAUCE

COMMENT ON METHOD

Escoffier really set the culinary world twittering in 1907 when he released his famous *A Guide to Modern Cookery*. In this work he commented upon the use of pure starch in the preparation of a roux for sauces. He said, "It is only habit that causes flour to be still used as the cohering element of roux . . . with a roux made from the purest starch . . . a sauce Espagnol' may be made in one hour . . . and be clearer . . . and better than that of the old processes

To make just under 1 pint of sauce

Step 1
Melt 3 tablespoons butter over a moderate heat and add 7 tablespoons flour. Stir well until sandy in texture.

Step 2
This step shows the roux in the making. Always use a wooden spoon and keep the roux constantly moving while it cooks together. About 2 minutes should be sufficient for a white sauce.

217 Cheese Sauce

RECIPE TO PRODUCE 1 PINT	U.S.A.	IMPERIAL	METRIC
Butter	4 tbsp.	2 oz.	60 grams
Plain flour*	½ cup	2¼ oz.	67.5 grams
Milk	2 cups	16 fl. oz.	455 milliliters
Clove	1	1	1
Onion	½ oz.	½ oz.	15 grams
Bay leaf	1	1	1
Parsley stalks	2	2	2
Salt, white peppercorns	To season	To season	To season
Mustard	1 tsp.	1 tsp.	1 tsp.
Cheddar cheese (matured)	3 oz.	3 oz.	85 grams

*If gluten-reduced flour is available, use quantities shown in basic recipe.

METHOD OF PREPARATION

Sift flour—tie clove, chopped onion, bay leaf, and parsley stalks in muslin bag—measure milk, butter, mustard. Grate cheese.

METHOD OF COOKERY

1. Make roux with butter and flour; stir in milk off the heat, returning to heat after each addition.
2. Beat and add herb bag to sauce. Stand over a very low heat to infuse for 15 minutes.
3. Remove herb bag, season, add mustard, and stir in grated cheese until sauce is smooth.

which needed three days at least to despumate." In this recipe I have used the new gluten-reduced flour, a flour specially processed to remove the gluten content. It is not the pure starch to which Escoffier refers, but it does do the job that he specified sixty odd years ago when this modern flour process could not have been anticipated.

Step 3
Remove saucepan from element and add 2 cups milk in three equal lots. When the first third has been added, stir and bring back onto heat to combine. Take off the heat again to add the second third and so on. Stir well each time so that the sauce remains perfectly smooth.

Step 4
Place 1 clove, 2 slices medium onion, 1 bay leaf, and 2 chopped parsley stalks into a muslin bag, beat the bag with a rolling pin (to bruise items to release flavor). Place bag in the sauce and leave on low heat for 15 minutes. Taste, season with salt and freshly ground white peppercorns. Remove herbs and serve.

218 Toheroa* Wine Sauce

RECIPE TO PRODUCE 4 PORTIONS	U.S.A.	IMPERIAL	METRIC
White Sauce (pp. 256-57, rec. 216)	2½ cups	1 pint	570 milliliters
Toheroa paste (usually tinned)	5 tbsp.	5 tbsp.	75 grams
Lemon juice	1 tbsp.	1 tbsp.	15 milliliters
Dry white wine	2 tbsp.	1 fl. oz.	30 milliliters
Indian saffron	¼ tsp.	¼ tsp.	¼ tsp.
Monosodium glutamate (msg)	¼ level tsp.	¼ level tsp.	¼ level tsp.

METHOD OF PREPARATION
Make white sauce—measure paste, lemon juice, wine, saffron, and msg.

METHOD OF COOKERY
1. Stir all ingredients into white sauce—reheat and serve.
2. Usually placed over poached fish, but is fabulous when spooned over Broiled Lobster Tails (p. 63, rec. 44).

*Toheroa is the world-famous New Zealand green clam unlike anything else in the world. It is a great delicacy and can be ordered at good stores.

219 BROWN SAUCE

COMMENT ON METHOD

Bread and brown sauce—not really a gastronomic pair, but they have something in common in this modern day and age. We very seldom make our own bread—it is now conveniently baked for us. A good brown sauce, including the preparation of an excellent stock, can take

To make 1 cup of sauce

Step 1
Melt 2 tablespoons clarified butter in a saucepan and add ½ cup tomato that has been skinned and pipped. Fry at quite a high heat, scraping off the bottom all the time so that it darkens in color but does not actually burn.

Step 2
When the tomato is well colored, measure out 1 pint of 30-minute Beef Stock (pp. 26-27, rec. 15). Mix in well.

220 New Zealand Sauce

RECIPE TO PRODUCE 4 PORTIONS	U.S.A.	IMPERIAL	METRIC
Tomato sauce	¾ cup	6 fl. oz.	170 milliliters
Dry white wine	¾ cup	6 fl. oz.	170 milliliters
Garlic clove	1	1	1
Butter	1 tbsp.	½ oz.	15 grams
Parsley stalks	1 tbsp.	1 tbsp.	7.5 grams

METHOD OF PREPARATION
Measure tomato sauce, wine, butter—chop parsley stalks—peel garlic.

METHOD OF COOKERY
1. Melt butter in frying pan. Add crushed garlic.
2. Add sauce and wine. Reduce by boiling to sauce consistency.
3. Add parsley stalks.
4. Serve as required.

Note: Two ounces of mushrooms may be finely sliced, fried in butter with lemon juice and cayenne pepper, and tipped into the sauce just before serving.

up to 4 days to make. Some hotels and restaurants may still do this, but the modern home fights shy and has been forced to accept some processed product in lieu. I have developed this quick brown sauce, made in 1 hour maximum, as a *possible* alternative to science!

Step 3
Measure the depth and make a mark on a spoon exactly halfway between top and bottom. This helps to record the exact level wanted for a reduction by half. Boil vigorously until the level is reduced to this mark, skimming off foam from time to time.

Step 4
Add 3 teaspoons arrowroot mixed with cold stock or water. As it enters the boiling sauce, stir rapidly with a wooden spoon. When the sauce thickens and becomes clear, adjust the seasoning with salt and freshly ground black peppercorns and serve.

221 Mushroom Sauce

RECIPE TO PRODUCE 4 PORTIONS	U.S.A.	IMPERIAL	METRIC
Mushrooms	¼ lb.	4 oz.	115 grams
Shallots	4	1 oz.	30 grams
Butter	3 tbsp.	1½ oz.	45 grams
Tomato sauce	1 tsp.	1 tsp.	15 milliliters
Dry white wine	6 tbsp.	3 fl. oz.	85 milliliters
Chervil and tarragon leaves (or parsley stalks)	1 tsp.	1 tsp.	1 tsp.
Brown Sauce (above)	¾ cup	6 fl. oz.	170 milliliters

METHOD OF PREPARATION
Peel and slice mushrooms and stalks—finely chop shallots—measure butter, wine, and tomato sauce—chop herbs or parsley stalks—make brown sauce—heat frying pan.

METHOD OF COOKERY
1. Melt butter in frying pan. Shallow fry mushrooms, add the diced shallots, tomato sauce, and wine. Reduce liquid level by half through boiling.
2. Add brown sauce and simmer 5 minutes until sauce has thickened through reduction. No additional flour or starch thickening should be used.
3. Add herbs (or parsley stalks) and use as required.

222 BUTTER SAUCE

COMMENT ON METHOD

This lemon butter sauce is my favorite sauce. It is so smooth and buttery that I will pos-sibly endanger my health with its constant use, but one has to die of something—so why not

Step 1
Bring water to just under simmering heat—bubbles should be fixed to the base of the pan. Place on top a double boiler containing 1 teaspoon lemon juice, a sprinkle of salt, freshly ground white pep-percorns, and grated nutmeg. Add also 1 table-spoon water.

Step 2
Add 4 yolks of egg with 4 tablespoons softened butter and beat together with a whisk.

223 Quick Butter Sauce

RECIPE TO PRODUCE 4 PORTIONS

	U.S.A.	IMPERIAL	METRIC
Flour	3 tbsp.	3/4 oz.	20 grams
Butter	1 tbsp.	1/2 oz.	15 grams
Salted water	1 1/4 cups	10 fl. oz.	285 milliliters
Large egg yolk	1	1	1
Cream	2 tbsp.	1 fl. oz.	30 mililiters
Lemon juice	1/2 tsp.	1/2 tsp.	5 milliliters
Butter	2 tbsp.	1 oz.	30 grams

METHOD OF PREPARATION

Sift flour—melt butter—boil water—measure cream—mix yolk and cream.

METHOD OF COOKERY

1. Mix flour with melted butter.
2. Slowly stir in boiling salted water until thick, beating well to dissolve thoroughly. Do not boil.
3. Add egg yolk and cream, then lemon juice.
4. Beat well, add 1 ounce butter just before serving.

lemon butter sauce? The technique is really very simple, and when served with grilled crayfish (rock lobster) tails, it is pure heaven.

Step 3
When incorporated, add another 12 tablespoons butter in three lots of 4 tablespoons, beating each in completely before adding the next. The sauce will by this stage have thickened considerably. After the last addition, remove the top pan, and whisk away from the heat for 1 minute.

Step 4
Return sauce to very low heat and add lemon juice to taste. Keep at this heat until ready to serve. It doesn't keep well, so serve it quickly! If it does separate during preparation, just add a tablespoon of hot water and whip well.

224 Orange Butter Sauce

RECIPE TO PRODUCE 4 PORTIONS	U.S.A.	IMPERIAL	METRIC
	2	2	2
Egg yolks			
Butter	½ cup	4 oz.	115 grams
Water	½ tbsp.	½ tbsp.	10 milliliters
White wine	¼ cup	2 fl. oz.	60 milliliters
Shallot	1	¼ oz.	5 grams
Salt	To season	To season	To season
White peppercorns	To season	To season	To season
Nutmeg	To season	To season	To season
Cayenne pepper	To season	To season	To season
Orange rind	½ orange	½ orange	½ orange
Orange juice	½ orange	½ orange·	½ orange
Tomato paste	½ tsp.	½ tsp.	5 milliliters

METHOD OF PREPARATION
Soften butter and divide into 2-ounce pieces—finely dice shallot—grate rest of half small orange and squeeze juice from this half—measure wine.

METHOD OF COOKERY
1. Place wine and shallot together. Reduce by boiling to 1½ teaspoons wine. (This may sound stupid, but it's necessary.)
2. Place wine, water, seasoning in top of double boiler over simmering water. Add tomato paste.
3. Add orange zest and juice to yolks. Beat together and add to wine in double boiler.
4. Beat in first 2 ounces of butter—when smooth, add remaining butter. Remove from heat and beat.
5. Return to heat and beat until smooth and thick.
6. Add 1 teaspoon hot water if it curdles.
Note: Try this sauce on lamb cutlets or fried fish—it's deliciously different.

COMMENT ON METHOD

When the famous author, gourmet, and world president of the Wine and Food Society, André Simon, dined at my home (I was terrified!), I gave him a hideous meal, but he did ask for a second portion of my mayonnaise. This pleased me immensely because I have taken some trouble to develop a good recipe. Here it is.

Step 1
It is **essential** to start off by warming everything that you need to use to make mayonnaise. You will also note a bowl full of whipped white of egg. This is insurance against curdling. If it does separate, a spoonful of egg white whipped in will solve the problem.

Step 2
Place 2 large egg yolks in the warmed basin with ½ teaspoon dry mustard and a pinch of salt. Beat together thoroughly.

226 Blue Vein Salad Dressing

RECIPE TO PRODUCE 4 PORTIONS	U.S.A.	IMPERIAL	METRIC
Mayonnaise (above)	1¼ cups	12 fl. oz.	340 milliliters
Lemon juice	2 tsp.	2 tsp.	10 milliliters
Blue vein cheese	¼ cup	2 oz.	60 grams

METHOD OF PREPARATION

Prepare mayonnaise as shown above—weigh cheese—measure lemon juice.

METHOD OF COOKERY

1. Mash blue vein cheese with lemon juice and add a spoonful of mayonnaise—mix to a smooth paste.
2. Blend paste into remaining mayonnaise.
3. The dressing will keep well. In fact, it tends to improve with age.

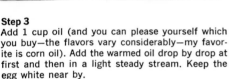

Step 3
Add 1 cup oil (and you can please yourself which you buy—the flavors vary considerably—my favorite is corn oil). Add the warmed oil drop by drop at first and then in a light steady stream. Keep the egg white near by.

Step 4
When the mayonnaise is thick and creamy add 1 tablespoon boiling water. This helps to keep the sauce. You can fold in the beaten white and make a very light-textured mayonnaise, but be sure to add more seasoning when you do.

227 G.K. Salad Dressing

RECIPE TO PRODUCE 8-10 PORTIONS	U.S.A.	IMPERIAL	METRIC
Tarragon wine vinegar*	1 cup	8 fl. oz.	230 milliliters
Olive oil	½ cup	4 fl. oz.	115 milliliters
Dry mustard	½ tsp.	½ tsp.	½ tsp.
Cayenne pepper	½ tsp.	½ tsp.	½ tsp.
Onion	1 medium	1 medium	1 medium
Garlic clove	1	1	1
Sugar	1–2 tbsp.	1–2 tbsp.	15–30 grams

METHOD OF PREPARATION
Measure vinegar—mix and add fresh tarragon sprigs—measure oil, mustard—finely dice onion—crush garlic.

METHOD OF COOKERY
1. Mix all dry items with oil.
2. Add vinegar and shake well immediately before dressing a salad so that oil and vinegar can emulsify.

Note: Dress salad at last possible moment or it wil go limp and slimy. For a quick dressing method, see p. 246, rec. 207, Step 4.

*Or use 1 fluid ounce 33⅓% diluted acetic acid and 13 fluid ounces dry white wine.

228 CLARIFIED BUTTER

COMMENT ON METHOD

Here it is—my favorite culinary ingredient! I sometimes worry about my constant reference to *clarified butter* but this is always pushed under by the satisfaction I get from using it. This method is very simple and the butter produced will not burn until it reaches 400° F. This should be hot enough for all your kitchen work.

Step 1
Place a small saucepan on a low heat and add 1 pound of butter

Step 2
After 10 minutes skim off the foam that accumulates on the surface. You will see here that the sediment has formed cloudlike concentrations under the surface.

229 Coconut Stock and Cream for Curries

RECIPE TO PRODUCE 4 PORTIONS	U.S.A.	IMPERIAL	METRIC
Coconut flesh or desiccated coconut (unsweetened)	1⅓ cups	4 oz.	115 grams
Water for cream	1¼ cups	10 fl. oz.	285 milliliters
Water for stock	2½ cups	1 pint	570 milliliters
Muslin	2 feet	2 feet	60 centimeters

METHOD OF PREPARATION

If using fresh coconut, grate the flesh finely. Or measure desiccated. Measure water for cream and stock —measure muslin.

METHOD OF COOKERY

Cream:
1. Boil 1¼ cups water and pour over coconut. Cover tightly and allow to infuse (like tea) for 30 minutes.
2. Pour entire contents into muslin and squeeze out moisture. This is the cream.

Stock:
3. Boil 1 pint water and pour over squeezed coconut used to make the cream. Cover tightly and infuse— again for 30 minutes.
4. Strain and squeeze through muslin. This makes the stock.

Uses: Stock used as cooking liquid for curries. Cream used to finish the curry (p. 164, rec. 120).

Step 3
Very gently pour the clear butter through muslin into a small jar or sauceboat. I find this sauceboat excellent—especially when the butter has to be used melted. You can put it straight onto an element.

Step 4
Pour the sediment into the skimmings and use this for buttering potatoes and vegetables.

230 Curry Side Dishes

Dark raisins—soaked first in water
Chopped chives
Chopped baked ham
Shredded Bombay duck (dried fish)
Pickled walnuts
Mango chutney
Peanuts and shredded coconut
Chopped lemon peel
Chopped lime peel
Chopped egg yolk
Sweet pickled onions
Crystallized ginger
Peeled sliced banana
Diced pineapple
Salted almonds
Fresh chopped chilies
Fresh chopped green peppers
Fresh chopped green tomatoes
Deep-fried or grilled poppadums (wafer thin Indian biscuits)
Diced cucumber in sour cream, with crushed garlic and fresh-grated ginger
Mix chopped apple, sliced bananas, 1 tablespoon chives, 1 teaspoon lemon juice
Sliced onion rings
Shrimp slices—deep fried
Sliced mushrooms fried in butter, flavored with garlic

METHOD

Step 1
Buy your beans freshly roasted at least once a week. Place them into an airtight jar and keep them in the refrigerator. By doing this you stop the natural coffee oil from going rancid. Invest in an electric coffee grinder—it is well worth the money and eliminates repetitive non-creative labor.

Step 2
Everything used in coffee making must be perfectly clean and well rinsed in cold water. The coffee **must** be accurately measured every time, so must the water.

Step 5
Iced coffee is made with double-strength coffee. In this case the recipe is for 2 pints. Bring 1 pint of milk to the boil and add 30 drops (½ teaspoon) of natural vanilla essence. You can add brown sugar if you like your coffee sweet.

Step 6
Pour the milk into the coffee and place in the refrigerator to become thoroughly chilled. It is best when almost frozen.

Step 3
I have chosen this type of percolator because it makes the best coffee. You will note that the water boils and travels up the center stem; by the time it reaches the coffee it is under boiling point. It is "boiling" that ruins coffee.

Step 4
Some makes of this type of percolator take an infernally long time to filter back into the bottom flask. You can bring these down by wrapping a wet cloth around the bowl.

Step 7
Whip some cream. You need ½ cup for 4 large glasses, with a light dusting of freshly grated cinnamon. Fill the glasses to within ½ inch of the rim and then pipe in the cream.

Step 8
Serve with straws and give the cream a final garnish of grated cinnamon. Just the thing for the summer or at a party when things are a little hot!

About Desserts

Every cook has an area of total relaxation, a branch of the kitchen in which he just sloshes about and has fun—generally with total lack of concern.

This is mine!

It all started when an important sponsor of our television show requested (gently) that we incorporate desserts. Hitherto I had considered sweet dishes as strictly (and literally) for the "birds." I fell upon each program with complete abandon. I'd teach that sponsor to intrude on sacred ground!

I enjoyed myself—time and time again I had a ball. The recipes worked brilliantly (well... quite satisfactorily)!

After a periodic mail count I was advised that desserts ran a close second in popularity to the main dishes—I was horrified!

I was hoisted by my own petard; desserts are now a standard part of the show—regardless of sponsorship.

The odd thing is that I've begun to get interested in them—even though, at home, I seldom serve a dessert other than fresh fruit and cheese.

Here then are a few of those that interest me.

CONTENTS OF SECTION

232 Iced Rice Hawke's Bay

RECIPE TO PRODUCE 8 PORTIONS	U.S.A.	IMPERIAL	METRIC
Chinese gooseberries	8	8	8
Strawberries	12 large	1 punnet	1 punnet
Crème de menthe	2 tablespoons	1 fl. oz.	30 milliliters
Long grain rice	¾ cup	3½ oz.	105 grams
Superfine granulated sugar	½ cup	4 oz.	120 grams
Milk	2½ cups	1 pint	.5 liter
Vanilla bean	1	1	1
Cream	1¼ cups	½ pint	240 milliliters
Gelatin	1 envelope	½ oz.	15 grams

METHOD OF PREPARATION

Remove skin from Chinese gooseberries—cut 6 into halves—leave 2 whole—hollow out a little of the center of each gooseberry—hull strawberries—measure rice and cook in boiling water for 6 minutes—measure milk and heat with vanilla bean until boiling. Measure sugar. Whip cream. Place mold (with hole in center) in refrigerator.

METHOD OF COOKERY

1. Place rice in milk and simmer 20 minutes. After this period add the sugar and simmer another 5 minutes. Remove vanilla bean.
2. Soften gelatin in a little cold water and whip into hot rice. Let thicken either over ice or in the refrigerator. When cool and thickened fold in whipped cream. Rinse mold with iced water and fill with rice mixture. Refrigerate for 2 hours.
3. Place a few drops of crème de menthe in each half gooseberry center and place a strawberry on top of each gooseberry.
4. Place mold in hot water for a few seconds and unmold onto a serving dish. Place the two whole Chinese gooseberries in the center of the mold and place the halves around it.

233 Angaston Rum Cake

RECIPE TO PRODUCE 8 PORTIONS	U.S.A.	IMPERIAL	METRIC
Flour (all-purpose)	2½ cups	10 oz.	300 grams
Wet yeast	½ oz.	½ oz.	15 grams
Butter	½ cup	4 oz.	120 grams
Salt	Pinch	Pinch	2 grams
Superfine granulated sugar	1 tbsp.	1 tbsp.	15 grams
Warm water	½ cup	4 fl. oz.	120 milliliters
Eggs	4 large	4 large	4 large
Walnut halves	8	8	8
Syrup:			
Water	1½ cups	12 fl. oz.	360 milliliters
Granulated sugar	1¼ cups	10 oz.	300 grams
Rum (overproof)	½ cup	4 fl. oz.	120 milliliters
Green gingerroot	Small piece	Small piece	Small piece
Filling:			
Cream (whipped)	1¼ cups	½ pint	300 milliliters
Rum	2 tbsp.	2 tbsp.	30 milliliters
Cinnamon	2 tbsp.	2 tbsp.	30 milliliters
Syrup for Glazing:			
Granulated sugar	½ cup	4 oz.	120 grams
Water	½ cup	4 fl. oz.	120 milliliters
Candied fruits	3 cups	¾ lb.	360 grams

METHOD OF PREPARATION

Sift flour, melt butter, grease 8-inch springform pan with hole in middle—whip cream—peel gingerroot and slice thinly—measure ingredients for syrup—measure ingredients for glaze and finely chop candied fruits. Preheat oven to 400° F.

METHOD OF COOKERY

1. Make a well in the sifted flour. Dissolve yeast in 2 tablespoons of warm water and pour into well in flour. Add the eggs, salt, and sugar, and beat thoroughly, adding the warm water remaining gradually.
2. Pour warm melted butter into mixture and beat hard until the mixture is shiny and smooth.
3. Place the walnut halves on the base of the cake tin—spoon over cake mixture, cover with a floured cloth, and leave in a warm place for about 2 hours or until the mixture has risen to the top of the tin. Place the cake in the oven and cook 20 minutes—unmold immediately onto serving dish.
4. Syrup. Place sliced gingerroot in the water and add the sugar—bring to the boil—boil 3 minutes.
5. Prick cake all over with a fork and spoon syrup over cake, allowing it to absorb liquid. Continue in this fashion until all the liquid is used. Spoon over it the rum.
6. Decorate cake with the candied fruits.
7. Glaze. Place sugar and water in a saucepan and boil until syrup reaches 310° F. (clear toffee).
8. Glaze cake all over with toffee. Fill center with whipped cream flavored with rum and cinnamon.

234 Pears Dijonnaise

RECIPE TO PRODUCE 4 PORTIONS	U.S.A.	IMPERIAL	METRIC
Pears	4 large	4 large	4 large
Raspberries	10 oz. frozen or 10 oz. 1½ cups fresh	10 oz.	300 grams
Black currants	2 cups	15 oz.	450 grams
Lemon juice	1 tsp.	1 tsp.	4 milliliters
Heavy cream	¾ cup	6 fl. oz.	150 milliliters
Syrup:			
Water	5 cups	2 pints	1 liter
Granulated sugar	1 cup	½ lb.	240 grams
Vanilla bean	1	1	1

METHOD OF PREPARATION

Cut pears in half (without removing stalk) and remove core with a melon baller. Make syrup by bringing water, sugar, and vanilla bean to the boil and boiling 5 minutes. Poach pear halves in syrup. Allow to cool in syrup. If using tinned black currants and raspberries drain off syrup. Whip cream stiffly.

METHOD OF COOKERY

1. Remove cooled pear halves from syrup and place in serving dishes.
2. Mix raspberries and black currants and purée. Add the lemon juice. Place purée on the heat to thicken and reduce (about 5 minutes). Allow to cool.
3. Spoon purée over pear halves and garnish with whipped cream.

235 Barossa Fruit Tart

RECIPE TO PRODUCE 8 PORTIONS	U.S.A.	IMPERIAL	METRIC
Pastry:			
Flour (all-purpose)	3 cups	12 oz.	360 grams
Salt	Pinch	Pinch	Pinch
Butter	1 cup	8 oz.	240 grams
Superfine granulated sugar	4 tbsp.	4 tbsp.	60 grams
Eggs	2	2	2
Vanilla	To flavor	To flavor	To flavor
Filling:			
Cream cheese	1¼ cups	½ lb.	240 grams
Egg yolks	2	2	2
Sour cream	4 tbsp.	4 tbsp.	60 grams
Confectioners' sugar	1 tbsp.	1 tbsp.	15 grams
Kirsch	2 tbsp.	2 tbsp.	30 milliliters
Fruit for garnishing:			
Cherries (cooked)	½ lb.	½ lb.	240 grams
Prunes (stoned)	½ lb.	½ lb.	240 grams
Apricots (halved)	1 lb.	1 lb.	500 grams
Peaches (halved)	2 lb.	2 lb.	1 kilo
Glaze:			
Kirsch	2 tbsp.	2 tbsp.	30 milliliters
Fruit juice	2 tbsp.	2 tbsp.	30 milliliters
Red currant jelly	1 cup	8 oz.	240 grams

METHOD OF PREPARATION

Make pastry—separate eggs—measure ingredients for filling—prepare fruits—measure ingredients for glaze.

METHOD OF COOKERY

1. **Pastry.** Mix butter with flour and salt—add sugar and the eggs—mix until smooth and add the vanilla. Form the pastry into a ball and allow to stand in a cool place ½ hour. Roll out to fit 13-inch flan tin (the base of which has been lined with aluminum foil) and cook 25 minutes in a 375° F. oven. Allow to cool thoroughly.
2. **Cream cheese filling.** Beat cream cheese with egg yolks, sugar, and sour cream until smooth. Flavor with kirsch and spread on tart case.
3. **Garnish.** Place the fruits around the tart (peach halves, prunes, apricots, and cherries) in a decorative manner.
4. **Glaze.** Heat jelly and fruit juice until boiling. Add the kirsch and allow to cool 1 minute. Pour over fruit and allow to set.

236 Crème Brûlée

RECIPE TO PRODUCE 4 PORTIONS

	U.S.A.	IMPERIAL	METRIC
Heavy cream	2½ cups	1 pint	.5 liter
Superfine granulated sugar	½ cup	4 oz.	120 grams
Egg yolks	6	6	6
Vanilla bean	1	1	1
Superfine granulated sugar for toffee	1 cup	8 oz.	240 grams

METHOD OF PREPARATION

1. Separate eggs.
2. Measure cream and sugar.
3. Preheat oven to 300° F.

METHOD OF COOKERY

1. Heat cream until boiling with vanilla bean.
2. Beat egg yolks with sugar until well blended and then combine with hot cream. Place mixture back on a gentle heat and stir until the custard has thickened slightly (enough to coat the back of a spoon).
3. Pour mixture gently into an ovenproof dish standing in a pan of cold water and place in the oven for 1 hour. Remove and allow to cool, then refrigerate.
4. Cover the top of the "cream" with sugar. Place the cream in a pan and surround with crushed ice. Allow sugar to caramelize in a very hot broiler. Serve.

237 Lemon Mousse

RECIPE TO PRODUCE 4 PORTIONS	U.S.A.	IMPERIAL	METRIC
Eggs	4	4	4
Lemon juice	2 lemons	2 lemons	2 lemons
Superfine granulated sugar	1 cup	8 oz.	240 grams
Heavy cream	10 tbsp.	5 fl. oz.	150 milliliters
Gelatin	1 envelope	½ oz.	15 grams
Glacé cherries	8	8	8
Cream to garnish	10 tbsp.	¼ pint	150 milliliters

METHOD OF PREPARATION
1. Measure sugar.
2. Whip cream and divide into 2 equal portions.
3. Cut cherries in halves.

METHOD OF COOKERY
1. Beat the eggs with the sugar until thick.
2. Soften the gelatin in the lemon juice and add to the egg mixture.
3. Whip cream and fold into mixture. Pour into glasses. Allow to set in refrigerator.
4. Garnish with whipped cream and cherries.

238 South Australian Strawberry Pie

RECIPE TO PRODUCE 10 PORTIONS	U.S.A.	IMPERIAL	METRIC
Mincemeat:			
Beef suet	1 cup	½ lb.	240 grams
Raisins	3 cups	¾ lb.	360 grams
Sultana grapes	2 cups	½ lb.	240 grams
Apple (Granny Smith)	3 cups	¾ lb.	360 grams
Currants	3 cups	¾ lb.	360 grams
Brown sugar	1½ cups	¾ lb.	360 grams
Lemon and orange peels (mixed)	2 cups	½ lb.	240 grams
Almonds (blanched)	1 cup	¼ lb.	120 grams
Lemon rind	2 lemons	2 lemons	2 lemons
Lemon juice	2 lemons	2 lemons	2 lemons
Vanilla bean (grated)	1	1	1
Nutmeg, allspice, cinnamon	Pinch each	Pinch each	1 gram each
Coriander, ginger	Pinch each	Pinch each	1 gram each
Brandy	10 tbsp.	5 fl. oz.	150 milliliters
Pastry:			
Flour (all-purpose)	4 cups	1 lb.	240 grams
Butter	1½ cups	12 oz.	360 grams
Superfine granulated sugar	1 tbsp.	1 tbsp.	15 grams
Egg yolk	1	1	1
Iced water	8 tbsp.	8 tbsp.	120 milliliters
Strawberries	8 oz.	8 oz.	240 grams
Cream	1¼ cups	½ pint	300 milliliters

METHOD OF PREPARATION

Mix all ingredients for mincemeat together and moisten with the brandy—place in jars and seal—make 1 month ahead at least.

Pastry

Cut butter into small cubes, measure flour, and sift—hull strawberries and whip cream stiffly—preheat oven to 400° F.

METHOD OF COOKERY

1. **Pastry.** Make a well in the sifted flour and place the butter in the well. Add the egg yolk, sugar, salt, and 2 tablespoons of the iced water. Combine all ingredients except the flour with the fingertips, and then work in flour to form a smooth dough, adding iced water as needed. Knead several times and place pastry in the refrigerator for 1 hour.
2. Roll out half the pastry to fit a 10-inch pastry ring standing on a baking sheet. Prick pastry base with a fork and cut a round of greaseproof paper to fit inside pastry case. Now fill with dried peas or rice—prick base again with fork and bake "blind" for 15 minutes. Remove paper and rice and allow pastry case to cool.
3. Fill cooled shell with mincemeat—roll out remaining pastry and place over mincemeat—crimp the edges and glaze with egg yolk. Place in 400° F. oven for 30 minutes or until golden brown.
4. Remove pie from oven—allow to cool. Cover with whipped cream and decorate with strawberries.

239 Chocolate Soufflé Trianon

RECIPE TO PRODUCE 4 PORTIONS	U.S.A.	IMPERIAL	METRIC
Dark chocolate	6 oz.	6 oz.	180 grams
Egg yolks	4	4	4
Egg whites	6	6	6
Butter	2 tbsp.	2 tbsp.	30 grams
Almonds (blanched)	2 tbsp.	1 oz.	30 grams
Grapefruit zest	1 tsp.	1 tsp.	2 grams
Whipped cream	1 cup	8 fl. oz.	240 milliliters

METHOD OF PREPARATION

Separate eggs—slice blanched almonds into thin slivers—slice grapefruit rind into very fine slivers and place into boiling water for 1 minute—drain. Whip cream stiffly—grease and sugar 4-cup soufflé dish and collar with 3-inch piece of buttered brown paper.

METHOD OF COOKERY

1. Preheat oven to 400° F. Place chocolate in a saucepan and cover with hot water—allow chocolate to stand until softened to the touch, then pour off water.
2. Add the butter to the softened chocolate and combine to smooth paste.
3. Add egg yolks to chocolate mixture—stir over a low heat until combined. Remove from heat and add grapefruit slivers and almonds.
4. Beat egg whites stiffly and fold them carefully into the chocolate mixture.
5. Pour soufflé mixture into soufflé dish and bake in oven 20 minutes.
6. Remove paper from dish and serve immediately, accompanied by the whipped cream.

Index

Mmmmh!

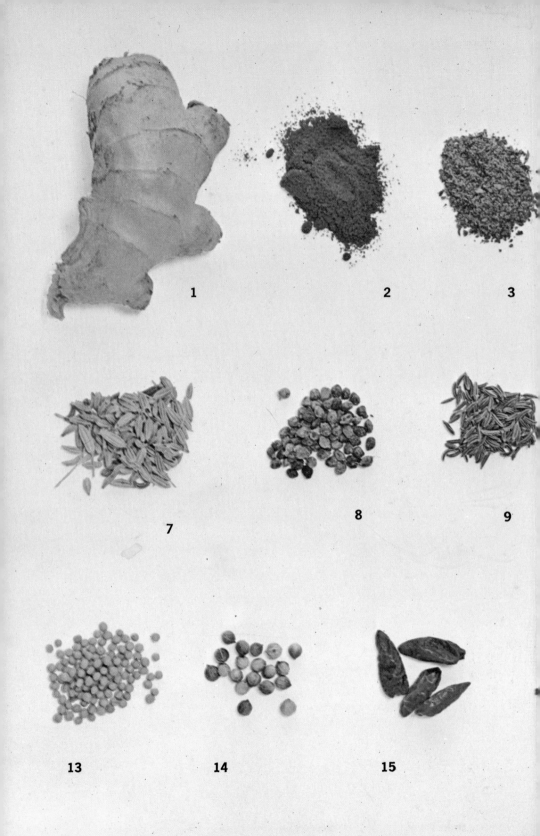

1   2   3

7   8   9

13   14   15